ADHD FOR SMART ASS WOMEN

ADHD FOR SMART ASS WOMEN

HOW TO FALL IN LOVE WITH YOUR NEURODIVERGENT BRAIN

TRACY OTSUKA

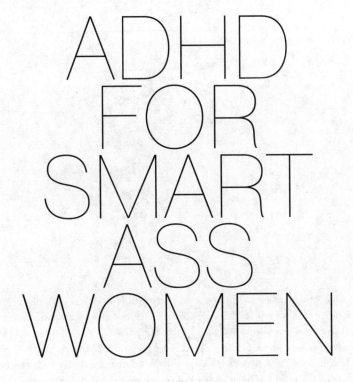

WILLIAM MORROW
An Imprint of HarperCollins*Publishers*

This book contains advice and information relating to health care. It should be used to supplement rather than replace the advice of your doctor or another trained health professional. If you know or suspect that you have a health problem, it is recommended that you seek your physician's advice before embarking on any medical program or treatment. All efforts have been made to assure the accuracy of the information contained in this book as of the date of publication. The publisher and the author disclaim liability for any medical outcomes that may occur as a result of applying the methods suggested in this book.

ADHD FOR SMART ASS WOMEN. Copyright © 2023 by Tracy Otsuka. All rights reserved. Printed in the United States of America. No part of this book may be used or reproduced in any manner whatsoever without written permission except in the case of brief quotations embodied in critical articles and reviews. For information, address HarperCollins Publishers, 195 Broadway, New York, NY 10007.

HarperCollins books may be purchased for educational, business, or sales promotional use. For information, please email the Special Markets Department at SPsales@harpercollins.com.

FIRST EDITION

Designed by Elina Cohen

Library of Congress Cataloging-in-Publication Data has been applied for.

ISBN 978-0-06-330705-6

23 24 25 26 27 LBC 5 4 3 2 1

To my linear-brained banker man

Hiring that pilot to fly that plane that trailed that banner that I absolutely could not afford was the best impulsive decision I've ever made.

XO, Scootles

And to my beautiful Mama

It was the honor of my lifetime to be your daughter. Hummingbirds, butterflies, frogs, and the color yellow— you are here, there, and everywhere.

CONTENTS

Dr. Edward M. Hallowell

Gerard Manley Hopkins's poem "Pied Beauty," written in 1877, begins:

> *Glory be to God for dappled things—*
> *For skies of couple-colour as a brinded cow;*
> *For rose-moles all in stipple upon trout that swim*

And like the sensibility of Tracy Otsuka, it is timeless, out of time, ahead of its time, bare, free, and without guile, pretense, or subterfuge.

Hopkins's poetry aims to celebrate life, to find all the beauty the poet can seize upon, and to call the reader to join in the resulting delight. Hopkins was drunk on life, spellbound by beauty, romantically in love with the transcendent, and called from beyond to proclaim to all the world the "couple-colours" he found beneath the shroud.

I'm a child and adult psychiatrist by training and a writer courtesy of muses unnamed. Fred Tremallo, my twelfth grade English teacher, saw some talent in me and gave me my head. Ever since then, I've been in love with stories and words, a love that sustains me in both of my jobs—one as a doctor, the other as a writer—and has led me to publish nearly two dozen books, mostly about the ADHD brain.

Tracy felt a calling herself, although she didn't label it that. She felt a sense of sacred presence firing within her before she knew what it was that caused her heart to skip a beat or a lump to come into her throat for no reason. She didn't know why she'd want to cry over nothing but would want to cry nonetheless. She didn't know why she wondered what made a turtle a turtle instead of a worm or a robin when others never wondered any such silly thing.

As if living a waking dream, she spent years experiencing life off-handed, neither left nor right, just her way, which, thanks to kind spirits like her parents and others she met on their journeys through life, she never knew as strange or odd or wrong, just her way, Tracy's way. She delighted in her childhood, loving yellow as a little girl, and all things like yellow, such as the sun, her mom, and Doris Day. Using the treasure-finder of an eye she was born with, she found the special, the eccentric, the speckled, and the hidden in every moment of every day. Her inner Geiger counter registered earthquakes of delight all the time.

She didn't notice until later that not everyone else took to life the way she did. She performed the tricks we ask our ambitious young to perform, and she put the letters after her name that garner the world's respect. But she wanted something else, something more. However, it wasn't the *more* that greedy or superficial people crave. It wasn't a yearning for yachts, $250,000 cars, or the adulation of crowds that she sought.

She sought a mission commensurate with her capacity to imagine one. She needed to make a difference in a unique way, in Tracy's way, and for that there was no blueprint, no agent, no important person's favor to curry.

So she relied on what she'd always relied on. She let her intuition and instincts be her guide. She stopped being realistic and pledged loyalty to her vision and imagination, as well as the values she naturally loved. She threw caution to the wind.

The rest reads like a fairy tale, and, as I told Tracy many years ago, she has become the Fairy Godmother of ADHD. She trusted what her special eyes could see, and she trusted what her deep sensibility could feel.

She then bravely shared her vision with the world. Bravely, because she risked ridicule, rejection, and defeat. But those were just words to her. What pulsed through her veins was a serum of conviction, vision, and passionate desire to give others the liberating knowledge she'd found.

I've seen similar characteristics of curiosity, courage, drive, and the need to do things their own way in other women with ADHD. For the thirty-plus years I've practiced as a psychiatrist, I've always had a special interest in girls and women with ADHD because they represent the most misunderstood and underdiagnosed group of all my patients. I also have ADHD and dyslexia, which I view as traits, not disorders, because if they're managed properly, they can become superpowers. And Tracy, more than others I know, has learned how to turn her own ADHD into a force that can help others who struggle with ADHD worldwide.

Today, she spends her life opening up the world to some very lucky people, mostly adult women, by teaching them about a way of being misleadingly called ADHD. Tracy discovered it sleepwalking, by which I mean she discovered it in random daydreams she can't even recall.

Some sleepwalk! Without training, preparation, or pedigree she stepped out a leader in ADHD, a freer of trapped minds, a validator of forgotten dreams, especially in women who had ADHD but didn't know it until Tracy spoke to them in a way they could hear and understand.

Like Hopkins, Tracy saw what others couldn't see, and she felt an ecstasy others didn't feel. She made it her mission to share what she saw so others could see it too, and to share what she felt so others could tremble with the same jubilation that fired through her every nerve.

Long before others saw through the sackcloth and ashes that drape the conventional view of ADHD, Tracy beheld the beauty beneath, as well as the yearnings of the women trapped by society, upbringing, and most of all, total ignorance of what this misunderstood condition really is.

Tracy became the best kind of expert. She lived her knowledge into coming alive. She learned by watching, inspecting, listening, and inquiring. She didn't blindly accept what the experts said. She learned from the women who came to her gatherings, soon to be called podcasts, much of which she put into this book.

What's here emerged from the laboratory of lived lives. Tracy, wide-eyed, took it all in. Tracy, ears opened, listened especially to what was not said, what people held back, but Tracy could intuit. In so doing, she applied the talent she was born with but a talent even she didn't know she had.

She was born a seer, a visionary, a healer, but she knew none of this. Growing up, she thought of herself simply as a happy little girl who lived in a loving family in a nurturing and encouraging community. She doesn't even remember the flashes of insight and intuition that came to her so often she thought everyone possessed such a sixth sense.

One day she wrote to me, "I'd really love to hear your perspective on what makes me different (if you see a difference) from others in the ADHD space. I'm not a medical doctor, psychologist, or therapist but somehow, I've been able to change lives when often [the professionals] haven't been able to. Maybe it's my blind, irreverent optimism? I'm not quite sure. I do love people and I always see the best in them."

The unadorned innocence and humility in those words point up how naturally Tracy came upon her gifts, and how much she strove to help others grow into their best selves.

It is one of the many conundrums in life with ADHD that we tend to have great talent embedded in great struggle. Until recently only the struggle got much attention. The "deficit disorder" model of ADHD—pathology written into its very name—reinforced the image of ADHD as an affliction with few, if any, saving graces. This model of the condition only made the condition worse, much worse. To this day, mothers tell me that the doctor who told them about their child's ADHD presented it almost as if it were a fatal illness, or at best a chronic, debilitating disease that had no cure.

But Tracy knew better. She knew about dappled things and stipple trout that swim and she knew that by paying attention to those parts of a person's life, the dappled, stipple parts would grow and begin to crowd out the sickly cells.

She asked me if it was her "blind, irreverent optimism" that gave her the power to change so many lives for the better, lives that professionals with far more advanced training had failed to bring out of the doldrums.

I'm certain her optimism helped her. Her optimism is not the feeble-minded, lily-livered, look-on-the-bright-side-of-life attitude it's usually depicted as, but rather it's a muscular, trained-in-the-trenches-of-life, bring-it-on-baby confidence that proclaims for all the world to hear that we can handle whatever life throws at us.

But even more, it was her inborn instincts that led her outside the conventional and restricted views of ADHD to the truth, as so many have verified.

An angel of trust kissed her at birth. She trusted her voice within. She listened to what people told her and put their stories before what was written in the textbooks. Now, thanks to her and others, the textbooks are being rewritten.

She perceived the beauty in disarray. She saw the potential greatness in a mess. She could hear the harmony gathering within the cacophony. She could find the love in hatred and find value in a feud.

No, she is neither a dainty violet nor an orchid in need of special care. She's more a hearty weed, part East, part West, able to be buffeted about and come up smiling. She's smart as a whip, but modest as a monk.

That she loves people has helped her, but that people love her, and reveal themselves to her fully and without disguise, has helped her to help them even more.

As you read this book, please know that Tracy Otsuka had one purpose in mind in bringing you these words. She wanted to bring the truth about a condition incorrectly called ADHD to as many people as she could. She's focused on women because she is one; she knows women well; and the need is great as adult women represent the single most undiagnosed group.

She was born to deliver a message. You will see it bursting out on every page. You will see how well she understands the many nooks and crannies of ADHD, or to cite words at the end of the poem we started out with:

> All things counter, original, spare, strange;
> Whatever is fickle, freckled (who knows how?)
> With swift, slow; sweet, sour; adazzle, dim; . . .

Tracy knows the pied beauty, the myriad contradictions, the counter, spare, and strange of ADHD as well as, if not better than, anyone.

But most of all, what she brings to you here, and wherever she goes, is the well-disguised (so as not to put anyone off) but unmistakable gift called love. Tracy's own—vintage, bonded, and unsurpassed—love.

How I Became the Fairy Godmother of ADHD Women

"Your number one job as his parent is to reduce his expectations, so he won't be disappointed in life."

The child psychologist looked me straight in the eyes as she leaned forward and hooked her pewter hair behind one ear. I stared back blankly.

"Ms. Otsuka, do you have any questions?" she asked.

Yes, I had a million questions about what she had just told me about my son, Markus. Reduce his expectations for life? At age twelve? Simply because he had ADHD? Her words burned through the air.

But I didn't ask any questions. She had her mind made up, and I wasn't going to change it. Instead I just shut down.

Markus had been diagnosed with attention-deficit/hyperactivity disorder, or ADHD, by a clinical neuropsychologist after enduring a battery of psychological, visual, and educational tests and undergoing various therapies for much of the last three years. My husband and I were confused by the diagnosis, so we had been working with this psychologist to learn more. She had come highly referred as *the*

ADHD expert, but after she harshly scolded Markus and my daughter for playfully pushing each other in one of our sessions, I started to question her approach. Now she was suggesting we lower his expectations in life. Who in their right mind would ever suggest limiting a child's potential for any reason whatsoever?

She clearly didn't know Markus. Charismatic, confident, and incessantly curious, he wouldn't stop until he had answers to all the questions that interested him. He feared nothing (except bugs) and walked around like an explorer staking his claim in the New World. He was driven and spent hours a week researching potential careers and the universities that would prepare him for those careers (starting at the age of nine). He had big dreams and high aspirations. Why would I ever quash his ambitions?

But this wasn't what I asked the psychologist. Instead, I gathered my bag, walked out of her office, and never looked back.

Eight months later, my world changed again when I received the same diagnosis: like Markus, I also had ADHD. I received this diagnosis only after learning everything I could about the condition once Markus was diagnosed, eventually seeing in myself many of the same symptoms, then proactively seeking out an adult ADHD specialist to confirm my suspicions. This is how I realized that ADHD is often passed down from parent to child and that the condition doesn't primarily affect boys and men, as plenty of doctors still believe. Just as many girls and women have ADHD, and they often go undiagnosed for years or are misdiagnosed with mental health conditions like depression, anxiety, or bipolar disorder.

ADHD also manifests differently in everyone, and you don't have to exhibit the stereotypical symptoms that many people, including doctors, associate with ADHD—like fidgeting, misbehaving, or doing poorly in school. I was gobsmacked. How could I have made it through four decades of life and never considered that I might have ADHD? Pretty soon, I learned I wasn't alone: as many as 75 percent of girls and women with ADHD go undiagnosed.

Once I realized how many misconceptions there were about ADHD and how many women were undiagnosed or misdiagnosed—or were diagnosed, then told to lower their ambitions as a result—I decided to make it my mission to change the conversation around the condition. Because I was certain that I've been successful in life because of my ADHD, not despite it.

The truth is, I've felt different my entire life because I was always "too much." I was "too chatty," for example; my parents called me the "Burlingame Blab" after my hometown, Burlingame, California, because I'd tell family secrets to anyone who'd listen. I was also "too intent" on challenging the status quo. On a lark, I met my husband through a personal ad well before there was online dating. Despite telling him I wasn't interested in anything serious, I was the one who proposed because when I know what I want, I'm driven to make it happen—and what I wanted was to get married in a very specific place and I didn't want to wait another year to reserve it (see page 112 for more of this story). I'm "too ambitious" and "too willing" to say exactly what's on my mind, like when I recently told a Zoom Room full of college professors that their teaching methods were terrible for neurodivergent students. Yikes. (*Neurodivergent* describes a person's brain, like mine, that processes or learns differently from what's considered "standard.")

Thinking through my diagnosis more carefully, I made an important connection: some of what others perceive as my ADHD "weaknesses" are exactly my greatest strengths. And my son is no different. You see, we're not hyperactive, just otherworldly energetic. We're not distractible, just incessantly curious. And yes, we can be impulsive, but some experts believe that creativity is simply impulsivity gone right (and one reason why many believe that Leonardo da Vinci, Vincent van Gogh, and Pablo Picasso all had ADHD). My ADHD diagnosis confirmed that I had been right about Markus and his big ambitions: given the right environment, he could accomplish his wildest dreams because I had. With two graduate degrees, I've passed the bar, worked as an attorney, and started three different companies. I have a thirty-year successful marriage and have remained happy and healthy throughout life. Today, I can see that my personal drive is a great form of hyperactivity and that my interpersonal intuition is the reason I can walk into a room and read how people feel before anyone utters a word, which has helped me successfully predict the mood of a group and ensure that everyone feels heard.

It's not that I don't have weaknesses. I'm never on time for anything that's not business related, and I'm incapable of washing a load of laundry just once, because I forget about the wet clothes in the dryer for days. The smoke alarm is the only reason my house hasn't burned to the ground, and I cannot balance a checkbook to save my life.

But despite my issues with time, memory, and money, I shouldn't be pathologized for having a brain that works differently—and neither should you. The more I learned about ADHD, the more frustrated I became with how many misconceptions and roadblocks there are for those of us who are neurodivergent. At the same time, I was meeting so many accomplished, successful, and brilliant women with ADHD. How come no one was talking about and celebrating us?

This is how I decided to start the podcast *ADHD for Smart Ass Women*, so that I could help us all better understand our brilliant, creative brains. I had an additional motive to meet more women with ADHD. And what better way to find my people than by letting them know that I am their people? What I didn't realize at the time, however, was just how many of "my people" were out there: in a little over a year, my podcast was ranked in the top half of 1 percent of all podcasts in the world on any subject. Clearly, there were many other women and some men who resonated with my strengths-focused view of ADHD.

Even more surprisingly, I started to receive messages from psychiatrists, psychologists, neurologists, therapists, and other medical professionals from around the world who commended me on the quality of my work and told me that *they* were learning about ADHD from *me*. Some also said they had referred their ADHD patients or clients to my podcast. Then, one of the country's leading ADHD experts, psychiatrist and former Harvard Medical School professor Dr. Edward M. Hallowell—whom I interviewed on my podcast—called me "a marvelous fairy godmother liberating women from their negative labels and helping them lay claim to the wonderful life they can have." This is how many women started calling me their fairy godmother, a title that has stuck.

With time, I began to realize the immense value of belonging to a community of like-minded ADHD women. My podcast, along with the online programs I subsequently launched for women with ADHD, was helping them recognize their own brilliance by seeing the same traits in other incredible women. Today, our community of ADHD women includes professors, scientists, doctors, lawyers, CEOs, entrepreneurs, contractors, artists, restaurateurs, writers, and everyone else who wants to tap into the strengths that ADHD has to offer and rewrite their own script. Meeting these women is inspiring and motivating. Throughout the pages of this book, I'll introduce them to you because it's important you meet them too.

What these women have in common is the shared belief that they are successful because of their ADHD, not despite it. They know that, given the right environment, they can take advantage of their natural strengths and interests. Many of these women are also action-oriented: They don't think about what they can't do or wish they could do. Instead, they go out and do it. And because they do it, you can do it too.

In my quest to learn all I could about ADHD, I eventually became an ADHD coach, which is a trained professional who helps people with the condition better manage their lives and symptoms. While there is no one regulating body that certifies coaches, most educational institutions that offer ADHD coach training have robust and specific criteria people must follow before becoming a coach. Some of the world's leading coaching organizations, like the nonprofit International Coaching Federation, certify ADHD training programs to help add credibility. Research shows that people who work with ADHD coaches end up improving their motivation, concentration, time management skills, self-esteem, and satisfaction with their school or work, in addition to other aspects of their daily function and life. This is one reason that many psychiatrists, psychologists, pediatricians, and other medical experts recommend working with an ADHD coach. In the epilogue, I'll give you guidelines on how to find a good ADHD coach.

I started taking ADHD coaching classes to better understand how my brain worked. While I never set out to become a coach myself, once I started taking the classes, I couldn't stop: I was so interested in putting together my own personal ADHD puzzle and understanding what makes my brain tick that I wanted to keep learning as much about the condition as I could. I also finally understood why life coaching had never worked for me: It wasn't that I was "uncoachable," as I had believed after my less-than-satisfying experience with a top life coach (see page 199), but that I wasn't being coached in the right ways, for my differently wired brain. At the same time, I began to see just how effective ADHD coaching can be and what a difference the right coach can make when added to our overall toolkit, which can also include medication, exercise, mindfulness, and other treatments and therapies. I also saw how often ADHD doctors insist their patients partner with ADHD coaches because these medical professionals understand the value of ADHD coaching.

After I became a coach and started working exclusively with female clients, I saw how quickly they improved after realizing the reason they'd been struggling their whole lives wasn't because they were flawed or not smart enough: they simply had ADHD. It was no longer an excuse, just a reason. Once this clicked, they were able to develop new workarounds and strategies that better leveraged their symptoms rather than allowing themselves to remain hamstrung by their traits. Through my podcast and the other ADHD groups I created, my clients were also able to connect with other successful, happy women with similar symptoms, which did the most work to dissipate the shame many felt. By seeing themselves in other successful women, many of my clients have finally been able to acknowledge and accept that they're not broken and they don't have some character flaw or moral failing. Instead, we women with ADHD have a unique brain that runs on a different operating system, like being a Mac in a Windows-driven world.

> *Instead, we women with ADHD have a unique brain that runs on a different operating system, like being a Mac in a Windows-driven world.*

Inspired, I started offering free workshops, like my 5 Days to Fall in Love with Your ADHD Brain. That's when it became even clearer to me that teaching ADHD women how their brains work can greatly reduce shame, help overhaul self-image, and change their belief in what they think they're capable of—sometimes in just a matter of days. And this is possible for you, too, even if you've lived with ADHD for years or have already tried multiple sessions of traditional therapy or life coaching.

For all these reasons, I knew that I had to write an ADHD book for women that didn't just disperse the same old or traditional advice, like to keep a to-do list and write everything in your planner, which may or may not work for you. Since the Covid-19 pandemic, medical professionals who don't understand ADHD have chided women who've diagnosed themselves with the condition by using TikTok (a real phenomenon, chronicled by *Good Morning America*, *Time* magazine, and many other eminent media outlets). The reason women have turned to TikTok to get help with ADHD is because we haven't felt heard or seen and we've been undiagnosed, misdiagnosed, or, worse still, told that it's all in our head. Other times, when doctors believe we have ADHD, we're given a prescription or a bunch of literature highlighting how we're disordered or defective when, in reality, our brilliant brains just work differently.

Recently, while reading the latest research on ADHD, as I often do, I stumbled on a large study conducted by scientists at the University of Toronto that found 42 percent of all adults with ADHD are in excellent mental health. Excellent mental health? Nearly half of us? I was floored. Why wasn't everyone talking about this study? I began to wonder what would happen if, instead of pathologizing ADHD, we looked at what these 42 percent of people were doing to live successfully with ADHD and leveraged their strategies for ourselves.

Discovering what your best life can look like with ADHD isn't always a straight path forward, and it may mean upsetting the applecart in places as you step into the brilliance of your extraordinary brain. Those of us with ADHD think differently, and not everyone likes different. I don't have tips on how to fit in because I don't believe we need to fit in. Instead, I believe we should embrace our unique brains so that we can work with our biology, not against it, to be truly successful and happy. This is what I want to teach you, how to work with your exceptional brain so you can do things your own way and live the life you were meant to live.

> ## *Those of us with ADHD think differently, and not everyone likes different.*

If you're struggling with your ADHD, one reason may be because you're still "trying harder" to do things society's way. A lot of ADHD women think they're broken because they live outside the status quo, but instead of kicking it to the curb (where it belongs), they end up trying to improve the areas of their brains that society tells us need shoring up. I strongly believe, however, that there are far better ways to spend your time, like embracing what makes you special and living up to your potential. You don't have to fit a square peg into a round hole—in fact, you can go ahead and ask why the damn hole needs filling in the first place.

This book is not packed with incomprehensible, confusing, or pathologizing medical jargon. It's written the way most of us speak: simply and directly, with a sense of humor. You can also start the book wherever you want. Take a look at the table of contents to see what interests you. You have my permission not to finish a chapter if it doesn't resonate with you.

I want this book to feel fun and easy so that you feel good about reading it—and keep reading it. What I want to foster in you with this book is positive emotion—when we feel satisfaction, success, happiness, or joy—because that's exactly what our ADHD brains need to feel inspired to keep going.

One of the most important lessons I can impart to you is, start to get curious about what works for you. Whether you realize it or not, you already have systems and procedures in place that function best with your ADHD brain. Together, we'll get curious about *your* systems and how *you* can leverage and implement them. That's the big secret with ADHD: you are already the expert on you. No one knows what will work best for you other than you. And while many of us may have stopped believing in ourselves years ago after being told we were "too much," I'm here to teach you how to start trusting in yourself again.

I have never met a person with ADHD who wasn't truly brilliant at something. Not one. That includes you, me, and my son, Markus, who has been my greatest teacher. He's now in his junior year at New York University and was recently offered a summer internship at an international bank after beating out 870 applications for one of fifteen spots—not bad for a kid who was told to lower his ambitions.

Markus taught me that often our creative ADHD brains need more structure, not less. By finding the right environment and surrounding himself with people who believe in him, my son's sky has become limitless. And so can yours.

Markus didn't need to have his expectations lowered—he needed them raised. Once he knew how his different brain worked and understood how smart and capable he was, hope took hold.

Hope is the bridge to our success. It fuels our intentions, drives our determination, and gives us the confidence to soar.

Hope is my promise to you.

PART I

UNDERSTANDING YOU AND YOUR ADHD BRAIN

What ADHD *Really* Is

Monday morning, 6:30. I head downstairs to the spin bike we keep in the garage. I adjust my bike seat, look down at my wrist, and remember that the watch I use to track my workouts is in the kitchen on its charger. I totter back up the wooden stairs in my bike cleats to the kitchen, where my bossy Shih Tzu, Mo, greets me with a face that says, *I need treats.* "OK, Mo," I say, reaching into the cannister and handing her a biscuit. She crinkles up her nose. She wants a different kind of treat, the kind I keep in the garage. Not only is she bossy, she's also demanding.

On my way to the garage, I see flies in the hallway. *Gross,* I think, *who left the door open?* I go back to the kitchen, grab a fly swatter, and begin to swat insects. After getting rid of enough flies, I head back to the garage to get Mo's biscuits, scooping up an unopened UPS package I see on the floor. Then it's back to the kitchen, where I slip and almost fall on the hardwood floors (I'm still in the damn bike cleats). I notice the postmark on the package: Even though it was mailed to me weeks ago, I decide now is when it must be opened! I start searching for scissors. Mo has given up on her treats. She's hovering at the kitchen door, asking me to let her out. I do so, then go back to the package.

While opening the package, I spot the hydrangeas that my mom and dad brought when they came for dinner the night before. If you're a gardener, you know how fussy hydrangeas can be—I see these ones are already wilting so I drop the scissors and start rummaging around for garden clippers to trim the hydrangea stems when another fly whizzes by. *Where's that swatter?* I think. I hear my cellphone ding with an email. I hesitate, but it could be important, so I may as well take a look, right?

Several minutes later, I see Mo out of the corner of my eye at the door again, begging to come in. I look up at our big kitchen clock. *How in the hell is it 7:15 a.m.?*

"Oh no, my workout!" I mindlessly grab the half-opened package, throw it on the kitchen island, and head down the stairs to the gym . . . without my fitness watch.

Believe it or not, this story only includes about 60 percent of the distractions I faced that morning. But as true as it is, the opposite is also true. If I'm really interested in something, I often hyperfocus, which happens frequently to those of us with ADHD. We "lock" onto a specific task and won't easily shift our attention elsewhere. We can concentrate on one thing so intensely at times, in fact, that it's enough to make all the surgeons, trial lawyers, and professional athletes out there jealous of our ability to keep our eyes on the prize (although many of them have ADHD too—and in the instance of elite athletes, experts even attribute their success to the condition). There are stories of those with ADHD writing entire books on round-trip plane rides and studies showing that hyperfocus allows those with ADHD to get into a "flow" state or "in the zone," where we can easily complete tasks because we're so immersed in them. Of course, we can also hyperfocus on things that aren't positive, like the negative thoughts we may have about ourselves or our situation. When we hyperfocus, we can forget to eat, sleep, or take care of ourselves in other ways. We can also lose all track of time and forget important things, like picking up our children from school (wait for this story).

In short, ADHD is a mixed bag. We may have trouble focusing our attention at times, but in other instances, we can home in on an activity better than anyone else. We may be disorganized and impulsive, but we may also be more resilient and creative than those who are *neurotypical*, which describes people with typical neurological patterns and behavior. People with ADHD are considered to be *neurodivergent*, meaning our brains work differently than the standard.

It might sound kind of confusing, but it doesn't have to be. You picked up this book because you have ADHD, believe you have ADHD, or want to help someone else with the condition. Either way, the first step in our journey together is to understand what ADHD actually is because there are a lot of myths and misperceptions out there. So, let's get started.

ALL ABOUT ADHD

ADHD is one of the most common brain developmental conditions in children, according to the CDC. But the condition doesn't just affect children. Many adults also have ADHD, although most don't know it: less than 20 percent of adults with the condition are aware that they have it, and for reasons we'll cover in this book, girls and women are more likely to go undiagnosed than boys and men, with up to 75 percent of all girls with ADHD remaining undiagnosed. While ADHD is just as likely to occur in either sex, 5.4 percent of American men have received an ADHD diagnosis while only 3.2 percent of women have. Just keep in mind these statistics are low, researchers say, because ADHD is underdiagnosed in adults, especially women.

Before we get into what ADHD is, let's talk about what it's *not*. Technically, ADHD stands for *attention-deficit/hyperactivity disorder*, but I don't find this name helpful or even accurate. (By the way, if you're wondering what the difference between ADHD and ADD, or attention deficit disorder is, ADD is just an outdated term, replaced by the ADHD diagnosis in 1987.)

ADHD is *not* a deficit of attention—it actually can produce a surplus of attention in those who have it, and when we're interested in something, we can hyperfocus on that event, task, or topic. The condition also doesn't necessarily mean that everyone who gets diagnosed is externally hyperactive in the way most people think of the word. For many women with ADHD, we may be able to sit still but we can't stop moving through our never-ending thoughts.

ADHD is also *not* a "disorder"—those of us with ADHD are far from defective. We just have a different brain that requires an alternate owner's manual. By developing positive emotion, which we'll talk about more in chapter 6, and new strategies that emphasize our strengths rather than our weaknesses, we can uncover our brilliance and become highly successful, not in spite of our ADHD but exactly because of it.

ADHD is also *not* overdiagnosed. This misperception has cropped up in recent years, especially as diagnoses among adults in the United States have increased four times faster than those in children. But as we just covered, researchers believe ADHD is underdiagnosed, especially in adult women. This is partly because the diagnostic criteria for ADHD was developed for children, not for adults, as we'll talk about on page 12.

ADHD also has nothing *to do with intelligence.*

ADHD also has *nothing* to do with intelligence. While those of us with ADHD may struggle to focus on school, work, and other structured activities, that doesn't mean we're not smart. Far from it. In fact, those of us with ADHD are usually intensely curious, persistent, and lifelong learners. While students with ADHD do have a higher incidence of learning disorders like dyslexia, the condition itself is *not* a learning disorder. When we find a learning strategy that works for us, we can be excellent students, especially if we're interested in a certain subject, since then we'll usually want to know everything about it. If we're not interested in a subject but have to learn it to satisfy a school or work requirement, we can struggle. In my experience, when ADHD students pursue university or graduate degrees where they can tailor their classes to their interests, they do much better. I often hear stories from women with ADHD who struggled through grade school but went on to receive a PhD and graduated with highest honors.

Finally, ADHD is *not* a made-up condition. Both the existence and impact of ADHD have been validated for decades by the country's leading medical organizations, including the National Institutes of Health, the US Surgeon General, the American Medical Association, and the American Psychiatric Association.

NOW THAT YOU know what ADHD is not, let's talk about what it *is*. ADHD is a neurodevelopmental condition, which means it affects how different areas of our brain develop and work. One of the primary areas affected by ADHD is the prefrontal cortex, which controls what is known as *executive function*. Executive function includes a number of mental skills, such as the ability to plan, organize, focus, self-motivate, regulate emotions, show self-restraint, manage time, problem solve, and retain working memory, which helps us recall temporary information like a phone number, email address, or the details of a story while listening to it. Because we face impairments to executive function, our ADHD brains can struggle with things like starting tasks or remaining focused on them, maintaining an even emotional state, regulating our actions (i.e., impulsivity), recalling information, and keeping track of time.

It's important to note, though, that ADHD looks differently in everyone—one reason it's difficult to diagnose. Experts also think that ADHD is a spectrum condition, meaning there's a wide range in the type and severity of symptoms that people can experience. Some of us may struggle with time while others can live by the clock but often procrastinate or can't remember what we've just been told. What's more, some people have such slight symptoms that they're not consistently impaired by them, even though they may still feel deficient or atypical in some way. No matter the degree of our ADHD, whether our symptoms are mild, moderate, or severe (how practitioners classify the condition's severity), learning about the symptoms and how to turn our weaknesses into strengths can be game-changing.

The degree of our ADHD symptoms can also be affected by whatever trauma or traumatic stress we faced when we were young. *Childhood trauma* includes what most people think of the term, like physical, emotional, or sexual abuse or the death of a parent or sibling. But it also encompasses less obvious factors, like socioeconomic problems, racism, emotional neglect, or if a parent abuses drugs or alcohol or has a mood disorder like depression. I've noticed firsthand in the women I've worked with how those who struggle the most with their ADHD symptoms faced substantial childhood trauma. We'll talk more about ADHD and emotional trauma in chapter 6.

ADHD is highly heritable. Research shows that around 40 percent of children with ADHD have at least one parent with symptoms. In addition, environmental factors like prenatal alcohol and drug use, childhood chemical exposure, and nutritional choices may influence who develops the condition.

I'm not sure who I inherited my ADHD from. Both of my parents were fiercely independent, which is a trait I've seen in many with ADHD. My mother was twenty-one when she left her native Germany with my father, whom she met while he was stationed there as a dentist and captain in the US Army.

My father, who is Japanese American, was born in Hawaii but moved to the mainland to go to college, attending dental school at Northwestern University. When he left the army and moved to the San Francisco Bay Area, he opened his own dental practice rather than work for anyone else. Nature has always been the cornerstone of his life, and for as far back as I can remember, he's spent much of his life outside, hyperfocusing on gardening.

At eighty-eight, my father is now retired but still spends hours every day in his garden. He also walks several miles daily and reads everything and anything. He is endlessly curious—an ADHD trait, as we mentioned earlier—and has a brilliant, sardonic wit. When I was a freshman in college, he wrote me letters and funny poems, which helped me get through a very difficult first year. He's also a stickler for commitment: if he tells you he'll do something, you can bet he'll do it—except he won't be on time because he has no sense of time, another common ADHD characteristic.

When I was young, I was lucky enough to have a stay-at-home mom, who raised me and my three siblings. She did everything for us, including cooking, cleaning, and driving us to school, all while learning English. When we were older, she volunteered as the vice principal of a local German-language school and then worked as a Realtor, still continuing all her motherly roles. She always had a lot of energy and taught me how to cook, sew, crochet, and knit.

My mom and I are very different—there's no question that I'm more impulsive—but we're also very similar. Like me, when she's interested in something, she doesn't just learn it, she immerses herself in it. For example, despite four young kids at home, she started playing the violin and often snuck off to the San Francisco Symphony to watch rehearsals, even though the concert hall was an hour away. She taught herself how to cook watching Julia Child on PBS and mastered the French recipes from Julia's cookbooks. Today, my mother's knitting is so intricate that it looks like the handiwork you'd find in a Connemara sweater from Ireland. Unlike my father, she is fastidious about time, which provided a lot of the structure in my daily life as a child. But we celebrated my brother's birthday on the wrong day for years, and she also bought Christmas presents early every year, and then forgot where she hid them. Like me, she has a poor working memory.

While neither of my parents was officially diagnosed with ADHD, I can see today that they both have many traits of the condition, which means I may have inherited my ADHD, too, just like my son had. For example, I have my father's entrepreneurial spirit, time blindness, love of nature, need for movement, and sense of humor, while I have my mother's empathy, crafty creativity, and sociability. I share both my parents' drive for excellence in our respective areas of interest. I also see the ADHD traits of drive, empathy, and creativity in my three siblings.

My experience is not universal. Being an able-bodied, cisgender, straight woman who grew up in a two-parent household in a middle-class suburb with many advantages, including higher education, was a privilege. This privilege means that my experience with ADHD has been much less arduous than it would be for marginalized women. I believe that it is my responsibility to do whatever I can to help ADHD women who have not been afforded the same access and resources that I have.

THREE TYPES OF ADHD

In the introduction, I promised to speak simply and straightforwardly and stay away from pathologizing scientific jargon, or medicalese. I still plan to honor that, but we need to start with a common reference point, which is understanding the clinical symptoms of ADHD. These symptoms come from the American Psychiatric Association's *Diagnostic and Statistical Manual of Mental Disorders, Fifth Edition,* or *DSM-5,* which is what doctors rely on today to diagnose ADHD.

According to the *DSM-5,* ADHD is characterized by a persistent pattern of inattention or hyperactivity and impulsivity that interferes with functioning or development. The *DSM-5* also specifies that there are three subtypes of ADHD:

- **HYPERACTIVE AND IMPULSIVE.** Those with hyperactive and impulsive ADHD are often restless and impatient and may talk a lot, interrupt, blurt out, or struggle to control their emotions. Boys and men are more likely to be diagnosed with this subtype.

- **INATTENTIVE.** Those with inattentive ADHD are often quiet, shy, easily distracted, and may have difficulty focusing on tasks, organizing, and paying attention to detail or instructions. Although inattentive types often appear quiet and calm, their brains are usually moving a mile a minute—in other words, the hyperactivity is in their minds, not their bodies. They may struggle more with ruminating thoughts and lose things more easily because they're overthinking, not remaining in their bodies in real time. They may also process information more slowly and less accurately and have trouble following directions. Girls and women are more likely to be diagnosed with the inattentive subtype, although girls with inattentive ADHD often go undiagnosed since they're not disruptive in the classroom, unlike boys with hyperactive and impulsive ADHD. As adults, women with inattentive ADHD are often misdiagnosed with anxiety or depression, as the symptoms can look similar.

- **COMBINED.** Those with combined ADHD, which is the most common subtype, have symptoms of both hyperactive and impulsive and inattentive ADHD.

Experts used to believe that children outgrow ADHD. Today, we know that most kids don't—studies show that only 10 percent of children diagnosed with ADHD overcome it. Instead, our symptoms evolve and change as we get older. For example, hyperactivity in a child can manifest as fidgeting in school or running around the classroom while, in adults, it can look like obsessing over thoughts or routinely dealing with distracting thoughts. Similarly, if we have ADHD as adults and suffer from impulsivity, we may be able to wait our turn or refrain from grabbing something out of a friend's hand, as we may have done as children, but we suffer from verbal impulsivity or make rash decisions.

According to the *DSM-5*, there are nine symptoms of inattentive ADHD and nine symptoms of hyperactive and impulsive ADHD (combined ADHD includes symptoms from both subtypes):

INATTENTIVE SYMPTOMS

- Makes careless mistakes/lacks attention to detail
- Has difficulty sustaining attention
- Does not seem to listen when spoken to directly
- Fails to follow through on tasks and instructions
- Exhibits poor organization
- Avoids/dislikes tasks requiring sustained mental effort
- Loses things necessary for tasks/activities
- Easily distracted (including unrelated thoughts)
- Is forgetful in daily activities

HYPERACTIVE AND IMPULSIVE SYMPTOMS

- Fidgets with or taps hands or feet, squirms in seat
- Leaves seat in situations when remaining seated is expected
- Experiences feelings of restlessness
- Has difficulty engaging in quiet, leisurely activities
- Is "on-the-go" or acts as if "driven by a motor"
- Talks excessively
- Blurts out answers
- Has difficulty waiting their turn
- Interrupts or intrudes on others

For adults to be diagnosed with any subtype, they need to: (1) display at least five of nine symptoms for at least six months; (2) some symptoms must have been present before age twelve; and (3) the intensity of symptoms must cause suffering or impair their ability to function in school, work, social or romantic relationships, and/or manage finances.

One reason so many adults, especially women, go undiagnosed or are misdiagnosed is that the *DSM-5*'s criteria was developed from research conducted on children—primarily male children—not women with ADHD. While you may be able to relate to the idea of "often unable to play quietly"—one of the *DMS-5*'s symptoms for hyperactive and impulsive ADHD—women aren't normally asked to play quietly in day-to-day life. But if we reword the symptom to something like "often can't relax on vacation or always needs to be busy," you may be able to see yourself there. Or we can sit still as adults, but we fidget in other ways, talking a lot, biting our cuticles, or constantly touching our hair.

I also agree with many experts that the *DSM-5*'s diagnostic symptoms are limiting in other ways. Many feel that they should be expanded to include problems that affect executive function, like issues with working memory or motivation and the inability to gauge or pay attention to time, stay on task, or reach goals.

As for the *DSM-5*'s requirement that someone with ADHD has to show some symptoms before age twelve, I've heard from so many women that they don't remember their childhood (hello, poor working memory or trauma!)—or even if they do, they're not sure if their behavior was atypical. Many women with whom I work have also shared that their most pressing symptoms arrived during puberty. I know mine did. I could memorize hour-long scripts for plays in English and German before puberty, but after age thirteen, I couldn't seem to memorize even one line of a chorus in my favorite Olivia Newton-John song.

Finally, I agree with Dr. Russell Barkley, a former professor of psychiatry who has devoted his entire career to ADHD education and research, that ADHD should be diagnosed if four, not five symptoms, are present in adults. In my experience, ADHD women will mask or suppress their symptoms as long as they can and carry on until they can't carry on anymore.

This much is clear:

- Just because you weren't diagnosed as a child doesn't mean you don't have ADHD.

- Just because you may have less intense symptoms today than you may have had as a child doesn't mean you don't have ADHD.

- Just because you don't know or can't remember if you had ADHD symptoms before age twelve doesn't mean you don't have ADHD.

- If you clinically have only four out of the nine possible symptoms, chances are, you may still have ADHD.

BEFORE WE GET into the next chapter, I want to emphasize that everyone has unique ADHD symptoms and traits. I also promised you a story on how ADHD caused someone to forget to pick up children from school. That story is my story, and it illustrates my unique symptoms and traits.

My friend Martina was on the other end of the phone. I could barely hear her. "I'm still in court," she whispered. "This is going a lot longer than it was supposed to. Will you please pick my boys up when you go to get Markus? I'll swing by the house and pick them up just as soon as I can."

At the time, Martina was going through a contentious divorce. And I was happy to help—her oldest son, Marco, had been best friends with my son, Markus, since kindergarten, and her youngest son, Lucas, often tagged along with them. I told her I would pick all three of them up, no problem at all.

It was 2 p.m. I still had an hour before pickup time and a pile of papers on my desk. Besides, I was never on time for pickup, as I refused to waste ten or fifteen minutes circling the school. The trick was to arrive just before the supervising teacher marched the kids who hadn't been picked up yet back into the building.

I left my office on time, proud of myself, figuring that I'd take the boys out for a snack before we came back to my house. At least that was the plan. I pulled into the pickup line and saw Markus standing with Marco and Lucas. At the time, I remember thinking how nice it was to see the three of them together, how polite they always were, and how cute they looked on that particular day. I rolled down the passenger window, waved, and shouted, "Hello, boys!" as my son got into the car. Then I drove away.

I left Martina's boys standing in the pickup line. They had no idea that they were supposed to come home with me, and I didn't even realize that I had forgotten them until an hour later, when Martina called me to find out what had happened.

To this day, I can't figure out how I forgot to pick up her kids in an hour's time, especially after seeing Martina's boys with my son when I pulled into the pickup line. I wish I could tell you that that was the only time I forgot to pick up a child, but I'd be lying. At times, I've been so engrossed in work that I've lost all track of the clock, forgotten that I even have kids, and arrived too late for pickup.

The interesting thing is that many ADHD women I work with will tell you that they've never been anything but early to pick up their kids and that they're never late. But these are the same women who say they constantly lose their phone or struggle to keep their home clean and organized. Other clients tell me that they don't struggle with any of these issues but can never get administrative tasks done at work.

Everyone's ADHD brain regulates attention, stimuli, and behavior differently. But what is consistent is that we're either utterly obsessed or completely uninterested. Let's keep learning how our ADHD brain works, specifically the brains of women.

Why Women Struggle to Get Diagnosed and What to Do About It

Danielle didn't find out she had ADHD until she was thirty-two, even though she clearly had symptoms as a child. "I couldn't ever sit down and do my homework like the other kids," she told me. "I was also incredibly talkative. I was so obviously ADHD, but no one caught it." Instead, Danielle felt confused and worse and worse about herself, especially after a teacher started calling her "rattletrap" because she allegedly rattled on in seventh-grade study hall. "There was quite a bit of shame for me associated with that nickname," she admitted.

Danielle's story sounds like those of many women I know who didn't get diagnosed until later in life or were misdiagnosed altogether and suffered a lot of confusion, shame, and low self-worth as a result. Another one of my clients, Jackie, was told by her doctor that she couldn't have ADHD because she can "focus on things she enjoys." Another client, Rachel, heard from her doctor that she couldn't have ADHD because she wasn't fidgeting during the appointment. I even have a client who's a doctor herself and was told by another physician when she went to get a refill on her ADHD medication that she, as a fellow physician, "should know you outgrow ADHD as an adult." That was in 2013.

For every woman who has a positive diagnosis experience with a knowledgeable practitioner, there are far more horror stories. Women are told that they can't possibly have ADHD because they're too smart, too educated, too successful, too depressed, too anxious, too bipolar, too borderline, too calm, too female, or too together. The fact remains that, while we've come a long way in other areas, girls and women slip through the cracks when it comes to ADHD diagnoses, oftentimes going undiagnosed or getting misdiagnosed, even though we're just as likely to have the condition as boys and men. In fact, American men with ADHD have a 70 percent greater chance of being diagnosed with the condition than women do—one reason why as many as 75 percent of girls with ADHD go undiagnosed. Girls and women are also more likely to be misdiagnosed with a mood disorder like anxiety and depression, which can trigger mismedication, increased suffering, and shame.

All these statistics point to an obvious fact: millions of women may have ADHD and not be aware of it.

In 2018, I launched the Facebook group ADHD for Smart Ass Women with the goal of creating a real-world community where women with the condition could share their strengths, strategies, and workarounds. Five months later, I launched a podcast with the same name after an overwhelming amount of interest and number of questions from Facebook members. Today, the group includes more than ninety thousand members, most of whom were diagnosed later in life, many only after their child was diagnosed. Researchers actually have a term for this—"the mommy factor"—which captures the number of women with ADHD who don't get diagnosed until they become mothers and their child is diagnosed. In my own experience with my son, Markus, it also helps with diagnosis to have a male child because far more boys than girls are diagnosed with ADHD, even though the condition occurs equally among sexes, for reasons

I'll discuss in a few pages. And for two-thirds of our members, their son was diagnosed with ADHD, not their daughter.

"The mommy factor" is troubling for a number of reasons, mostly because a woman's prognosis is far better the earlier in life she's diagnosed, as it allows for earlier treatment, in addition to the realization and awareness that there's a clinical reason for her perceived differences or struggles. But when girls and women with ADHD aren't diagnosed early and don't receive treatment, studies show that they often develop psychological, social, academic, and financial issues.

WHY ADHD IN WOMEN IS OFTEN OVERLOOKED OR MISDIAGNOSED

Here's why girls and women continue to face so many hurdles when it comes to getting diagnosed with ADHD.

Gender-biased research has created gender-biased stereotypes around ADHD

Let's start with the biggie: The research establishing the diagnostic criteria and rating scales for ADHD was originally based primarily on boys with hyperactivity (diagnostic criteria are always being updated, but that doesn't erase decades of gender stereotypes and gender biases in proper diagnosis). This, in turn, has created and fueled many long-lasting stereotypes about what ADHD should look like—mainly that those with the condition need to be climbing up the walls, racing around rooms, picking fights, and generally engaging in disruptive or unmanageable behavior. But most girls and women with ADHD don't exhibit this kind of behavior, leading teachers, parents, doctors, and women with the condition to rule out ADHD. What's more, teachers and school administrators are often the ones most likely to suggest the possibility of ADHD to parents and healthcare providers, so if educators aren't informed of how girls manifest symptoms differently, the girls often go undiagnosed.

Women are more likely to internalize their symptoms

Boys and men with ADHD are more likely to "externalize" their symptoms, meaning they might break rules, engage in aggressive behaviors, or mouth off. They act out. Girls and women with the condition, on the other hand, are more likely to "internalize" their symptoms. They live with their symptoms in their head. Girls and women are also more likely to suppress feelings of anger and frustration, and many times are too fearful to share with others what they're going through. Instead of reaching out for help—or receiving it passively because they display disruptive behavior like boys often do—girls and women develop negative thought patterns when dealing with their symptoms. This exacerbates low self-esteem, anxiety, and depression.

Women express hyperactivity differently

Hyperactivity is perceived to be a hallmark of ADHD. While men often manifest hyperactivity in physical, aggressive, or disruptive ways, as we've discussed, women are more likely to show our hyperactivity by talking too much or excessively ruminating (in addition to picking our cuticles, bouncing our foot up and down, or constantly repositioning ourselves in our chair). The problem with this, however, is that being chatty is typically seen as a common characteristic of women, not necessarily a specific sign of ADHD, though excessive talking is typical in adults with ADHD. When women do it, however, it's perceived as socially acceptable, even charming, not as a warning flag that we have a neurodevelopmental condition. If we happen to also excessively ruminate, the symptom is ignored because it's not apparent to those around us or disrupting anyone else.

Women are more likely to have the type of ADHD that gets overlooked

As we know from chapter 1, of the three subtypes of ADHD (hyperactive and impulsive, inattentive, and combined), girls and women are more likely to have inattentive ADHD than boys and men. Women with inattentive ADHD are often withdrawn, dreamy, and perfectionists—traits that don't prompt people to automatically think of ADHD.

"I have so many memories of adults waving their hands in front of my face, trying to get me out of my reverie and daydreaming," says Triin, who was diagnosed with ADHD at age forty-one. Growing up, she was a self-proclaimed "good girl" who never made trouble and always sat in the back of the class. Now an author and freelance writer, Triin can see how her inattentive symptoms manifested when she was young. "I stayed up until midnight after everyone had gone to bed so that I could finally do my homework in peace and quiet and read up on the class content at my own pace," she says.

Women with inattentive ADHD can also appear shy, forgetful, disorganized, and distracted. As children, they may have been the ones like Triin who spent most of their time in the back of the classroom, lost in their own fantasy worlds—not the ones acting out, blurting out, and interrupting. As adults, women with inattentive ADHD oftentimes look like the absent-minded professors: bright in certain areas but otherwise distracted. Girls and women with inattentive ADHD usually don't cause classic ADHD disruptions, allowing the condition to be overlooked as a diagnosis.

Coexisting conditions complicate an ADHD diagnosis

Both men and women with ADHD are more likely to have comorbidities than those without ADHD, meaning we have two or more medical conditions simultaneously. Common comorbidities for those with ADHD include depression, anxiety, obsessive-compulsive disorder (OCD), learning disabilities, executive function difficulties, and tic disorders (think Tourette's syndrome or a motor tic). But recent research shows that ADHD women are much more likely than men with the condition to have these comorbidities, including autism spectrum disorder, personality disorders, substance abuse, and suicidal behavior. Women with ADHD also tend to experience more "internalizing disorders" like anxiety, depression, and other emotional problems. These comorbidities can cause doctors to diagnose women with one of these conditions but not with ADHD, confident that their primary diagnosis explains their patients' symptoms. Additionally, women can be diagnosed with a comorbidity that they don't have, as providers often mistake common ADHD symptoms for a mood disorder. Oftentimes when girls and women are treated for ADHD, their depression or anxiety resolves as well.

Women are more likely to be judged for having ADHD

Despite a growing number of ADHD diagnoses among females, the condition is still primarily perceived as a male problem, perpetuating the myth that women don't "get" ADHD. Many people assume that girls and women are more compliant, organized, neater, and less aggressive than boys and men, so if a female has ADHD or exhibits traits that defy these gender stereotypes, she is more likely to be judged as atypical, meaning there's something really wrong with her. This bias has helped contribute to the fact that boys are more likely to be referred for treatment than girls, regardless of symptoms.

Women are more likely to overcompensate

I know many women who have been told by mental health professionals that they can't possibly have ADHD because they're a nurse, doctor, lawyer, business owner, or—heck—they graduated from college.

To succeed, it seemed to me that I had to work harder than everyone else. I didn't just read the materials and take notes to prepare for exams. Instead, I developed elaborate systems to stay focused, reading everything once with a highlighter, tabbing the important concepts, then reading it a second time and making notes in the margins. Next, I created an outline from my highlights, tabs, and notes and then made note cards to study from.

Stereotypes and gender norms often cause girls and women with ADHD to overcompensate to avoid being judged or ostracized. We often hide our struggles for as long as we can, or until the demands of school, work, or life in general exceed our ability to compensate.

Gail, one of our Facebook group members, told me that she made it through college by deliberately choosing a school where she didn't know anyone so that she wouldn't be distracted from getting her studies done by her social life. After college, she made a name for herself working in public relations for a Fortune 100 company, which she did, she says, by working harder than everyone else, especially after she had kids. "I'd work through lunch and every spare second that I could find," she told me, adding that she'd routinely wake up at 5:30 in the morning to catch up and open her laptop and work for another four hours after putting her kids to bed at night. "I always felt behind," she said. At age fifty-seven, she was finally diagnosed with ADHD. "That's only when everything I had done for decades started to make sense," she said. "There wasn't anything wrong with me other than I wasn't treating a condition I'd had for years." Once she started learning techniques to manage her ADHD, she stopped working incessantly. "I could finally put in normal hours and still get things done without feeling like I'd let the other shoe drop."

Doctors don't receive adequate training on ADHD

Ninety-three percent of adult psychiatry residency programs include no training in ADHD. In fact, there aren't even any questions about ADHD symptoms on the board certification examination for adult psychiatrists. In one research effort, when psychiatrists were told that they were part of a study on ADHD, 60 percent refused to believe that it could be a coexisting condition. There are also some doctors who don't believe in ADHD at all, as if the condition is a conspiracy theory, even though it's been recognized by all major medical groups.

Some practitioners also mistakenly believe that ADHD exists only in children and manifests primarily as hyperactivity, which people outgrow. But as we know from chapter 1, while both boys and girls can experience hyperactivity as kids, girls and women are more likely to internalize hyperactivity with racing thoughts and emotional dysregulation, which describes an inability to regulate or control our feelings. This often leads doctors to incorrectly jump to a diagnosis of anxiety, depression, OCD, bipolar disorder, or borderline personality disorder, even if they're only part of the diagnosis. What's more, many healthcare providers aren't fully educated on how ADHD looks in girls and women. Instead, girls and women who show symptoms are often diagnosed with depression or anxiety, which may be present at the same time as ADHD, but it's actually the ADHD that's causing the depression or anxiety.

GETTING PROPERLY DIAGNOSED

Now that we've covered the diagnostic hurdles, let's focus on solutions. Psychologists, psychiatrists, neurologists, family doctors, nurse practitioners, therapists, and/or clinical social workers can all theoretically diagnose you with ADHD. But just because they can doesn't mean that they will—even if you have the most obvious symptoms.

For all the reasons just discussed, many ADHD women remain un-diagnosed or misdiagnosed. This is why it's so important to find a provider who specializes in ADHD, especially ADHD in women (if the practitioner is a woman, even better).

Once you are diagnosed, however, you will still need a physician, a nurse practitioner, or a physician's assistant (under the supervision of a physician) to prescribe ADHD medications if in fact it is determined you need them. To add to the confusion, laws for how prescriptions for ADHD are handled vary by state, since the medications fall into the category of stimulants.

If you have a friend or colleague who was recently diagnosed, consider asking them for a referral, or talk with your primary care doctor to see if they can recommend a practitioner. Online resources such as Children and Adults with Attention-Deficit/Hyperactivity Disorder (CHADD), ADDitude, or GetADHDHelp.com all contain professional directories that can help you find a local expert. If you can't find a practitioner in your area, consider a virtual diagnosis by a highly trained clinician you can find in one of the directories mentioned above. In some instances, like with Diagnostic Learning Services (a group that provides comprehensive virtual testing for ADHD), you will be provided with a report that you can then give to a local physician or psychiatrist to help you with treatment strategies.

Even if you're able to meet with a practitioner experienced in ADHD, I highly recommend learning everything you can before your appointment, including how the condition manifests in women so that you can advocate for yourself. If you find it helpful, bring books like this one, articles, or even studies to show to your provider and to help make your case about why you suspect you have ADHD.

It's also helpful to make a list of your symptoms to take with you to your appointment. A list in hand will help organize your thoughts and remind you to share all your relevant symptoms with your doctor.

Knowing what your appointment might look like can also help. First, there is no single medical, physical, or genetic test for ADHD. There's also no standard procedure for diagnosing ADHD. Instead, a practitioner will gather your personal and medical history using multiple sources, including symptom checklists or behavior rating scales. Practitioners can use assessment tools to rate your symptoms that may be filled out by you and those who know you well, like a spouse, roommate, parent, or teacher. According to Laurie Peterson, founder of Diagnostic Learning Services, those of us with ADHD may not be able to perceive our own symptoms, which is why having others rate our traits can be helpful.

Some practitioners also require standardized testing like an IQ test to measure how your working memory and problem-solving skills compare to those of others your age. Another standardized test that may be ordered is something known as the QbTest, short for Quantifiable Behavioral Test, a computer-based test that measures activity, inattention, and impulsivity.

The fact that there is no standard diagnosis for adults with ADHD can make the process frustrating. I know some women who have been diagnosed after multiple lengthy appointments based on their current and past functioning, standardized test results, symptom checklists, and behavior rating scales. Others I know were diagnosed after a brief same-day office visit in which providers used only a single checklist or online video consultation. Others still were diagnosed by their primary care doctor after going in with concerns about a separate condition altogether.

In my case, I met with a psychologist who asked me questions about my childhood, including how I did academically and whether I ever got in trouble for talking or disrupting classes. She also asked if anyone else in my family had been diagnosed with ADHD, what I felt were my past and current challenges, and if I thought my symptoms had worsened over the years. Both my husband and I took home rating scales to help measure my symptoms, which I brought to my second visit a week later. As I sat waiting, the psychologist looked over my rating scales, made some calculations, and diagnosed me with the combined subtype of ADHD on that day. All in all, the entire evaluation lasted several hours.

When my son, Markus, was diagnosed, the doctor asked his school's principal, his primary teacher, and my husband and me to all fill out behavior scales. Markus also underwent a battery of cognitive tests (which weren't required for my adult diagnosis) that looked for giftedness, learning disabilities, strengths, and weaknesses. Federal law for elementary, high school, and college accommodations require more robust ADHD evaluations and may sometimes mandate a medical doctor's sign-off, although the doctor may not do the actual testing.

After we discovered that Markus has dyslexia, I decided to get tested for that learning difference while getting retested for ADHD, which I did through Peterson's Diagnostic Learning Services. During the process, I took the adult version of the cognitive test that Markus had taken, something that's known as the Wechsler Adult Intelligence Scale (WAIS), which is designed to measure intelligence and cognitive ability. I also filled out a symptom checklist and a more detailed background form and completed the QbTest. I did score again for ADHD, but not for dyslexia.

ADHD WOMEN OFTEN share with me that getting evaluated and diagnosed is therapeutic. They feel reassured to finally have answers after years or even decades of struggling. In my own experience, retesting with the WAIS test boosted my self-esteem because it showed I was actually good at critical thinking and had strong visual-spatial skills, which are useful in advanced mathematics like trigonometry. This explained how I was able to do so well in trigonometry in high school while struggling to get Bs in other math classes. The WAIS test also showed that I had strong working memory, even though I had told myself for decades that I was deficient in this category.

The WAIS test, QbTest, and other advanced diagnostic tools can be expensive, however, ranging from five hundred to several thousand dollars, depending on where you live and how many specialists are available in your area. While my health insurance paid for my original diagnostic testing, it didn't cover this second round. But I felt both tests were well worth the price because they provided more insight into how my brain works and a confidence boost that I wouldn't have found elsewhere. These types of tests aren't necessary to confirm an ADHD diagnosis, but I believe they're a great investment for life, confirming or refuting preconceived notions you may have about yourself and your challenges.

According to Peterson, whichever way you decide to get tested for ADHD, it should be more comprehensive than one fifteen-minute appointment and a single test. "Client interviews and behavior rating scales are important, but the assessment should also include an objective measure of where your skills are in comparison to peers of your same age that doesn't rely on opinions or observations of others," she said. She recommends seeking out providers or practices that use standardized testing like WAIS that can assess your executive function skills as well as an additional objective measure like a QbTest.

If you're confident that you have ADHD but are told otherwise, get a second opinion. Those of us with ADHD often have strong intuition: trust it.

Those of us with ADHD often have
strong intuition: trust it.

WHAT ABOUT MEDICATION?

I'm not a doctor so I'm not going to discuss specific medications and what they do in this book. Plus, the absolute best place to get this kind of information is by meeting with a psychiatrist who specializes in ADHD and whom you can work with over time so they can get to know *you*.

Instead, I want to share my personal experience with ADHD medication and what I've observed while coaching thousands of women with ADHD. First, I want to say that ADHD medication can be life-changing. I think of Gina, one of my Facebook group members, who shared that she was suicidal before taking stimulant drugs. Then, there's Maria, one of my podcast guests, who was flunking out of law school before she was finally diagnosed with ADHD and prescribed medication—the following semester, she aced nearly all her classes. I've also heard from Marta, another member of my Facebook group, who felt anxious and judged because she couldn't get out of bed in the morning to help her four children get ready for school. After she was prescribed medication, however, she was able to wake up and seize the day with energy and motivation.

At the same time, I feel strongly that medication should not be the only treatment for ADHD. I've personally witnessed how much more successful medication is when combined with exercise, good sleep, healthy nutrition, and an understanding of how your brain works. I've also seen so many women who have successfully treated their ADHD using nutritional supplements and other modalities and with no medications whatsoever. The most important thing is being open to all types of treatment plans before making a decision.

What's more, not all medications work for all women all the time. For approximately 20 percent of ADHD women, medication doesn't work at all, causing negative side effects or exacerbating the symptoms of ADHD itself. Trust me, I know.

After I was diagnosed with ADHD, I met with a psychiatrist to discuss medication options. The appointment lasted no more than fifteen minutes, with no discussion of the different kinds of ADHD drugs, including stimulant versus nonstimulant meds, or nonpharmacological options. Instead, he handed me a prescription for Adderall, which immediately made me feel anxious and jittery—symptoms that got worse as the days went on. But I kept working with the same psychiatrist for several months, trying to find a different medication, when I realized that he didn't have anything other than Adderall and Ritalin in his ADHD toolkit. That's why I began to do research into the various ADHD drugs, telling him which medication I wanted to try next. It wasn't ideal, not by a long shot.

Ultimately, I ended up hiring a private psychologist who had run the women's mental health division for the largest managed care consortium in Northern California. We would talk about and decide upon a new medication for me to try, then I'd get a prescription through my healthcare plan's psychiatrist. After several months, however, I realized this approach wasn't helping either. While this psychologist was an expert in ADHD medications for women, just because something had worked for one of her patients in the past didn't mean it was going to work for me. Instead, I felt like a guinea pig in a very expensive science experiment.

By the end of my ADHD medication journey, which took almost two years, I had tried Adderall, Ritalin, Wellbutrin, Vyvanse, Strattera, and Focalin, along with BuSpar and Lexapro, which doctors had prescribed to help me manage the anxiety that can accompany stimulants. For some, these medications overhaul their symptoms and change their lives. For me, however, the end result was anything but. Yet I tried all of these different medications because I kept believing the outcome would change only if I kept trying. In the process, though, I lost sight of what it felt like to feel good. Instead, I felt on edge, overwhelmed, and at times depressed, completely unlike my normal optimistic self.

My story illustrates what I've seen firsthand in many other ADHD women. We try too long with medication because (1) we're desperate for solutions; (2) those of us with ADHD tend to be tenacious; or

(3) we were prescribed these meds by a doctor who must know more about our situation than we do. The thing is, however, *you* are the best expert on you. And if something isn't working for you, don't stick with it until, like me, feeling badly becomes your new normal.

Yes, your doctor may know a ton about different ADHD medications, how they work, and which ones patients similar to you have had the most success with in the past. But that doesn't mean your doctor knows you and how each particular drug will work for you. Only you know that, which is why you must pay attention to how you feel whenever you start taking a prescribed medication. I cannot stress enough how important it is to track in writing how you feel every single day while on a new medication. While it's difficult for anyone to remember how they felt last week, let alone five weeks ago, for those of us who struggle with time management and working memory (see chapter 9), it can be especially challenging to recall how long we've been on a drug, how long we've felt poorly, and whether it's getting better or worse.

In summary, if you have ADHD, seeing a psychiatrist to discuss different medication options is an important and potentially life-changing step. Just be sure to remember to *always* trust your instincts and your intuition.

3

Why ADHD Women Face More Issues

Let me tell you about the time I almost flunked out of college.

In high school, I decided that I wanted to become a dentist like my dad, even though I had zero aptitude or interest in taking the required classes to be a dentist. But *Dr. Otsuka* had a nice ring to it, and I didn't know any other female dentists, which was another plus. Besides, wouldn't becoming a dentist be proof to the outside world that I was actually smart? While I already knew I was intelligent, my brain's consistently inconsistent function made me aware that I operated slightly differently than most others.

This is how I started out in college as a biochemistry major. But by the end of the first semester of my freshman year, I realized that I had made a serious mistake, as I saw my grades in biochemistry and calculus tank. No number of all-nighters or caffeine pills helped me learn the material—I hated it all and felt so different from my class-mates, most of whom seemed to hone their diligence to get passing grades. I knew that if I didn't make some changes, I wouldn't gradu-ate with a GPA that would allow me to get into grad school, let alone graduate from undergrad. That's when I made an appointment to see the college guidance counselor. I told him that I wanted to switch my major to political science.

In my mind, I had only three career options: doctor, dentist, or lawyer. Since I lacked the interest (and thereby aptitude) to get into dental school, I figured that medical school was also out of the question. That's when I started to think that my interest in people, justice, and discourse—not to mention my love for reruns of *Perry Mason*, which I watched with my mother—might make me an ideal candidate to study law. Plus, a doctoral degree in law was still a doctorate, which would still mean that I was "smart." I decided that I should become an attorney.

When I explained all this to the counselor, he looked at me like I had three heads. "That's not how you choose a major, Tracy," he said. *Maybe that's not how* you *choose a major, but it's how* I *do it*, I thought. Later that day, I became a political science major.

The only problem was that I was now a semester behind as a political science major. I realized I'd have to go to summer school to make up classes and repair my ailing GPA. Ironically, though, summer school turned out to be a fantastic decision for reasons other than just boosting my poor grades and catching up on credits. For the first time in my academic career, I finally chose classes that really interested me, like creative writing and women's studies, rather than those I needed to take. To this day, these are the two classes I remember most vividly from my four years of undergraduate study. For the first time in my academic career, I could write about whatever I wanted in creative writing class, so I made sure it was irreverent, funny, and wholly inappropriate—something that only got me in trouble in Catholic high school.

The women's studies class changed my life. We didn't sit in rows of seats but in a circle, and our textbooks included issues of *Ladies' Home Journal* and *Playboy*. Unlike the students in my science and math classes, my classmates in women's studies were vocal and opinionated. Some shared traumatic stories of sexism. I listened closely, and began to question everything that I had experienced about gender roles and expectations growing up.

I thought about how upset I used to get when my mom would ask only my sister and me to help her clean the house, while my younger brothers laid around and made even more of a mess. I remembered how my mother would work a full day but would also be responsible for all the cleaning, laundry, childcare, grocery shopping, and cooking, while, by comparison, my dad's only contributions to the household's chores were gardening and making pancakes on Sundays. (In his defense, he did make a mean pancake and helped with the dishes, which is more than most of my friends' fathers did.)

After summer school, I considered majoring in women's studies. What dissuaded me, though, is that I had no idea how I would ever make a living as a feminist. And weren't there "smarter" things I could be? At the time, I never considered that because I was passionate about women's studies, I'd find a way to turn my passion into a profession. It's not lost on me that I've come full circle and have now made a career of fighting for ADHD women affected by gender bias and sexism.

While having ADHD is challenging no matter your gender, women struggle more due to a combination of factors, including gender expectations about the roles women should play, sexist norms about how women should act, increased feelings of low self-worth, and even a greater tendency toward self-harm due to the condition. We're also less likely to get properly diagnosed or treated, as you know from chapter 2. On top of all this, fluctuations in female hormones can worsen ADHD symptoms, as we'll cover later in this chapter.

GENDER ROLES AND ADHD

A lot of women with ADHD do a good job managing their symptoms through school, then hit a brick wall once they move in with a partner, get married, or have children. Suddenly, they're not just taking care of themselves but also a partner, household, and/or kids. Look, all people with ADHD have to manage themselves and their career, which is challenging enough, but society expects women to also be a chauffeur, chef, personal shopper, housekeeper, tutor, nurse, and social secretary. These roles require executive function skills: planning, organizing, motivating, scheduling, and time management—exactly what most women with ADHD lack.

Here's the truth. We may have come a long way since the days of June Cleaver, but housework, childcare, and eldercare are still considered women's work. Studies show that American women handle most of the essential household chores, including laundry, cooking, cleaning, childcare, and grocery shopping. Studies also show that women are more likely than men to care for elders and spend more time with aging parents. While women are unfairly expected to play these roles far more than men, ADHD women pay an even higher price.

Monica, a member of one of my online groups, and her husband, Bill, both have ADHD. When Monica first met her in-laws (while she and Bill were still dating), Bill's mother told her how happy she was that her son had finally found someone to keep him on track. "It only took a couple of forgotten dates and consistent late arrivals before my mother-in-law realized that I was a fraud," Monica quipped. "That's when she quietly took on the role of reminding both of us when something needed to be done." A decade later, Bill's mother gifted the two of them with a calendar filled with all the family's important events, like birthdays and anniversaries, already written inside. She even included the date that Bill and Monica should buy each other anniversary gifts.

"That ten-dollar calendar is my favorite Christmas gift ever!" Monica exclaimed. "I am lucky to have a mother-in-law who gave up her gendered expectations without any problems."

Most women, though, aren't as fortunate as Monica is. Research has found that women are more likely to be negatively judged for not upholding their gender norms, especially around housekeeping and other "female" responsibilities. One study, conducted at Emory University, showed more than six hundred people photos of a messy living room and kitchen, then a tidy version of the same spaces. When people were told a woman lived in the messy rooms, they judged it as dirtier than those who were told a man occupied the same space—participants also thought the woman was more likely to be viewed less favorably than the man. What's more, subjects thought the woman should be responsible for cleaning the spaces, even if she was in a heterosexual marriage and both were working full-time. These kinds of gender biases are problematic for all women, but even more so for those with ADHD who struggle to plan, organize, initiate, and complete.

Unfortunately, what causes suffering and shame for ADHD women isn't just how others see us: it's also how we see ourselves for being ADHD women. Through my work as an ADHD coach, I've met so many incredibly accomplished women who don't believe they're successful because they can't keep a clean house or manage their husband or kids.

One of these women, Emerald, is a successful marriage and family therapist (MFT). She's also a wife, mother, PTA president, school counselor, community leader, and activist. While she's great at what she does—counseling others and being a loving mother and wife—she struggles to keep up with household chores and other "female" duties like picking up and dropping off her kids. For years, she felt inadequate, questioning her abilities as a mother, wife, and even a therapist. In Emerald's mind, it didn't matter how brilliant she was as an MFT or a mother, she couldn't acknowledge it because it was overshadowed by the fact that she'd shown up late to pick up her kids or couldn't get dinner on the table on time.

When we met, I encouraged Emerald to focus on her strengths rather than her weaknesses. By doing so, she identified that she was driven in many tasks, fearless in her pursuit of social justice, and a creative, out-of-the-box thinker who continually identified new solutions for clients. Focusing on her strengths rather than her weaknesses helped Emerald recognize that she is, in fact, an amazing mother and wife. Maybe she was late to pick up her kids and get dinner on the table, but she was ingenious at supporting her husband

and children, introducing them to new experiences and causes, being present when they spent time together, and providing consistent love.

Emerald's story highlights the power of channeling positive emotions, which are pleasant, desirable, or "happy" emotions that can help women with ADHD overcome the shame so many of us have around our ADHD symptoms. We'll talk more about positive emotions in chapter 6.

GENDER NORMS AND ADHD

Prevailing social and cultural norms around what's considered "appropriate" behavior for each gender make it more difficult for women with ADHD. After all, it's not seen as "feminine" to interrupt, show up late, be messy, or blurt out insensitive comments. Because of these gender stereotypes around behavior, many girls and women are ashamed of their ADHD symptoms, which don't trigger the same reaction in boys and men. Just like it's more socially acceptable for men to keep a messy home, men are more likely to get a pass for being impulsive, disorganized, and energetic.

Courtney, thirty, still tears up when she talks about how her messiness and disorganization were the butt of family jokes. "To this day, I'll never fit the mold of the feminine and organized woman," she said. "Relatives gave me signs to hang on my bedroom door that said, 'It's Not Dirt. It's Angel Dust!' and books like *How to Not Be a Pack Rat* or *Organization for Teens*, which just led to more shame because they didn't do anything to help me understand how to fix the problem. None of their strategies worked for my brain."

What made it even more difficult for Courtney was that her brother, who was also diagnosed with ADHD, got a pass to be as messy as he wanted. "It didn't matter what his bedroom looked like," she observed. "In fact, they saw his disorganized room as evidence of a gifted brain—he would just need a good secretary when he got older to keep himself organized and on schedule. Meanwhile I was expected to become a doctor *and* a good secretary. As a child, I'd play it off, but deep down, all those instances of being told how messy you are really affects you."

LOWER SELF-ESTEEM AND MORE SELF-HARM

ADHD is often compared to an iceberg. Above the water, at the top of the iceberg, the world sees all our symptoms: the forgetfulness, the dreaminess, the missed appointments, a messy home. But what they don't see, what's under the water, is far worse: the learned helplessness, the imposter syndrome, the perfectionism that develops after years or even decades of feeling like we're too much and all wrong.

Numerous studies confirm that ADHD women are more likely to suffer from low self-esteem, low self-worth, and overall negative self-perception. Many of us struggled in school when we were young or we do in our careers now. Research also suggests that ADHD women are more likely to berate and blame themselves for their symptoms. Some of us may feel like a failure as a partner, wife, or a mother because we can't fulfill the roles society has placed on us or feel like we're flawed because we have more stereotypical "masculine" traits like impulsivity, assertiveness, and disorganization. Finally, it's been shown that many ADHD women are hypercritical of themselves and have a difficult time accepting positive feedback.

For all these reasons, combined with the fact that ADHD women have higher rates of anxiety, depression, and other mental health issues, women with the condition have a greater propensity toward self-harm and suicide than the general population. One surprising study conducted in Canada even found that approximately 23 percent of ADHD women have attempted suicide, compared to 8 percent of ADHD men and 3 percent of women without the condition. Women who have combined ADHD or the hyperactive and impulsive subtype are believed to be more at risk because they are more impulsive, as the diagnosis implies, making them more likely to make impetuous, ill-fated decisions.

FEMALE HORMONES AND ADHD

I discovered the hard way just how much female sex hormones affect ADHD—like the *I went to five different doctors before anyone told me* hard way. So let me tell you what I learned so you don't have to go through it too.

It was a Tuesday in the middle of the winter, two years before I was diagnosed with ADHD, when I parked my car outside the hospital and headed to the neurology department. I was there because I had complained to my primary care doctor about brain fog, memory lapses, and changes in my penmanship. My right hand wasn't totally steady either when I had to do anything with fine motor skills, like thread a needle or button a blouse. As I watched an elderly woman in the waiting room pull herself up with her walker, I panicked. Always the optimist and in true ADHD fashion, I hadn't thought about the possibility that I could have Parkinson's disease or something more serious, which explained why I showed up to this appointment alone.

"Tracy Otsuka?" The nurse interrupted my fear-filled daydream. "The doctor is ready to see you." She led me to a small, windowless examination room and closed the door behind her. *She's going to tell me I have Parkinson's*, I'd tell myself one second, followed by *Don't be ridiculous* the next second. The doorknob clicked, and the neurologist walked in. She started by asking me a bunch of questions about my symptoms, then tested my muscle strength and watched me walk up and down the hall several times. Back in the examination room, I sat nervously as she wrote. Looking up with a reassuring smile, she said, "I don't think you have Parkinson's, but let's get an MRI just to confirm it."

When I finally got the MRI results—negative for any degenerative cognitive condition—I felt like I had won the lottery. But while I was elated, the results didn't help me identify what was causing my brain fog, memory lapses, and the feeling of overwhelm that literally left me physically spinning. I was also struggling to read contracts—something I was well-trained to do as a lawyer—and had recently left a client's home with all their doors and windows wide open (all of them) because my brain was so checked out. At the same time, I couldn't relax mentally until all my work was done, which meant I had begun routinely taking phone calls at all hours of the evening, during the weekend, and even once at a friend's birthday dinner, where I was the only guest.

After the neurologist, I went back to my primary care doctor, who told me to see my gynecologist because I was now "a woman of a certain age" and my symptoms could be related to perimenopause (turns out, she was partially onto something). My gynecologist suggested I try hormone replacement therapy, but after the medication made me feel bloated, sluggish, and a hundred years old, I went to see a hormone specialist. That specialist told me it was my thyroid (it wasn't) and recommended a prescription drug and hundreds of dollars of supplements, all of which made me so anxious that one afternoon after a minor problem, I had to talk myself out of smashing my brand-new iPhone on my patio. I decided instead to meet with a psychologist. "Do I have anxiety?" I asked. "And what about this feeling of malaise? I've never felt like this ever. I'm used to running circles around everyone, but I no longer even know where the circles are."

"You're fine. It's likely just an Asian thing," the psychologist, who was Chinese American, told me in reference to my Japanese American heritage. "As Asians, we have such high expectations, and as we get older, the bloom comes off the rose and nothing is as exciting as it used to be. What if you just accepted that?"

What ridiculous advice is this? It sounded a bit like my son's doctor, who advised my husband and me to reduce Markus's expectations so he wouldn't be disappointed in life. No one had been right about anything yet, so I set out on my own quest to figure it out myself. Six months later, I was diagnosed with ADHD, and the condition's symptoms were only now flaring because I was entering perimenopause.

Unfortunately, very little research has been conducted to date on how female sex hormones affect ADHD, in part because women have been historically excluded from clinical trials investigating new drugs and medical treatment and also because most ADHD research has been done on prepubescent boys. What we do know is that the hormonal fluctuations we experience as part of our monthly menstrual cycle, as well as over the course of our lifetime, do in fact influence ADHD symptoms and the medications commonly used to treat the condition.

Let's start with the good news: Estrogen increases levels of the feel-good brain chemicals serotonin and dopamine, both of which can improve mood, concentration, motivation, the ability to sleep, and emotional regulation. Higher estrogen levels are also associated with increased cognitive and executive function and may even improve the efficacy of ADHD medications. In short, estrogen seems to be a good thing for women with ADHD.

> ## *In short, estrogen seems to be a good thing for women with ADHD.*

The problem, however, is that our estrogen levels aren't always high—they plummet during the last two weeks of our monthly menstrual cycle and during perimenopause and menopause. When estrogen levels are low, it can create a double whammy for ADHD women already struggling with impaired executive function and low dopamine levels. This is why ADHD women during times of lower estrogen may experience intensified symptoms like difficulty concentrating, poor memory, and impaired emotional regulation, in addition to all the other symptoms associated with low estrogen, including depression, anxiety, moodiness, and flagging energy. ADHD women are also more vulnerable to hormone-related mood disorders like premenstrual dysphoric disorder (PMDD)—a severe version of PMS—as well as postpartum depression.

Lower estrogen levels during perimenopause and menopause may also explain why so many women suffer from anxiety, depression, sleep difficulties, inattention, and increased problems with working memory and verbal fluency during these hormonal transitions, whether or not they have ADHD. One survey of 1,500 women with ADHD found that 94 percent felt their symptoms intensified during perimenopause and menopause. If this sounds familiar, speak with your doctor about possible treatment options, including nonpharmaceutical interventions like exercise and nutritional changes.

The impact of estrogen loss during menopause is not a given, however. Some women struggle with it mightily while others do not. Unfortunately, we just don't know how many ADHD women are impacted by menopause because no research exists on the phenomenon.

Here's another trick out of the ADHD playbook that I learned from firsthand experience, as well as after speaking with hundreds of women as an ADHD coach: many women aren't diagnosed with the condition until they go through perimenopause or menopause. While we may experience some ADHD symptoms beforehand, we're able to manage just fine until our estrogen levels drop precipitously. I call this "midlife onset ADHD." I suspect many women, like me, have had ADHD symptoms since puberty but didn't seek professional help until later in life, as their symptoms became more pronounced or problematic. What makes the puzzle even more complicated is that menopause symptoms like forgetfulness, mood swings, and sleep problems overlap with ADHD symptoms.

Regardless, it's critical for ADHD women to know that our sex hormones, primarily estrogen, affect our dopamine levels and overall symptom patterns. When we're aware of why we may be struggling to a greater degree at certain times of the month or in a specific period of our lives, we can mitigate the shame that oftentimes accompanies these struggles. If we can accept that our brain's biology, not a character flaw or moral failing, is driving our symptoms, we can stop or limit the self-blaming and -berating. We can also reschedule important meetings or wait to make major life decisions, for example, so that they don't occur during the last week or two before our period, when possible.

HORMONAL SOLUTIONS FOR ADHD WOMEN

If you feel you're suffering from aggravated symptoms during low estrogen times of your monthly cycle, the following interventions may help by increasing your sense of agency and control, boosting dopamine and serotonin levels, or calming your nervous system:

- Cognitive behavioral therapy

- Mindfulness and meditation

- Other nonpharmaceutical interventions like exercise, sleep, and hydration

- Hormone replacement therapy

- Low dose of estrogen-only medication

- Changes in stimulant medication dependent on cycle or life transition

- Antidepressants to treat low mood

Talk with your ADHD treatment team to learn more.

Turning ADHD Traits into Superpowers

When I was a young lawyer, I had a short and truly memorable conversation with a colleague. She was upset because she had agreed to meet a friend for dinner, and he had gone ahead and made a reservation at a restaurant she'd never been to before, without consulting her. This, in her opinion, was both rude and selfish. Here's how it went:

"Everything always has to be his way!" my colleague whined.

I saw her point but didn't agree. "It could have been worse: He could have made a reservation somewhere you have been and don't like," I countered. "And who knows? The place he just booked could end up being your favorite new restaurant! Besides, you should be grateful that you didn't have to do the work of picking a place and booking a table."

My colleague looked at me and rolled her eyes—this wasn't the first time I'd responded to one of her complaints with overwhelming optimism. "You're so irritating!" she quipped. "Why do you always have to make lemonade out of lemons?"

For as long as I can remember, I've been an optimist, which, as it turns out, is a common trait among people with ADHD. While our optimism can sometimes cause us to be unrealistic, it can also help us turn everything from a friend's dinner reservation to our issues with ADHD into things to embrace rather than circumstances to get upset about. When we tap into it, our optimism can often lower our stress, increase our enjoyment of life in general, and help us keep searching for solutions when others give up. Our optimism is also one of our many ADHD superpowers.

Don't get me wrong. As much as I'm an optimist, I'm also a realist. If I could take only the ADHD traits I consider to be superpowers while leaving behind the ones that don't serve me, you better believe that I would—in a heartbeat. I'd love a working memory, for example, that lets me memorize just one phone number or email address. Or the ability to speak without jumping from tangent to tangent. And don't get me started on anyone who starts a conversation with "my uncle's brother-in-law's niece": Without a whiteboard and a marker, my nonlinear brain won't be able to figure out who this person is.

But I know that my brain isn't defective: it's just different. The better I understand my brain and develop strategies that work with it rather than against it, the happier and more successful I am.

Our optimism is also one of our many ADHD superpowers.

Perhaps the best description for ADHD I've heard comes from a book written by Drs. Edward M. Hallowell and John Ratey, two of the world's leading experts on ADHD: "ADHD is a term that describes a way of being in the world. It is neither entirely a disorder nor entirely an asset. It is an array of traits specific to a unique kind of mind. It can be an advantage or a curse, depending on how a person manages it."

This last sentence can help overhaul your life: *ADHD can be an advantage or a curse, depending on how a person manages it.* In other words, when you understand that your ADHD traits can be advantages and strengths, you have the power to turn your ADHD into an opportunity that you may not know you have. Throughout this book, I'm going to show you exactly how to do this by outlining strategies to help you better manage your ADHD. First, though, let's talk about how to start to see your ADHD traits as advantages rather than impediments.

WE MAY BE MORE CREATIVE AND BETTER ABLE TO PROBLEM SOLVE

If you have ADHD, you likely already know that your brain works differently than those without the condition—why ADHDers are referred to as "neurodivergent." But this doesn't mean our cognitive function is insufficient. At times, it can be exceptional. Unlike neurotypical folks, those of us with ADHD are more able to think outside the box. Research shows that people who are easily distracted, hyperactive, or impulsive—all ADHD traits—are more creative. In fact, "creativity is just impulsivity gone right," according to Dr. Hallowell.

Creativity doesn't only mean being good at the arts or at coming up with new ideas. We can also be creative in how we approach tasks, situations, and problems. Studies show that those of us with ADHD are better at tasks that require divergent thinking, which is a type of thinking that helps us generate multiple ideas or solutions around one topic or problem. This is one way our ADHD brains can help us solve problems, troubleshoot, and be resourceful.

Many women with ADHD have chosen creative fields in which they can make use of their imaginative minds. One of these women, Fran, who joined my ADHD for Smart Ass Women Facebook group, told me she got Cs, Ds, and even Fs in school in every subject but art, even though she knew she was smart. When she was young, while other kids were watching TV or talking on the phone in their free time, Fran was reading medical books, teaching herself shorthand, and writing pretend scripts for TV shows. She's now an award-winning actor, writer, producer, and director of theater, film, television, and digital media.

"Creativity is about how you think your way around issues," said Fran. "We think faster and can see ahead more than other people can. Sometimes, it's frustrating because I've already solved the problem, and while others are catching up, I'm onto the next issue. I have this ability to fast-forward in my head and see whether it's going to fail or not, which is a skill that I think all people with ADHD have."

WHEN WE'RE INTERESTED IN SOMETHING, WE CAN OFTENTIMES GET THINGS DONE MORE EFFECTIVELY AND EFFICIENTLY

While we can be easily distracted at times, those of us with ADHD can also laser-focus on the things we're interested in so effectively and intensely that fifteen minutes suddenly turns into five hours. This is our ability to hyperfocus. Hyperfocusing can derail us at times, but it also helps us get in the zone more quickly and efficiently so that we can build a business, learn a new skill or hobby faster than most, and get tasks done. The only caveat is that we must be interested in something to be able to hyperfocus on it. That's because our ADHD brains are wired for interest, not information. While neurotypical people are more easily able to concentrate on subjects or projects that they're interested in, studies show that they don't tend to hyperfocus like people with ADHD regularly do.

If you're able to identify and home in on what interests you, this can be a superpower. You can find hobbies, shape tasks, realign your career path, or launch a new business or side hustle that leverages those interests, thereby channeling your ability to hyperfocus and work effectively. You can also tactically choose not to hyperfocus on a task, hobby, or other activity before bed, meals, work, or a workout, so that it doesn't interfere with your sleep, nutrition, job, or other everyday responsibilities or acts of self-care.

WE MAY BE MORE DRIVEN

When I was first told that I had ADHD, I questioned whether the diagnosis was accurate. Sure, I struggled with time, working memory, and procrastination, but I was also so driven, ambitious, entrepreneurial, and tenacious. And when I pop into hyperfocus, there's no stopping me. At the same time, I struggle to relax—you'll never see me doing nothing, not even on the beach while on vacation. So how could I have ADHD if I was always doing, working, and building?

What clinched my willingness to claim my ADHD diagnosis was when I discovered that hyperactivity can lead to extreme restlessness and feelings of always being on the go, as if driven by a motor. Being driven is a form of hyperactivity, which makes many of us with ADHD classic go-getters. Maybe there are times we should give up, but we don't. We often see possibilities where others only see problems.

I met Raquel when she signed up for my online program Your ADHD Brain Is A-OK. She has a driven, go-getter attitude, propelled by her hyperactivity. In college, she discovered that she loved to travel so much that she went on a moneymaking mission to fund her trips while also taking a full course load. She already had a part-time job on campus but was looking to make some serious cash, and quickly. She remembered that she had helped to promote a friend's band in high school and was good at it, so she decided to call the biggest music promoter in her area. That's when he told Raquel that he had scheduled a two-day concert but couldn't book the bands for personal reasons, and so she agreed to take over even with no formal experience or training.

When Raquel was done, she had booked twenty-one bands,

extending the duration of the music festival to four days to accommodate them all. "No one could believe it and that included me!" she recalled. "I had bands I loved that were calling me. I'd answer the phone in a calm, professional manner, then jump up and down in my dorm room, which was now the concert hotline. MTV even covered that festival!" Even better, she earned enough money through concert promoting to spend summers traveling throughout her time in college. She also held down a campus job. And graduated summa cum laude! She hyperfocused on her travel goals and fueled her tenacity with hyperactivity that allowed her dreams to come true.

WE MAY TAKE MORE RISKS IN OUR CAREER AND LIVES AT LARGE

Numerous studies have found that those with ADHD are more likely to engage in risky behavior when it comes to decisions around sex, finances, substances, and even our own safety. Researchers believe we're more likely to take risks because we can be impulsive but also because we may overestimate the payoff of our decision. One study published in the *Journal of Attention Disorders*, for example, asked nearly one hundred adults with ADHD to fill out questionnaires about risk. When participants perceived a greater benefit to a risky decision, they were more likely to opt for it despite the outcome.

But being more likely to take risks isn't always a bad thing. When we apply our impulsive tendencies to our careers, relationships, hobbies, or other positive interests or challenges, the trait is a bonus. I know so many successful ADHD women who have challenged themselves in roles that other women might have shied away from. Look at Pulitzer Prize–winning journalist Katherine Ellison, who routinely put her life on the line to cover human rights violations and other atrocities. Or Olympic gold medalist Cammi Granato, who chose to pursue a gender atypical sport—hockey—and became one of the best in the world.

In my work as an ADHD coach, I've collaborated with so many incredible women who have taken big risks to challenge themselves, the status quo, or both. One of these women is Rene, a guest on my podcast who is a certified canine behavior consultant, meaning that she helps train aggressive dogs. When we first met, I asked her how she chose this career. "I had just gotten out of the army and was trying to rehabilitate pound dogs into service dogs for veterans with PTSD—except I didn't realize what I didn't know," she said. "One day I ended up in the middle of a seven-dog pit bull pack fight in my living room."

The next week, when Rene met with a canine trainer who was helping her, he noticed she was riddled with bite marks from the dogs. "The trainer told me right then and there that I had two choices," Rene recalled. "One, I could euthanize the dogs. Or two, I could become an aggression expert. So I became an aggression expert."

Rene and other impulsive ADHD women are attracted to the challenge of overcoming frightening tasks or ambitious situations. She did not let fear stand in her way. This trait can also help us handle crises better than those without ADHD for several reasons. Imaging studies show that people with ADHD produce more relaxing theta brain waves than the neurotypical population, which helps our brains stay calm and focused in a crisis. We can also hyperfocus on a task at hand and come up with nonlinear solutions that neurotypical people might not be able to consider in the moment.

WE CAN BE NONCONFORMISTS

Whether or not we take risks, many of us with ADHD follow the beat of our own drum, refusing to do things the "normal" way. We already think differently, and most of those with ADHD I've worked with don't like to follow rules—especially rules for rules' sake. It's no surprise then that people with ADHD also have a higher likelihood of developing oppositional defiant disorder (ODD), a behavioral disorder marked by disobedience, and conduct disorder (CD), which occurs when someone doesn't adhere to traditional social conduct. Yet even in the absence of these disorders (which are more common in ADHD men), many women with ADHD have a lower tolerance for repetitiveness and monotony. And if we grew up feeling different or separate for any reason—whether we had a different learning style in school than the other kids, for example, or we got easily distracted during after-school activities, or we couldn't remember or follow directions like most of our friends—we may have felt like an "outsider." Research that has interviewed people with ADHD has found many of us end up adopting an "outsider's identity," meaning we feel as though we don't fit into the mainstream. This outsider's identity can also propel many of us to become nonconformists: if we don't fit in, we'd rather embrace and even celebrate our identity outside the mainstream.

But being a nonconformist can be a great thing. Multiple studies, for example, show that being a nonconformist in the workplace can help spark innovation, improve performance, and increase personal status. Outside the office, nonconformity can boost our self-efficacy and well-being, and may even make us sexier to other people, as per one survey. American conservationist Aldo Leopold once said that nonconformity is "the highest evolutionary attainment of social animals." Right on!

One ADHD maverick whom I met as a guest on my podcast is Taylor, a well-known immigration attorney who was diagnosed with ADHD after she started law school. What I love about Taylor is that she began to practice law six years before officially becoming an attorney, thanks to a loophole in the federal law that lets those with an alternative law license practice immigration law as an accredited representative. Taylor was so passionate about helping people that she couldn't follow the traditional path that most take to become an attorney.

Like Taylor, when those of us with ADHD can accept and get comfortable being ourselves, speaking our minds, and being outsiders, we're often able to happily step into our true passions.

WE WILL OFTEN DO BIG, HARD THINGS

When Jayne was young, she didn't believe she could do much of anything. She struggled so much in school that she convinced herself that she was "just a lazy, bad kid." She was a fourteen-year-old dropout. Fast-forward to when, through my podcast, I met Jayne as an adult. The high school dropout is now the owner of two successful hair salons, the founder of an international hair-styling educational business, and the brains behind a successful Instagram account. Even though her academic experience led her to believe that she wasn't very smart, she invented a new way of cutting hair into shags that drew a cult following. In a matter of just a few years, Jayne became a sought-after hair educator traveling by private jet. When the pandemic hit, instead of closing her salons like many others did during lockdown, she intelligently began to teach people how to successfully cut their own hair at home, which won her worldwide renown. Thousands of students now routinely show up for her sold-out hair-cutting classes.

"It actually makes me cry because, for so many years, I just beat myself up," Jayne lamented, comparing her current success to her early struggles. "The mere idea of opening a piece of mail, reading it, following the directions, writing a check, putting a stamp on it, and putting it in the mailbox felt so far beyond my ability. It gave me so much stress that I would put it off and put it off and put it off until my car [would be] towed or my electricity would get turned off. I thought I was just an irresponsible adult."

Turns out, Jayne wasn't irresponsible, she just faced the same struggles that I've heard so many other ADHD women have faced. They find it difficult to do the small things in life like paying a bill, but they have no problem accomplishing big feats, like creating a brand-new business plan or continually reinventing themselves.

As we've already discussed, the key to our success is our interest. When we're interested, like Jayne was in hair styling, we can hyper-focus on our passions and do even seemingly impossible things.

WE ARE OFTEN MORE EMPATHETIC

When I was young, my family watched Disney movies together every Sunday evening. All these movies upset me: the baby deer who lost its mother, the father who had to leave his family, the cat who died. I was traumatized by it all.

As a teenager, I couldn't see scary movies with my friends. When I did show up, I'd always hide behind my hands or the popcorn bag, with a huge knot in my stomach. When we decided to go see *The Shining*, I chickened out at the box office, calling my mom at the last minute to come pick me up. Today, I haven't seen classic movies about human suffering like *Schindler's List*, *12 Years a Slave*, and *Slumdog Millionaire* because I know I'll react poorly. In fact, I joke that if a movie wins an Oscar and is actually worth seeing, I haven't seen it—I'm just too sensitive. But if we met, I bet that you would never describe me as sensitive. I'm irreverent and have no trouble speaking my mind.

No matter our outward personality, hypersensitivity is a common trait among people with ADHD. Those of us who are hypersensitive can be more susceptible to physical stimuli (like flashing lights, itchy fabrics, and loud noises) and emotional stimuli (like other people's feelings, human suffering, or media designed to evoke an emotional response).

Researchers also believe that ADHD women are more likely to struggle with hypersensitivities like sensory overload, which occurs when we receive more input from our senses than our brains can process. You see, our ADHD brains don't filter information in the same way as most neurotypical brains. Similar to how we might find it difficult to edit what comes out of our mouths at times, we may also have a tough time screening the onslaught of information around us. When everything feels important, we can end up paying attention to all of it, taking in everything we see, smell, touch, hear, and feel, as well as taking in other people's emotions.

But taking in or feeling others' emotions isn't always a bad thing, especially when we're aware of our tendency to do so. Many experts believe people with ADHD are more empathetic than those without the condition, meaning that we're better able to feel and relate to others' emotions. Empathy is not only critical to having healthy relationships, but it can also help us be better partners, parents, daughters, friends, managers, entrepreneurs, and negotiators, as we're able to see and understand the inner worlds of those around us.

Recently, I asked Taylor, the immigration lawyer who came on my podcast, how she can do the work she does—helping asylum-seeking families who are often faced with unbelievable hardship, possible separation from their loved ones, and constant racial discrimination—if she's so empathetic. She responded, "I'm very empathetic in a way that others are often not. I can feel my clients' emotions, and this makes me a better advocate for them."

WE TEND TO BE JUSTICE SENSITIVE

Taylor's story points me to another one of our ADHD superpowers: We fight for others. Studies show that justice sensitivity, or the tendency to notice wrongdoing and have a more visceral reaction to perceived injustice, is more pronounced in people with ADHD, especially in those with the inattentive subtype.

Fran, the award-winning film writer, producer, and director who tapped into her own creativity to become successful despite a history of poor academics, created a rape activist initiative called Believe Women that championed the Bill Cosby survivors. Emerald, the therapist from chapter 3 who channeled her strengths to realize that she was an amazing mother and wife, is a social activist for BIPOC communities. And Taylor noted she chose her profession exactly because she is so justice sensitive: "I cry in court sometimes, which is very embarrassing, but the intensity and importance of what I'm doing also drives and motivates me. I feel this extreme need to do the work and to continue to pursue justice."

WE MAY BE MORE INTUITIVE

I've always had the ability to walk into a room and know what's going on without hearing a word. That's because I can read the energy of those around me. While the concept of intuition may sound woo-woo to some, it's been researched and documented by scientists for decades, with studies showing that we often improve our decision-making when we rely on our intuition.

Intuition is that gut feeling you get about a person, event, situation, or choice. According to experts, people with ADHD are oftentimes more intuitive than neurotypical people. Our brains tend to focus on the connections or relationships between things rather than on specific bits of information, which helps us to see a more comprehensive picture of what's going on around us. We also tend to lean on our intuition for decision-making because our executive function isn't all that great. Our tendency to be hypersensitive can also increase our intuitive powers.

In my work as an ADHD coach, I've met many successful psychiatrists, psychologists, therapists, and personal development coaches with ADHD who use the trait to intuit how others feel, which helps them fill in the blanks for all the things left unsaid. Isabelle is an ADHD coach and one of the community mentors for my online group Your ADHD Brain Is A-OK. "I have learned over time to trust my intuition," she observed after being diagnosed with ADHD at fifty-nine. "I can tell the stressed people, the happy people, and the nervous people. I also notice if someone moves their hand to the right every time they're not telling the truth or how they always look to the left when I say something that makes them uncomfortable."

People with ADHD are oftentimes more intuitive than neurotypical people. Our brains tend to focus on the connections or relationships between things rather than on specific bits of information.

When I discovered the link between intuition and ADHD, I identified so strongly with the trait that I stopped second-guessing myself and all my decisions, realizing that my intuition would help guide me to make the right choices. I also stopped trying so hard to make myself understood once I knew that many around me couldn't see or feel everything that I saw and felt. I began to truly trust and honor my intuition. You can too. When we learn to quiet our minds and listen to our bodies, we are better able to connect to our inner rudders and become our own best guides.

5

How to Find Yourself, Your Passions, and Your Purpose

If you have ADHD, your path through life may feel all over the place, not only to others but also to yourself. You're not alone. Many people with ADHD don't follow a linear life path. Instead, we zigzag through transitions or from job to job, or we stay in the same job but do so in a nontraditional way. This can be true of people without ADHD, of course, but in my experience, those of us with the condition are more likely to continually question ourselves and others about what we want or should do with our lives, both professionally and personally.

I grappled with these questions for decades. While I've always been ambitious and driven, I spent years perpetually worried that I would never live up to my potential. I changed jobs and directions many times, going all-in on a path I found exciting for a few years before growing bored and getting distracted by a brighter, shinier idea. I knew I wanted kids, but there was so much life I wanted to experience that I couldn't decide when I should become a mom. When I left law, I started a women's wear company, even though I had no training or experience in fashion. After I had children, I worked in traditional real estate, then bounced to nontraditional real estate, partnering with banks to sell distressed properties, which was risky and often dangerous but more exciting to me than selling residential homes still owned by the homeowner. It took me decades before I finally found my true passion and purpose: helping ADHD women on their paths of self-discovery and self-actualization.

Before I finally found my purpose, I had read numerous self-help books, took countless personality tests, and hired a career counselor and a life coach. But none of this helped me connect the dots. I was interested in so many things. And quite competent when I applied myself. But as I learned, just because we're good at something doesn't always mean we should pursue it.

Most everyone wants to live a life of meaning and purpose. But for those of us with differently wired brains, our drive for meaning and purpose may be more pronounced—according to psychiatrists, we experience life more passionately than neurotypical people do. This is in part because our brains don't filter out sensory information as well as neurotypical folks, and many of us are always thinking, noticing, and moving, as our brains never rest, resulting in a full-on, nonstop sensory experience. As I came to know more ADHD women, I saw this over and over again to the point where I decided to do my own anecdotal research. I polled women in my ADHD Facebook group asking if they felt that they needed to live a life of meaning and believed that they cared more about living up to their potential than their neurotypical peers did. Of the 159 respondents, 98 percent believed they cared more about fulfilling their potential and purpose than those without ADHD.

To help me personally clarify who I really was and what was really important to me, I developed the six-step program you'll find in the following pages. Once I realized how well it worked, I broadened it and eventually had it patented to help other women do the same. This program is designed to help you, the reader with ADHD, determine your personal values, strengths, skills, passions, and purpose. The program will help you develop a plan to create the life you want by leveraging these attributes.

Getting clear on who you are by identifying your values, strengths, skills, passions, and purpose is also critical to helping you feel you're living a life of meaning, allowing you to make major life decisions based on who *you* truly are. You may have climbed the highest tree, but if you're in the wrong forest, you likely won't feel happy or fulfilled (and may not even know why). But if you're able to identify your values, strengths, skills, passions, and purpose, you can pursue work, activities, or ambitions that align with who you truly are. Plus, when we're interested and passionate about what we're doing or pursuing, we can leverage our ADHD brains to be successful by using our ability to hyperfocus.

The following six steps have been used by hundreds of ADHD women to help them build a life of meaning and purpose. Take your time with these steps, journaling your answers to help you remember them.

1. FIND WHAT YOU VALUE

Values are the principles, beliefs, and ideas that are important to you. Your values will usually drive your personal and professional decisions, influence your relationships, and can help you understand your ambitions and dreams.

While most of us think we know our values, many of us can end up adopting and following values that more closely align with those of our family, friends, or community. For those of us with ADHD, we're more likely to do so because we stopped trusting ourselves after being told for years that our way is the wrong way. But when we live other people's values, we live other people's lives, which won't make us feel fulfilled, happy, or satisfied.

Tonya, one of my students, was raised in a religious family that rejected science. When Tonya started examining what was important to her, she discovered how much she loved science. As a child, she was always outside in nature, lying in the grass or gazing up at the stars. Tonya valued nature because it generated positive emotions—a common experience among many people with ADHD, in part because spending time in nature has been shown to reduce stress for anyone and limit ADHD symptoms.

Unfortunately for Tonya, she adhered to her parents' beliefs even into adulthood, and instead of pursuing her interest in science or working in the natural world, she wasted years in retail without ever understanding why she was so unhappy. After she got clear on what was important to her and her own well-being, though, she finally gained the confidence to go to college and study astronomy.

Getting clear on what is important and meaningful to you can help eliminate second-guessing your track in life. How to identify what you value, though? Consider the following list of values, and for each one, think about whether you always value, often value, sometimes value, or never value it:

Adventure	Fun
Appreciation	Gratitude
Authenticity	Honesty
Beauty	Humor
Connection	Intuition
Creativity	Justice
Curiosity	Kindness
Excellence	Living to potential
Fairness	Nature
Family	Optimism
Fitness	Originality
Freedom	Simplicity

The values you identify as "always value" represent the principles, beliefs, and ideas most important to you. They represent what you stand for.

Another way to determine what you value is to think about how you plan to spend your time and money. Sometimes, this can help illustrate a value you think you have but aren't following. For example, you may believe that achieving financial success will lead to lasting happiness, that a formal education is important, or that family is one of your highest priorities, but if you put your friends and work first, you may not value spending time with family as much as you think. You may also find it helpful to identify what you *don't* value by asking yourself what you struggle to accomplish in a timely manner. These activities or pursuits may represent things that aren't important to you but that you may have been socialized to believe are of value.

2. KNOW YOUR CHARACTER STRENGTHS

Many of us with ADHD can identify our weaknesses, but we don't know or can't recognize our strengths. Some of us may even believe that we don't have any strengths. Hogwash! We all have strengths! Identifying your signature character strengths will help you better live by your values.

Character strengths are the positive parts of you and your personality. Creativity, courage, and love are qualities that other people admire and respect. Note: The difference between a value and a character strength is that a value is what you hold important while a character strength is a quality that comes naturally to you. You may not be living your values right now, but you are always using your character strengths.

When you show or use your character strengths, they create positive emotions in and around you. And when who you are (your values) aligns with what you do and how you act (your signature character strengths), you're more likely to be happier and feel more inspired.

A simple way to identify your character strengths is by taking the VIA Character Strengths Survey offered by the VIA Institute on Character, a nonprofit organization that provides resources and spearheads research on character strengths. You can access the website and take the organization's ten-minute survey completely free of cost. I encourage all my students to take the VIA test, and many tell me the insight they gained by doing so has helped them better live their values. Like values, our character strengths can change over time depending on what's going on in our lives, which is why you may want to take the test every several years.

3. GET CLEAR ON YOUR TALENTS AND SKILLS

Talents are the activities, hobbies, or abilities for which you have a natural gift. Talents become skills when you dedicate time to practicing or pursuing them. For example, you can have a natural talent for piano or dance, but if you don't practice, you won't build your skills.

Oftentimes, we struggle to see our talents and skills because we think that we're not special, that everyone can do what we do. This prevents us from capitalizing on our superpowers. Alicia, a member of my A-OK program, described herself as "mediocre" when we first met, so I asked her to put together a list of her talents and skills. When she couldn't come up with anything, she asked her mother for help, who reminded her that she had published four novels, was ten units away from completing a degree in psychology, and worked as a research assistant to a professor who adored her. She also has three young kids, is highly creative, a great cook, and loves people.

Alicia is a perfect example of what happens when you're good at a lot: nothing you do seems special. This is why I encouraged her to write down all her accomplishments so that she could see exactly how incredible she is. Because many of us with ADHD struggle with working memory, we can also forget the many talents and skills we have.

To identify your talents and skills, consider which aptitudes or abilities come naturally to you and which you may be better at than most people. If you're like Alicia and struggle to recognize your talents and skills, ask your parents or close friends to weigh in. Your talents and skills can include things like athletic prowess, entrepreneurial instincts, or the ability to see others' potential, along with what you may have identified as one of your values or signature character strengths like creativity, connection, intuition, or curiosity. The more overlap between your values, signature character strengths, and natural talents or skills, the more you know what to lean in to.

4. FIND YOUR PASSIONS

For those of us with ADHD, identifying our passions is crucial. Since our brains are wired for interest, when we're able to pursue our passions, we generate positive emotion, pop more easily into hyperfocus, and are able to succeed beyond our wildest dreams. If we're not pursuing what we're passionate about, however, we may feel distracted, bored, and as though we're not reaching our full potential, and switch from hobby to hobby or job to job, limiting our potential for success.

Passions come from within. They are what you love to do, could do all day, every day, are good at doing, or are willing to make a fool out of yourself trying to be good at. To discover your passions, think about what you can do for hours on end that puts you in a flow state, where time just flies by.

As a child, Katelyn, a guest on my podcast, knew she was smart but still struggled in school. She had difficulty with reading and couldn't understand why. Somehow, she got herself to college. The first two years of university were challenging until Katelyn figured out that she was passionate about special education and wanted to help students like herself learn how to read so they didn't have to go through what she had gone through. Identifying her passion and pursuing it allowed her to be successful. She graduated top of her class with a master's degree in special education and is now the author of a children's book on ADHD and the host of a podcast for kids with the condition.

Although Katelyn made a career out of her passion, you may find that your passions serve you better as hobbies. And sometimes the best way to remain passionate about something is to keep it as a hobby. Only you know what's best for you.

5. CHOOSE A PURPOSE

It's easy to assume that once you begin to practice your passion, you'll find happiness, joy, and meaning in life. But this is how you can end up putting all your stock in the passion basket only to discover years later that you're unhappy, despite doing something you love. This is where your purpose comes in.

For most of us, our purpose is one of our many passions that we can leverage to help others or further a cause that we care about. Our purpose may be helping other women in some way, for example, or taking steps to make our neighborhood, community, or school a better place, or working with animals or environmental causes. These kinds of purposes can help give our lives meaning and provide us with direction.

For many with ADHD, the purpose that motivates us the most is the one that allows us to help others who face the same struggles we did or do. By making our purpose personal, it can help provide meaning to our past and allow us to come to terms with and better appreciate ourselves. Katelyn is a good example: while her passion is special education, her purpose is helping children with ADHD learn to read and succeed in school.

If you're not sure what your purpose is, consider each stage of your life and write down what has made you joyful and proud of yourself.

Next, ask yourself what these joyful or proud moments have in common. Were you connecting with other people, doing something with animals, or furthering a cause of importance to you? This exercise can help provide clues.

I suggest choosing a purpose, then experimenting with how it feels to help others or be part of a greater cause in this way. By experimenting and not settling immediately on any one thing as your "life's purpose," you remove the intimidation factor. Our purpose can also grow in action, and if we begin to work within the neighborhood of our purpose, we can often find positive emotion, joy, and motivation to fine-tune it. I also believe that we don't need to search for our purpose: when we find it, we can step into it because it's always been there inside of us.

6. FIND THE OVERLAP BETWEEN YOUR VALUES, STRENGTHS, SKILLS, PASSIONS, AND PURPOSE

One of the best ways to make the right decisions for you in life is to pick the choice that converges with as many of your values, character strengths, talents/skills, passions, and purpose as possible. This overlap is where your intention and positive emotion will be greatest and where you'll best be able to connect who you are with what you're doing. When you find this overlap, write it down. Cherish it.

We don't need to search for our purpose: when we find it, we can step into it because it's always been there inside of us.

In the glow of a new idea, I can forget what I know about myself, which is why I developed a way to tidy my overactive brain and keep this information front and center. I listed my values, signature strengths, talents/skills, passions, and purpose on one piece of card stock and had it laminated. I call it my Intelligence Report, and I keep it in the top drawer of my desk, where I refer to it weekly. You could even frame yours and keep it on your desk!

When I'm trying to decide if I should entertain a new "idea," I pull out my Intelligence Report and ask myself, "Does this new idea integrate my top values, signature strengths, talents/skills, passions, and purpose? Or is it exciting to me only because it's new?" If the answer to the first question is no, I shut it down immediately. If the answer is yes, I may continue. Reminding myself of what's important to me calms my brain and helps me make connections I otherwise might not see. It also notifies me when I'm out of my lane and not living by my values, using my signature strengths, recognizing my skills, pursuing my passions, and following my purpose. It explains why I can second-guess myself and feel uninspired. And no matter what, it serves to connect my mind with who I am and what I want to do while reminding me that I am always my own best expert.

PART II

ENHANCING YOUR ADHD BRAIN WITH SMART ASS SOLUTIONS

Big Emotions, Trauma, and How to Better Manage Both

Dear Tracy,

I just want to say thank you! I am a thirty-year-old second-year law school student who was diagnosed with ADHD about a year ago. All my life I've been told that I'm too emotional, too sensitive, too much. It didn't matter what happened because even little things would send me into full-on panic mode. Out of nowhere, I would suddenly feel certain that everyone hated me. I'd feel criticized, rejected, and devastated. Even when I objectively knew that what I was thinking could not possibly be true, it didn't matter: My whole day would be ruined. There was nothing I could do to stop that feeling because I couldn't control it. Then the shame would set in, and I'd blame myself, thinking there was something wrong with me, wondering why I couldn't be like everyone else.

After listening to your podcasts, I've realized that I have suffered from rejection sensitive dysphoria [a condition found in many with ADHD] for my entire life. I'm so grateful that I finally know what it is, which has provided an amazing sense of relief. I'm now obsessed with finding my ADHD superpowers and reshaping the way I see myself. Could it be that all my feelings also explain my vast reserves of empathy? Could I turn my rejection sensitive dysphoria into one of my greatest strengths?

Thank you again,
Carly M.

I received this email from a listener after I published a podcast episode on rejection sensitive dysphoria (RSD). RSD is a condition that causes people to be acutely sensitive to what others say and do or to constantly be fearful of criticism or rejection. RSD is strongly associated with ADHD and one of the ways that emotional dysregulation, which often occurs alongside ADHD, can manifest. Emotional dysregulation is the inability to control, manage, or accept your emotions or emotional responses. I often say on my podcast that those of us with ADHD have big emotions, which is another way of describing emotional dysregulation: we may feel a lot, but we can't always control how we respond to what we feel. Our tendency toward emotional dysregulation doesn't just apply to our negative emotions: we may also have trouble controlling our response to positive emotions, which can lead us to be more easily excitable. I often joke that I'm a "gusher" because I'll rave, refer, and effervesce over a product or the work someone else does when I'm pleased.

Back to the email from Carly M. When I first read it, I thought about how relieved the women I work with always feel when they discover that their emotional dysregulation isn't due to a character flaw or moral failing but is because of their neurodivergent brain. Once their shame dissipates, they can then begin to explore strategies to help manage their emotions.

While there are many ADHD traits that we can and will discuss throughout this book, I'm dedicating a whole chapter to emotional dysregulation because it affects ADHD women so profoundly. Women have "significantly greater rates" of emotional dysregulation than men with the condition, which can cause us to ruminate, feel overwhelmed, or be ashamed of our emotional outbursts or other behaviors. Emotional dysregulation can also lead to RSD, depression, anxiety, and other mental health issues, and accounts for one reason why up to 80 percent of all people with ADHD are also diagnosed with a mood or personality disorder or substance abuse problem. Emotional dysregulation is such a common trait among people with ADHD that it was listed as a primary symptom for the condition in the American Psychiatric Association's diagnostic criteria for years. Now many experts want it added back to the diagnostic guidelines, including one group of researchers who found emotional dysregulation present in 73 percent of nearly 1,500 study participants with ADHD.

Of course, plenty of people without ADHD also struggle with emotional dysregulation. But those of us with ADHD are much more likely to be unable to self-regulate and control our emotional responses, even to what can seem like minor grievances or issues. One reason is because we respond to external stimuli more quickly, more intensely, and for longer periods of time than neurotypical folks. Our brain's prefrontal cortex, which helps control our executive function, like emotional regulation, works differently, and the connection between the prefrontal cortex and the amygdala, which helps drive our fear and stress responses, is also divergent from the norm. And while all humans have a natural negativity bias—that's our tendency to register and dwell on negative information more than we do on positive input—those of us with ADHD are more likely to have a negative bias memory, which means that we're more apt to remember the negative things people say and do. What's more, because many of us are also impulsive, we have less patience, have lower tolerance for frustrating events, and are more emotionally excitable in general. All of this creates and increases our risk of emotional dysregulation.

In the programs I offer, women ask me about emotion more than any other subject. Most aren't even aware that emotion is part of their ADHD or that RSD exists. When they discover that what they've been struggling with all along is a symptom of ADHD, they want to learn everything about it. For many women, it's a huge aha moment and a relief to learn that they're not broken or flawed—their brain biology is just different.

While I've come to a place where I rarely apologize or feel bad for my big emotions, I know many ADHD women do. But when these women discover that their outsize emotions are just another part of their ADHD and may even be responsible for some of their strengths like empathy or justice sensitivity, they can begin to reduce any feelings of shame.

Learning how emotional dysregulation can manifest in those of us with ADHD can help us lessen the stigma that we may suffer because of our big emotions. Later in this chapter, I'll provide strategies to help you better manage emotional dysregulation, trauma, and their emotional health sidekicks: depression, anxiety, and RSD.

THE ROLE OF TRAUMA IN ADHD

Before we talk about how emotional dysregulation manifests, I want to cover trauma, which can cause emotional dysregulation. Many of the women I've worked with who struggle the most with ADHD have experienced significant trauma, either as children or as adults. Many of them also have RSD.

Trauma is a broad term that includes life-altering events, like rape, incest, physical abuse, serious illness, and the incarceration or death of a loved one. But trauma also encompasses what psychologists call "small *t* traumas," including exposure to overly critical loved ones, repeated failure in school or at work, divorce and other relationship conflicts, and similar stresses. For our purposes, you can think of trauma as any stressful or upsetting event that takes a toll on a person—and what's traumatic to one individual may not be traumatic to another. Research reveals trauma can cause nervous system dysregulation, meaning our brain can't function properly, in addition to symptoms like difficulty concentrating, poor memory, anxiety, depression, poor sleep, impulsivity, and a tendency toward substance abuse—all symptoms of ADHD.

Exposure to stressful or upsetting experiences at any time in our lives can cause trauma, but the stress we experience when our brains are still developing is the most impactful. Childhood trauma includes whatever we experienced as kids, including those events that occurred when we were too young to even consciously recall. The human brain stores all memories from infancy onward, including those implicit memories. If we didn't feel safe in infancy or as young children for any reason, we may have difficulty regulating our emotions and emotional responses as adults. If our early care wasn't consistently stable and nurturing, we may have learned that others can't be relied upon or trusted, resulting in feelings of unworthiness—otherwise, our parents would have provided the care and safety we needed. These beliefs threaten to affect our self-esteem and emotional regulation skills for the rest of our lives. They can also become self-fulfilling prophecies: when we feel the world is unsafe, it impacts how we behave around others and how they ultimately respond.

The link between ADHD and trauma is complex. Some research shows that childhood trauma can increase the likelihood of developing ADHD while people with ADHD are more likely to have experienced childhood trauma. Thirty-four percent of women with ADHD, for example, say they were sexually abused before the age of eighteen while 44 percent of ADHD women say they experienced physical abuse in childhood compared to just 21 percent of neurotypical women. This link can be confusing, however, because the symptoms of trauma can mimic ADHD and impact the same areas of the brain affected by ADHD, causing similar traits like emotional dysregulation, lack of verbal and behavioral impulse control, and increased reactivity.

Untreated ADHD can also cause trauma. If you were constantly admonished for being lazy, disorganized, and stupid, that likely triggered feelings of shame and low self-worth, which take a toll. Unresolved, those feelings can last a lifetime.

Rumination

Rumination is one way that emotional dysregulation and trauma can manifest. ADHD women often show their hyperactivity by being active in their minds, constantly ruminating or dwelling on negative thoughts. While rumination is especially pronounced in women with the inattentive subtype, almost all women with ADHD whom I've met struggle with overthinking to some degree.

If you ruminate, your mind may resemble a hamster wheel, with the same thoughts going around and around in your head that don't help you get anywhere. Because many of us with ADHD also have the tendency to hyperfocus, once we start ruminating on a situation or something we said or did, it's hard to stop. Rumination has also been shown to increase the risk of depression, anxiety, insomnia, overeating, and substance abuse, in addition to other physical and mental health issues.

We'll talk more about rumination and specific strategies to limit it in chapter 7.

Depression and anxiety

Depression and anxiety are common side effects of emotional dysregulation, and women with ADHD are more likely than men to suffer from both. But it's not so straightforward. When we simultaneously have ADHD and emotional dysregulation, we can also be misdiagnosed with depression or anxiety instead of ADHD itself. Similarly, some of us with ADHD never get properly diagnosed with depression or anxiety because symptoms are blamed on our ADHD rather than a mood issue. What's more, feeling disorganized, constantly being late, and dealing with other executive function deficits can cause anxiety in itself.

If you suspect you may have depression or anxiety, it's important to see a trained mental health professional who understands ADHD and how emotional dysregulation can manifest. While ADHD, depression, and anxiety share similar symptoms, each is a separate condition that should be identified first, then treated independently.

Otherwise, you risk being prescribed antidepressant medication that you don't need, with possible side effects that you don't want. On page 85, I'll share tips to find qualified therapists who are also knowledgeable about ADHD.

Rejection sensitive dysphoria (RSD)

Do you feel extra sensitive to rejection, teasing, or criticism or always think you're a failure or deficient? You may have rejection sensitive dysphoria, or RSD. The condition isn't a clinical diagnosis. There's no official criteria that allow doctors to say if you have it, but its symptoms have been linked with ADHD. It's hard to pinpoint how many people with ADHD have RSD. Some experts believe up to 99 percent of teens and adults with ADHD are much more sensitive to rejection.

If you have RSD, you may perceive that others reject you or that you're disappointing them. The morning after a party, for example, you may feel certain you offended a friend, who now hates you. No matter what you actually said, you'll convince yourself that your friend is angry and the friendship is over. This is one way RSD affects our relationships. If you think people are always rejecting you, you will act as if they're rejecting you, which can turn your fears into self-fulfilling prophecies.

You may constantly feel disappointed in yourself, like you're a failure who can't attain the high standards or goals you set. As a result, many with RSD become perfectionists. A consequence of this perfectionism is that people may become reluctant to pursue their goals for fear of rejection or failure. They don't date, apply for jobs, or make new friends, limiting their potential.

I've spoken with countless women who were finally diagnosed with ADHD because they identified so strongly with RSD. Many of them are extremely bright and accomplished but felt perplexed as to why they couldn't reach their potential. Here's what I've heard from women in my Facebook groups about what it's like to live with RSD.

> *My RSD shows up as me being overly perfectionistic. I go after jobs that are "below" my abilities to make sure I don't screw it up or get rejected.*
>
> —ARTI

> *RSD has been the most debilitating part of my life. It has stopped me from committing to and trying things and going outside my comfort zone, all because I'm on high alert, waiting to be criticized.*
>
> —CHRISTINA

> *No matter what I do, I feel that it's never good enough. I always feel like I should have figured out a way to do more, whether it's with my work, home, kids, or something else.*
>
> —SUNNY

Obsessive-compulsive disorder (OCD)

Obsessive-compulsive disorder, or OCD, is a common neurological condition characterized by unwanted thoughts, obsessions, or the strong desire to do something repeatedly. Women are three times more likely to have OCD than men, and those with ADHD have an even greater probability of OCD than neurotypical people. While the common perception is that people with OCD are neurotic and spend hours on certain rituals like cleaning their homes, the condition can manifest in many ways, like obsessively tracking or counting things (think steps or social media likes), refusing to go outside their routines, or having to have everything "just right."

Body-focused repetitive behaviors

A condition associated with OCD is body-focused repetitive behaviors, in which you pick, pull, or tug at parts of your body to the point of physical damage, such as obsessively biting your nails or cuticles, picking at pimples or other skin imperfections, or pulling out your hair or eyelashes. Many of the ADHD women I work with engage in one or more of these behaviors, and experts suggest there's a link between the conditions. Many times, those with body-focused repetitive behaviors feel shame. "I bite the skin on my fingers even when it gets bloody," Taryne, part of my Facebook group, wrote. "It's ugly and burns sometimes when I wash my hands or cook—and it's worse when I'm stuck in traffic or really stressed."

While the cause of body-focused repetitive behaviors is unknown, most research suggests an inability to regulate emotions like anxiety. ADHD women also tell me that engaging in these behaviors helps them focus. Cognitive behavioral therapy and dialectical behavior therapy (a type of cognitive behavioral therapy that focuses on accepting difficult emotions, as we'll discuss later in this chapter) have been shown to help treat the condition. Chewing gum (see page 83) can also distract you from engaging in these behaviors.

Oppositional defiant disorder (ODD)

While males are more likely than females to be diagnosed with oppositional defiant disorder, or ODD, new research shows that oppositional defiant disorder—marked by angry, argumentative, defiant, or vindictive behavior that occurs for at least six months—is also common among girls and women, especially those with ADHD: one study found 42 percent of girls with ADHD had ODD compared to just 5 percent of girls without ADHD. Adults with the condition may be short-tempered or defensive, tend to blame others, and defy rules.

Borderline personality disorder

Borderline personality disorder severely impacts one's ability to regulate emotions. Women with the disorder have an intense fear of abandonment and don't easily tolerate being alone. At the same time, they often push people away with bouts of explosive anger, impulsiveness, and mood swings. This can lead to unstable relationships, self-destructive behaviors, and self-harm. They may also struggle with rejection sensitive dysphoria, which can cause them to slip into a cycle of sabotage-and-amend within their relationships.

Borderline personality disorder is diagnosed more frequently in women than men, even though research suggests that the condition exists equally in both sexes. ADHD and borderline personality disorder also share symptoms, like impulsivity, inattention, and emotional dysregulation, which can complicate a diagnosis for either. Many with borderline personality disorder also have a history of trauma, which is true of ADHD.

Dialectical behavior therapy, a type of cognitive behavioral therapy that is designed to help people manage intense emotions (see page 81), is often viewed as the gold standard to help people with borderline personality disorder manage emotional dysregulation.

Bipolar disorder

Bipolar disorder is a mental health condition that causes extreme mood swings, mania followed by periods of deep depression, trouble with concentration, and the inability to make decisions and complete everyday tasks. In most people, bipolar disorder develops in their late teens or early adulthood, and the condition affects both men and women equally. Just like ADHD, there is no blood test or standard exam to confirm a bipolar diagnosis.

Up to 20 percent of people with ADHD have bipolar disorder. The two conditions have overlapping symptoms, like emotional dysregulation, impulsivity, inattention, and mood swings, which can lead to misdiagnosis. In my experience, women are often misdiagnosed with bipolar disorder when, in reality, they have ADHD.

This is exactly what happened to Fran, our award-winning film writer, director, and producer who forged her own creative path: She was misdiagnosed twice with bipolar disorder. She was prescribed bipolar medication, which made her feel suicidal. She didn't feel like herself until after she was diagnosed with and began to treat her ADHD.

How can you tell if you also have bipolar disorder? If you have ADHD, your mood swings are usually contextual, meaning that they depend on what's going on around you. You can feel really down, but if your situation shifts or someone says something nice, you feel lifted. With bipolar disorder, you often can't pinpoint why you feel depressed, and no change brings you joy. If you think you have bipolar disorder, make an appointment to see a psychiatrist, psychologist, or other licensed mental health professional, preferably one who's experienced in both ADHD and bipolar disorder.

STRATEGIES FOR MANAGING EMOTIONAL DYSREGULATION AND TRAUMA

Just knowing that strong emotions and trauma symptoms may be part of your ADHD diagnosis can help mitigate some of the side effects these emotional issues can cause. Amanda, who joined my Your ADHD Brain Is A-OK program, told me that simply knowing she has RSD didn't solve the problem, but it has allowed her to put "a pause in between the event and [her] reaction" to remind herself what she believes may not reflect what's going on. In addition, the following strategies may help you better manage and control the side effects of emotional dysregulation and trauma and increase your quality of life with ADHD.

Psychotherapy

Psychotherapy can be life-changing if you have ADHD, helping you identify and work through trauma while addressing depression, anxiety, or other mood disorders. It can teach you to better regulate your emotional responses. While there are many types of therapy, cognitive behavioral therapy, dialectical behavior therapy, and eye movement desensitization reprocessing therapy have been shown to be especially effective in treating ADHD symptoms, in addition to emotional dysregulation and trauma.

As a reminder, I'm an ADHD coach, not a licensed mental health professional. Anecdotally, based on my experience with thousands of ADHD women, the following treatments have helped. But therapy is a very individual choice and a personal one at that. The right therapy for you is the one *you* find the most effective and in which *you're* the most likely to engage.

Cognitive behavioral therapy (CBT)

Cognitive behavioral therapy, or CBT, is a popular form of talk therapy that can help people with ADHD regulate their emotions and treat depression, anxiety, and other psychiatric conditions. One study found that just twelve sessions of CBT helped adults with ADHD improve their symptoms while changing the same regions of the brain that ADHD medication affects. Other studies have shown that CBT can help reduce hyperactivity, impulsivity, and inattention while improving depression and anxiety.

Cognitive behavioral therapy sessions are designed to be short and goal-oriented. During sessions, you'll work with a therapist to help identify negative thought patterns, also called cognitive distortions, and how these distortions affect your emotions, emotional responses, and other behaviors. Some examples of negative thought patterns include:

- **BLACK-AND-WHITE THINKING.** When you think in extremes or have an all-or-nothing mindset, like *I'm never on time, I'm a terrible partner,* or *I'm always disorganized.*

- **COMPARATIVE THINKING.** When you compare yourself unfavorably to others, like *She's a much better mother than I am* or *My friends are able to do X, Y, or Z so easily, but I never can.*

- **OVERGENERALIZING.** When you draw conclusions or make assumptions with limited information, like *I'll never get that job if I apply for it* or *I'm too easily distracted to ever write a book.*

- **MIND READING.** When you assume what others are thinking, like *My partner is judging me for my messy home* or *My friends think that I'm a flake.*

Many ADHD women develop negative thought patterns because they've felt unworthy or wrong their entire life, constantly thinking, *It's always my fault, I'm too loud, too unfocused, too much,* or *I'm not smart enough.* CBT challenges the truth of these unhealthy thoughts and can help you develop strategies to change them and ultimately your emotions and behaviors. Cognitive behavioral therapy works by retraining your brain and teaching you to be your own therapist—which is why CBT is also called cognitive restructuring. Cognitive restructuring can help shift how you feel about yourself and react to situations and boost your attention span and productivity.

Dialectical behavior therapy (DBT)

Dialectical behavior therapy is a form of CBT that focuses specifically on developing skills to improve how you regulate or control your emotions. DBT differs from CBT because it teaches you to accept uncomfortable emotions before trying to change them. DBT does this by using:

- **MINDFULNESS.** This teaches you how to be present and calmly accept what's happening (more on mindfulness on page 85).

- **DISTRESS TOLERANCE.** This teaches you how to self-soothe instead of losing your temper, ignoring negative feelings, or dissociating (when you shut down mentally or emotionally).

- **INTERPERSONAL EFFECTIVENESS SKILLS.** These teach you how to communicate needs in relationships in healthy ways.

- **EMOTION REGULATION SKILLS.** These teach you how to assess your feelings without immediately acting on them.

Like CBT, DBT has also been shown to help people with ADHD reduce symptoms of emotional dysregulation and other ADHD traits.

Emotional Freedom Technique (EFT)

Emotional Freedom Technique, which is almost always shortened to EFT or referred to as *tapping*, is a type of psychotherapy that's increasing in popularity. Patients report it reduces stress, helps them better manage their emotions, and treats their anxiety, PTSD, sleep problems, or other mood and emotional disorders. In my opinion, tapping is one of the most important therapies for ADHD women because it's available to everyone, regardless of individual resources. I use it daily, whenever I feel anxious, dysregulated, or find myself procrastinating or spinning through my thoughts. With tapping, I'm able to stop the uncomfortable feeling that comes when I think about starting a task (more on this in chapter 7). Tapping pushes me out of my head and stops me from ruminating over how difficult a task will be, connecting me with my body instead. After tapping, I feel as though I'm already in action instead of thinking about how

CHEW GUM TO EASE ANXIETY

Chewing gum can lower anxiety and help you focus to get things done. It works, researchers surmise, by giving people an outlet for their emotional tensions. One study found that chewing gum twice a day for two weeks significantly reduced the stress hormone cortisol, which works to also lower anxiety. The next time you feel anxious, are ruminating, or need to get something done, try it! As a bonus, gum may also improve your cognitive function by increasing alertness and oxygen flow to the brain.

to get into action—I'm suddenly able to focus on what I need to do. In my experience, tapping eliminates big emotions around traumatic thoughts in other ADHD women as well, even when those thoughts have been present for decades.

The practice of tapping relies on meridian points, which are specific places or pressure points on the body through which energy flows, according to traditional Chinese medicine. When you tap, you use your fingertips to lightly drum nine specific meridian points on your face, hands, and body in a specific sequence. Meridian points are also used in acupuncture, but with tapping, you use your own fingers rather than needles.

Before beginning to tap, it's helpful to identify a fear, anxiety, problem, memory, or emotion that you want to address with your practice. For example, you may feel anxious or uncomfortable about something you have to do, which you could choose to help mitigate through tapping. After you pinpoint a specific problem or emotion, rate its intensity on a scale from zero to ten, with ten being the most extreme. As you start to tap, continue to focus on the problem or emotion while repeating any phrase that helps you accept it, for example, "Even though I have X problem or feel Y emotion, I deeply and completely accept myself." After you finish tapping all nine points (this is considered one round and should take only a few minutes), rate the intensity of your problem or emotion again. Repeat this until your negative feelings have reduced to a three or lower on the intensity scale.

Studies show that tapping lowers rates of anxiety, depression, pain, and cravings while increasing happiness and boosting immune system function. The practice has also been found to lower the stress hormone cortisol, blood pressure, and resting heart rate. EFT has been used by Veterans Affairs to treat emotional issues like PTSD.

While there's no science on *how* EFT benefits ADHD, I've heard from women that it helps them control their emotions and anxieties. It's also easier to do than other therapies because you don't feel distracted or impatient when tapping, since you're in constant movement. "I love it because it's so simple and so fast," my client Candace told me. "I can't meditate, but tapping works for me because I'm not bored and forcing myself to sit still."

There are many online resources where you can learn to tap, or you can choose to work with an EFT professional.

Eye movement desensitization and reprocessing (EMDR) therapy

Eye movement desensitization and reprocessing therapy, frequently shortened to EMDR, forces you to do certain eye movements that can evoke painful memories and events and help you heal from trauma. When these memories and events come up, a trained EMDR therapist helps you reinterpret their meaning and transform how you feel about them. EMDR has been shown to reduce symptoms of trauma and PTSD, in addition to anxiety, depression, addiction, and other psychiatric conditions. Experts believe that EMDR helps lessen the symptoms of ADHD.

Lara, who was part of one of my earliest ADHD groups, credited EMDR with helping her limit RSD. "All those memories, all those times when I felt rejected—EMDR has helped me let go of that pain," she said. "It's helped with my emotional regulation so much."

HOW TO FIND A GOOD THERAPIST

People spend decades thinking the same thoughts, traveling down the same neuropathways, automatically and instinctually. To build new neuropathways, we all can use a little help. A good therapist can stimulate you to think differently by providing new perspectives, questioning your assumptions, and helping you track your progress.

In my experience as an ADHD woman, I think it's important to find a therapist who will leave you feeling positive and hopeful at the end of most sessions. You need to be able to be honest with your therapist so that they can push you to grow, which means some of your sessions may be uncomfortable. If you just feel like you're meeting an old friend who tells you what you want to hear, it might be time to find a new therapist. Most importantly, it's critical to see a therapist with an expertise in ADHD women. To find an ADHD-trained therapist in your area or with whom you can have virtual sessions, consult the online professional directory for Children and Adults with Attention-Deficit/Hyperactivity Disorder (CHADD), ADDitude, or GetADHDHelp.com. You can also call psychology clinics or psychology departments at universities in your area and ask for a referral to therapists who specialize in or have experience with treating ADHD women.

Mindfulness and meditation

When I started my journey to understand everything I could about my ADHD brain, someone recommended that I try mindfulness and meditation. At the time, I thought, *Oh no, that hippie-dippie, woo-woo nonscience?* Now I know *much* better that mindfulness and meditation are highly effective on the ADHD brain. Mindfulness and meditation can also physically change our brains through neuroplasticity, which describes the nervous system's ability to change and adapt during a person's lifetime. I love the idea of neuroplasticity because it means we're not stuck with the brain we were born with for life. Physical movement can also play a big role in neuroplasticity, which you'll learn about in chapter 11.

Mindfulness is the practice of focusing on the present without bringing judgment or expectation to the moment. Mindfulness requires us to slow down, which is the opposite of what our ADHD brains typically do. With mindfulness, we notice our thoughts and feelings without reacting to them. The most common way to practice mindfulness is through meditation. When you meditate, you focus on your breath or a repeated mantra as you allow your thoughts to pass without assigning them value or judgment.

Studies show that mindfulness can increase multiple aspects of self-regulation in people with ADHD, helping us improve our attention, cognition, emotional regulation, and stress management while even causing structural changes in the areas of the brain most affected by ADHD. Long-term meditators have been found to have thickened regions of the brain related to attention, self-monitoring, and emotional regulation. This brain-thickening benefit of meditation can even occur past age forty, fighting the typical cortex thinning that occurs over time. Finally, a consistent meditation practice can help you improve your attentional blink, which is the ability to focus on bits of information delivered one right after another. By using conscious attention, your mind can actually help to rewire your brain.

Meditation is a lot like exercise. If you don't use it, you lose it. Similar to exercise, it's better to build it into a routine, starting with five minutes daily, then adding more as you grow more comfortable with the practice—and the more you do, the more benefits you'll reap. The good news is, the effects come quickly. Just five minutes of meditation daily can help lower stress and improve mindfulness, while five consecutive days of practice is enough to improve your attention span.

Cold-water immersion

Several women with ADHD have told me that immersing their face or hands in cold water immediately reduces anxiety and can even stop a panic attack cold, no pun intended. Cold-water immersion has also been shown to snap people out of their ruminating thoughts by boosting dopamine and activating the parasympathetic nervous system—the branch of our brain that helps slow our heart rate and breathing, lower blood pressure, and relax the body. Early research also shows that cold-water immersion may help reduce anxiety and depression while improving mood and stress tolerance.

To try it, fill a large bowl with ice, add cold water, and plunge your face in the bowl for six seconds. Come up for a breath, then repeat for ninety seconds total, which is how long experts say it takes for negative emotions to pass.

FOOT MASSAGE

Studies show that receiving a ten-minute foot massage can help reduce anxiety, improve mood, and lower blood pressure, helping you to relax and calm your nervous system. Better still, you don't need to spend a ton of money to get a good foot massage. A scientist and ADHD coach in Switzerland recently turned me on to spiky massage balls, which are small, like tennis balls, and covered in hard spikes that you can use to massage any area of your body. I find using them jolts me out of my rumination and forces me to focus on my body and the present.

Grounding

Grounding is a self-soothing technique that can help calm you and regulate your emotions in real time whenever you feel overwhelmed or anxious. The exercise distracts you from uncomfortable feelings by taking you through a step-by-step process to help connect you with your surroundings and anchor your awareness in your body rather than your mind. Here's how to do it:

- Start by taking slow, deep breaths. Once you feel as though you can comfortably breathe, proceed to the next step.

- Name *five* things that you can see. Identify them out loud. (For instance, "I see my dog, the couch, the computer, the tea kettle, and my watch.")

- Name *four* things that you can touch. As you touch them, name them. ("I'm touching my hair, my shoes, the dirt, and this gray rock.")

- Name *three* things you can hear. ("I hear birds chirping, kids playing in the swimming pool next door, and water from the fountain.")

- Name *two* things you can smell. ("I smell roses and coffee.")

- Name *one* thing you can taste. ("I taste coffee from the espresso I drank earlier this morning.")

This should help you feel more present and grounded in your body.

Social connections

One of the best indicators of our mental health is the health of our relationships—one reason why I have a whole chapter on how to better navigate our relationships with others when we have ADHD. But if you're looking specifically to address symptoms of emotional dysregulation and trauma, working to form and maintain healthy social connections will go a long way toward helping you heal from either or both. I also believe it's important to seek out and create connections with other ADHD women. I've seen firsthand how developing a community of ADHD women can help us fall in love with our ADHD brains. Once we know one brilliant ADHD woman, then a second and a third, we start to realize that ADHD women are amazing and that by default, we're amazing too. Joining an ADHD network can also help you learn new strategies to manage and leverage your ADHD traits.

Look for communities online or find or create your own support group in your area. Catheryn, who oversees our Facebook team of administrators and moderators, started a support group using an online meetup platform after she moved to a new area of the United Kingdom. After several months, the group grew to ten members, who met regularly, became friends, and even went on vacation together.

Positive emotion

I talk a lot about channeling positive emotion throughout this book because I believe it's critical to helping ADHD women accomplish their goals and feel good. According to the American Psychological Association, positive emotion is any emotional reaction that helps you achieve a positive affect and occurs when you obtain a goal, mitigate or obviate a threat, or feel content with your current situation. Research shows that channeling positive emotions like pride, hope, interest, and enthusiasm increases emotional regulation and resiliency.

Negative emotions like frustration, anger, fear, and helplessness, not surprisingly, create stress, which weakens the prefrontal cortex—the same area of the brain affected by ADHD. Negative emotions can intensify ADHD symptoms, such as poor working memory, rumination, and procrastination. When we're worried or fearful, it becomes very difficult to notice anything else. This is why I refer to myself and the women I work with as "gold-star people," because we can and will flourish with encouragement and affirmation—these are our gold stars—while we can wither when criticized or rejected.

> *Research shows that channeling positive emotions like pride, hope, interest, and enthusiasm increases emotional regulation and resiliency.*

One of the best ways to channel positive emotions is to identify our individual strengths and accomplishments. Oftentimes, we're so focused on our weaknesses we can't see our strengths. Taking the time to recognize our accomplishments allows us to celebrate success, generate positive emotions, and fuel increased self-worth, self-regulation, and motivation.

Ways to End Overthinking, Overwhelm, and Self-Doubt

Early one Sunday several years ago, I was surfing the web when one link led to another and I accidentally ended up on Reddit, reading a thread about ADHD. As I scrolled through the comments, I saw my name and froze. They were talking about me on Reddit! I wasn't just being mentioned here and there either. Nope, I was the topic of conversation. About a hundred-plus posts were commending me for flipping the script on ADHD, but there were two negative posts that accused me of not believing in medication (completely untrue) and making it more difficult for people with ADHD since I refuse to pathologize our condition. (As I said in the beginning of this book, I believe that we can all choose whether we want to leverage our ADHD traits or buy into the traditional narrative that our neuro-divergences are flaws that will ultimately limit us.)

While someone else may have ignored the few haters and focused on all the positive posts, this was difficult for me. All I could think of were the two negative comments. Within minutes, I began to spiral down a tunnel of negativity, thinking about what had prompted the two users to rebuke me and wondering how many others agreed. The more I ruminated, the more trickles of self-doubt began to creep into my brain. Was I conveying my message aggressively enough? Was I too aggressive in my podcasts and programs? I decided to dedicate the next week's podcast to address the critics' comments. I sat down to outline the episode, but then, I started to overthink again: Why couldn't I just sit down and focus on outlining the episode? I had the time. *A neurotypical person wouldn't struggle with this*, I thought.

What happened to me that Sunday is a common ADHD phenomenon. We get stuck in our heads, in a mental short circuit. As a result, we have difficulty accomplishing simple, everyday tasks. These mental tendencies—overthinking, overwhelm, and self-doubt—can derail us more than other habits.

After sharing my experience with the Reddit comments on my podcast, I received an email from a listener from London:

> Your show—and your life—shows that ADHD is not a curse, there is nothing wrong or terminal about it, and it can actually be positive and fun. Because you tell us that we have a choice in how we respond to ADHD, some people who don't want to hear that message may try to make you feel like there's something wrong with you. You also imply that people are responsible for their actions and that they shouldn't just do or accept what they are told because the "rules" say so. . . .

So far, so good.

> You call your listeners "smart" and trust that we are intelligent, regardless of what grades we got, because you know what smart means in the real world. . . . I listen to your podcast because you are annoying and talk too much.

Did I still like this listener? Now I wasn't so sure, so I kept reading . . .

I listen because you model for me that my tendency to be annoying is also what makes me successful. You help me get out of my head and stop looping through negative thoughts about myself by reminding me that we all have a choice in whether we stay mired in negative thoughts and let ourselves feel overwhelmed—or we focus on the positive and use it to motivate us into action while we have fun along the way. All the best from London, Mikey. P.S.: Sorry, I listen to your podcast and I'm a guy.

I burst out laughing when I finished the email. Good on you, Mikey. Not only are you a maverick, you also just summarized what I had been feeling at the time: we can spend a lot of time in our heads, reliving and rehashing what we did, what others said, whether we were annoying to everyone else, why we were late, why we couldn't get something done—the list is endless because we as ADHDers tend to overthink, get easily overwhelmed, and doubt ourselves. When we engage in these mental habits too often or for too long, it can trigger a kind of paralysis that prevents us from getting anything done, which only works to make us feel more overwhelmed and as though we're no good or unreliable. But we do have a choice. There are workarounds to help limit overthinking, overwhelm, and self-doubt.

In this chapter, I outline ways to make the choice to get out of your head. You'll also find strategies and tools to fight the overwhelm we often feel when staring down small, nagging, or incomplete tasks.

HOW TO STOP OVERTHINKING

Many people believe we have no control over what we think, assuming our mind has free will and there's no way to intervene. Not true. The human brain thinks more than six thousand thoughts per day, and we can play an active role in deciding what those thoughts will be if and when we start paying active attention to them—something most of us don't do. Becoming aware of our thoughts and the times when we're ruminating, or thinking negative things about the past or present, can help shift our mindset and improve our emotional state. Watch your thoughts.

Because ADHD women are likely to express hyperactivity through our thoughts, we have a tendency to ruminate, overthink, and catastrophize. We replay worst-case scenarios in our heads, predicting which outcome will happen when we have absolutely no idea what will occur. We may believe that all our negative thoughts or worst-case predictions are true, even with no corroborating evidence.

One reason people with ADHD ruminate more than neurotypicals do has to do with a faulty connection between two areas in our brains: the default mode network (DMN) and the task positive network (TPN). If your eyes crossed at these acronyms or the idea of neurospeak in general, bear with me. Taking the time to understand how our brains work can help you embrace new strategies to end rumination.

The DMN is an interconnected group of regions in the brain that are active when we're not focused on a conversation, task, or what's happening around us. In short, the DMN is active when we're resting or letting our mind wander. It has some great properties, like generating creative thought and self-reflection, but the DMN can also mire us in rumination.

When we *are* focused on a conversation, task, or something happening around us, another interconnected network in our brains, known as the TPN, takes over. When our TPN is active, we don't have time to think about something that happened to us in the past or may happen to us in the future. We're engaged in what we're doing.

Our ADHD brains don't toggle so easily back and forth between the DMN and TPN. Instead, our DMN remains active for a longer period of time, and we can't easily engage our TPN, increasing the amount of time we spend in creative thought (great), as well as the amount of time we spend brooding and ruminating (not so great).

When ruminating, your brain is stuck in its DMN. And the best way to reengage your TPN is to do something that requires focus.

Go to the gym. Take a walk. Run, bike, or read a book. Call a friend. Just get out of your head.

Focused breathing helps too. You can do it anywhere, anytime. Specific breathing exercises or techniques can bounce you out of the DMN. Here's one called the 4-7-8 technique: Inhale through your nose for a 4-second count, then hold your breath for 7 counts before exhaling through your mouth for 8 seconds. Repeat until you feel calmer and more centered.

Here are other suggestions to stop ruminative thoughts:

- **QUESTION YOUR THOUGHTS.** The next time you start to ruminate over something, ask if what you're thinking is actually true. Do you have evidence? Are you sure your dire conclusions will happen? Have you ever imagined something similar that turned out that way? Chances are, you're catastrophizing. Take the time to recognize that your thoughts, predictions, and conclusions may be no more than your imagination. It can go a long way toward stopping the rumination cycle.

- **CHANNEL POSITIVE EMOTION.** Thoughts help drive our emotions, which trigger our actions and produce results. When we create positive emotions like satisfaction, contentment, inspiration, excitement, or joy, we are more likely to take action and get out of our heads. We can also generate positive emotion, putting our brains' natural tendencies to overthink to good use by ruminating on what makes us feel good. We can create positive emotion when we're ruminating on what makes us feel bad by engaging in tapping, grounding, breathing exercises, and the other feel-good techniques we've talked about.

- **ATTEMPT SOMETHING (SAFE) THAT INTERESTS AND SCARES YOU.** I'm constantly encouraging ADHD women to do things that spike our dopamine, which is low in people with ADHD. One of the best ways to boost dopamine is to try things that may scare or excite us. For example, I used to be afraid to appear live on camera. I overthought and wrung my hands at the possibility of adding live video content to my program for a year. I took classes in video presentation and invested in a professional setup before I even appeared in real time in front of a camera. Finally, I signed up for a class for online influencers. It required us to record a live video for thirteen days in a row. By day two, I realized I actually enjoyed it! Here I was, overthinking it for more than a year, when all I had to do to finally accomplish what I'd been avoiding was "just do it." Hello, positive emotion. Thank you, dopamine rush.

- **GET CREATIVE.** One way to engage our TPN is to focus on a creative task. One of my favorite ways to get creative when I'm ruminating is to pull out a sketch pad and a set of markers. I organize my thoughts in colorful pictures and bullet points, outlining the small steps I need to take to reach the goal or complete the task I may be overthinking. Once I've used my creativity to organize my thoughts, my ruminating brain starts cooperating, and I can take action.

- **CELEBRATE THE SMALL THINGS.** We often feel better when we're in action, rather than stuck in the DMN and repetitive thoughts. But many of us with ADHD have a hard time pausing what we're doing to recognize and celebrate our accomplishments. We often jump from one thing to the next. While this can propel our ambition, when we don't stop to celebrate, we can feel as though we haven't accomplished anything. It's so important to take the time to stop and acknowledge the wins. Many of us also suffer from self-doubt, imposter syndrome, and low self-worth. This makes acknowledging and celebrating ourselves difficult. I've learned that celebration is super important for my brain: it allows me to stop, decompress, reflect, and appreciate what I do, helping me realize how much I have accomplished and generating the positive emotion I need to stay focused and happy.

- **BELIEVE IN YOUR JOURNEY.** When you believe in where you're going and what you're doing, you won't feel as compelled to try to overthink. You can trust yourself and the outcome. If you can get clear on your values, strengths, skills, passions, and purpose, your actions will align with who you really are, and it'll be clear what you need to do next and why. This clarity allows you to believe in your journey and stay focused. Everything in this book, including my six-step program from chapter 5 that I designed to help you find yourself and your passions and purpose, can help you identify your strengths and superpowers and give you the clarity you need to find and believe in your journey.

COMBATING THE BIG O(VERWHELM)

Feeling overstimulated, overcome, or even paralyzed by our thoughts, emotions, to-do list, or life in general is so common among ADHD women that I've nicknamed the phenomenon the *Big O*. The Big O is that feeling of extreme overwhelm that rolls in from out of nowhere, causes us to spin—sometimes literally—and can lead to a whole truckload of procrastination, which often manifests as the inability to start doing whatever we need to do.

One reason we feel more easily overwhelmed is because our creative brains notice everything around us, all at the same time. We struggle to know what's important among the many thoughts, feelings, sensory information, and ideas that barrage our minds. We're so easily distracted, especially when we're bored, that we can jump quickly from one thing to another without pausing. This is why we often can't complete a task, finish a conversation, or rethink what may be really happening around us before we react.

Our poor executive function skills may also make planning, organizing, remembering, and completing tasks difficult, leading to an endless to-do list. With planning, for example, because we often have an altered sense of time, we don't have a straight-line progression to get things done like neurotypical people do, according to ADHD psychologist Ari Tuckman. We might also not think about the future until it's literally here, making planning that much more difficult.

What's more, we focus on what we find interesting at the moment, not what's pressing or what needs to be done. We're inclined to be bored with mundane tasks, which can make it hard to get anything done, increasing our sense of overwhelm. We may also feel like we can't control our attention span, so when the Big O shows up, we can start talking incessantly about how distracted, unproductive, and overwhelmed we are, making us feel even more distracted, unproductive, and overwhelmed. If we find it difficult to slow down, we might blame others as a defense mechanism due to the Big O.

There are also sociocultural reasons ADHD women may get more easily overwhelmed than others. Many of us were shamed in school, at home, or at work because we couldn't focus or keep up, and so we stopped trusting ourselves and our intuition. This sense of learned helplessness means we believe we're unable to control or change our situation, so we stop trying.

> *What's more, we focus on what*
> *we find interesting at the*
> *moment, not what's pressing*
> *or what needs to be done.*

I'm not immune to experiencing the Big O. I often feel overwhelmed when I have a busy day, an upcoming work deadline, or company coming over. When I do get overwhelmed, I use the self-soothing techniques I've talked about so far, like tapping, breathing, and spending time in nature, in addition to exercise. Experimenting with different forms of psychotherapy can also help you learn to better regulate your emotions so that you feel less overwhelmed in general. Building awareness of and understanding how ADHD impacts your relationships can help you feel more in control when you're with partners, family, or friends. Finally, taking the steps I just detailed to get out of your head when you're mired in a spiral of ruminative thoughts can help end those feelings of overwhelm.

Here's a real life example. When Christa first joined my 5 Days to Fall in Love with Your ADHD Brain workshop, she told me that she constantly felt overwhelmed by nearly everything in life. During class, she often misplaced the training materials, never knew what we were working on, and always felt behind. Outside the class, she felt like she was never doing enough at work or as a wife, mother, and friend. By focusing on everything that was wrong, Christa completely missed what was going right.

Through my program, she learned how to use the breathing techniques I discussed earlier in this chapter, along with tapping and spending more time in nature to calm herself in the moment and better regulate her emotions. These techniques allowed her to pause and consider a different perspective in real time: Was it really true that she was unfocused, scattered, and anxious? And what did she actually feel so anxious and scattered about?

After Christa began to question her thoughts and emotions, she also started to see that she didn't need to let the Big O take over her brain. Challenging her thoughts helped her see that she was empathetic, energetic, and trustworthy. She may not always be on time or able to remember a friend's birthday, but when it really mattered, she did show up for others as well as herself.

Through my workshop, Christa also learned the importance of using humor to defeat the Big O. I'm a big fan of learning how to laugh at our circumstances and even ourselves because it helps change negative emotions to positive ones. Christa, for example, learned to channel humor and laugh at her idiosyncrasies, including the time she showed up for a New Year's Eve party on December 30. "I was early!" she chuckled. "Normally I would have just berated myself, but now I laugh when I mess up. It's so much clearer to me where I'm really brilliant, so of course there are going to be things that I'm not so good at."

HOW TO STOP PROCRASTIVITY
AND GET THINGS DONE

Emotional overwhelm is one thing. But what about the Big O as a result of having so many things to do and feeling like we can't even get one task done?

Feeling overwhelmed by everyday tasks is common among ADHD women. Our brains struggle to focus, initiate tasks, and motivate (hello, poor executive function), all of which makes starting and finishing chores, projects, and other mundane tasks that don't hold our interest all but impossible. Many of us also grapple specifically with predictable or repetitive tasks, because our minds wander, glitch, and switch directions when faced with predictability and routine, as we look to get a hit of dopamine through novelty or the unexpected. Since our brains revolt against boredom, we'll look to do anything other than cleaning the kitchen or finishing that administrative task at work. This isn't because we're lazy, lack work ethic, or aren't smart. We're just easily bored and have poor executive function, which is needed for task completion.

In total, this can create what researchers call "procrastivity" in us ADHDers. We procrastinate boring tasks by using our tendency to be active and engage in more interesting things. This can look like putting off doing your taxes on April 14, for example, to spend the day redecorating your home instead.

My procrastivity shows up in different ways. Recently, for example, I signed up for a class in visual facilitation, which is the process of turning complex data or information into pictures (think infographics)—I prefer to think visually in pictures rather than words so I thought learning how to use images to express myself would be an amazing asset. The only problem was that I got so overwhelmed by what we were supposed to do *before* the class even started that I didn't do anything. We had to order special pens from Germany and a specific type of paper, and we also had homework. Homework!

Needless to say, I didn't do any of it. This wasn't because I was watching TV or eating metaphorical bonbons. I was exercising my procrastivity instead by doing other things, like researching online dog training programs and "procrasti-cleaning," which I consider to be one of the most productive forms of procrastination. When I went to the first class and realized everyone else had done the homework and had all the supplies, I thought, *Oh my god, how could I be behind after the first class?* In a matter of moments, I created a whirlwind of anxiety and negative emotion over ordering the materials and was so overwhelmed that I considered dropping the class that I had been so eager to take.

Whenever we feel the Big O around a certain task or set of tasks, it's easy to start beating ourselves up for feeling overwhelmed, which can trigger us to force ourselves to try harder, telling ourselves we just need to focus while questioning what's wrong with us. This reaction, however, while natural, sparks negative emotion and usually makes it more difficult to get things done.

Cecilia, who participated in my Your ADHD Brain Is A-OK program, has undergraduate and graduate degrees from two Ivy League schools. Despite her double Ivy credentials, she struggled for months to accomplish one relatively simple chore: moving the contents of a small storage space she had rented for years into her new home. She was so paralyzed by this one task that she kept paying the monthly storage fee even though she had enough space at home for everything inside, cursing herself at the same time for being wasteful with money she didn't have. Every time the monthly deadline drew near, she'd try to muster the motivation to clean out the space but never succeeded. Months of doing this made Cecilia feel unreliable, careless, and defective. *What's wrong with me?* she kept asking herself. Finally, she gave herself a one-week deadline, telling herself that she just had to suck it up, force herself, and get it done.

When Cecilia told me about her strategy, all the alarm bells in my head went off. This was exactly what so many ADHD women do when struggling to accomplish a mundane, everyday task, even though the approach is guaranteed to backfire and sow self-doubt and even low self-worth. While I applauded her for trying to complete the chore for once and for all, I suggested that she might instead want to use what I call "The Plan," a step-by-step method that I teach all my clients.

This plan, outlined below, relies on two factors:

1. *Creating an intention, inspiration, identity, and positive emotion around your tasks.*

2. *Trusting your own intuition and yourself that you know how to do things in a way that works best for you.*

Because so many of us were shamed in school, at work, or at home, we overlook or ignore our intuition and listen to everyone else's advice on what, why, or how we should do things. This can lock us further in task paralysis because other people's reasons, motivations, and ways of doing things don't work for us. The key to freeing ourselves and curbing the Big O in everyday tasks is to find or create your own intention, trust your own intuition, and make decisions that serve *you*.

THE PLAN

- **IDENTIFY OR REFRAME WHY YOU'RE DOING SOMETHING.** To get something done, it helps to set an intention, which is the reason you believe you want or need to get the task done in the first place. Ask yourself *why* you want to accomplish this specific chore or project. Is it important to you personally, or is it one that others want you to achieve? Does the task align with your values, strengths, skills, passions, and purpose? If it doesn't, is there a way to reframe the *why* so that it does align with your values, strengths, skills, passions, and purpose?

   For example, you may not want to clean your kitchen, but if you know that a messy kitchen will affect your ability to function or feel at peace throughout the day, you can reframe your intention to be that you want to be more productive and calmer—not that you should do it out of propriety or because your partner wants you to do it. Remind yourself of your reframe whenever you find yourself dreading or procrastinating this chore.

Sometimes, we do things other people want us to do rather than what we want to do. If we're not interested in a task, though, we won't follow through, which can make us appear unreliable. While there will always be chores and work tasks we don't like or want to do that we need to get done, reframing them to be in service of our health, livelihood, or professional path—rather than to make someone else happy—can help us initiate and complete.

To create your own intention, start with something small that *you* want to change and that *you* care about. Instead of focusing on how frivolous or "bad" a certain habit is, ask yourself why you want to make a change and what kind of person you want to be by doing so. For example, maybe you want to be the kind of person who doesn't view social media first thing in the morning because it makes you anxious, or maybe it causes you to feel behind the rest of the day. Creating an intention and identity around the kind of person you want to be, then reframing how you think about that habit with a positive intention can help you follow through on making change. You can tell yourself, "I am the kind of person who doesn't view social media first thing in the morning" or "I am the kind of person who values starting my day in a way that serves me."

When you stick to your intention, it shows you that you are the kind of person who *can* make and keep small promises to yourself, which can change your life. You realize that you can show up for you and are reliable and trustworthy.

- **IDENTIFY *WHEN* A BORING TASK HAS FELT APPROACHABLE IN THE PAST.** I guarantee that you have a system to accomplish boring, repetitive, or obligatory tasks: you just don't know that you have a system. Because we oftentimes don't do things the neurotypical way, we can believe that we lack any kind of plan to get things done. And whenever we do complete a task, we might think that we did so only through dumb luck or by accident. Your system may be unconventional, but it's worked for you before.

To identify your system, think about the last time you were able to accomplish something you didn't want to do. Maybe you were able to finally complete that arduous home mortgage application or file your taxes by getting a friend to come over and do their own work while you did yours. Or maybe you know you need a subtle distraction to get things done, like listening to music or keeping the television on in the background to keep you company. No matter how you got it done, if it's worked for you before, try to apply these strategies again to new situations even if they don't follow neurotypical rules.

- **ASK *WHAT* ADHD STRENGTHS YOU CAN USE TO MAKE THINGS EASIER.** Many of us are so used to thinking about what we perceive to be our deficiencies that we forget about (or are unaware of) the many strengths we have as neurodivergents. We know, for example, that we can hyperfocus on what interests us, which can be a huge asset when we want to get things done. Consider if there's a way to infuse a boring or obligatory task with something that interests you so that it triggers your hyperfocus. In the instance of cleaning your kitchen, if you love to dance or listen to music (or both), can you dance to some inspiring music while you clean to make it interesting and fun? Or if you tend to hyperfocus on science or politics, can you listen to a podcast on your phone while you do the dishes and wipe down the counters?

  I believe creativity is one of my signature ADHD strengths, so I like to use it to create new solutions. I'll regularly set timers and keep mental records to see if I can beat an old time in getting just about anything done, like getting to inbox zero or putting groceries away. This sort of a challenge, along with moving quickly and staying in action, keeps me going and makes even boring tasks fun.

- **ASK *HOW* YOU CAN SIMPLIFY IT.** Simple is easy, and easy is more approachable to any brain. To make things simpler, break the task into smaller steps. In the example of cleaning the kitchen, perhaps you can break it down into unloading the dishwasher, washing dishes, clearing everything off the counters, then wiping them down. For my visual facilitation class, I broke down the preparation process into printing out exactly what I needed from the online instructions, reading those instructions carefully, highlighting the action items, then ordering the pens, paper, and books. I listed each one of these actions as its own line on my to-do list rather than writing down the single entry of "order supplies," which is how I would have approached it in the past only to wonder why it sat there uncompleted for days. Breaking down tasks like this into their smallest components makes them much more doable and allows you to cross them off your to-do list, which will generate the positive emotion and dopamine that can fuel you to continue.

If you have a bigger task, like an important presentation or work project, divide it into microtasks and assign days or weeks in which to get them done. If you start feeling the Big O during these bigger tasks, stop and ask yourself if you can make their components even smaller to simplify the chore to a greater degree.

In Cecilia's case, we applied The Plan to make the mundane, yet seemingly impossible task of clearing out her storage space as simple and fun as possible for her. First, she set an intention and an identity: she wanted to do this for herself so that she would be the kind of person who has all her stuff in one space, which seemed like a nice, orderly objective, rather than her previous belief that she had to do it so as not to be so wasteful with money—something that only caused her to feel badly about herself. In the past, she had been able to accomplish chores that didn't take a lot of time—she could organize a bathroom closet, for example, if she knew it would only take her fifteen minutes—so we agreed that she would never spend more than twenty-five minutes at one time working in the space.

Next, to break down the task into the smallest steps possible, I asked her to take a clipboard, notepad, and pen into the space to inventory everything there. When she did, she realized that she had built it up in her mind to be a much bigger chore than it actually

THE SIMPLE TOOL THAT HAS HELPED ME
HACK TASK INITIATION

One of the best hacks I've found for helping start and finish tasks is my bamboo Datexx TimeCube. This brand-name, portable cube is a four-way timer, with four different countdown clocks on four sides of the cube. All you have to do is flip the cube over to the timer you want, and the countdown will start. When the time is up, a loud bell will ring. The TimeCube is available with different timer combos, including five, fifteen, thirty, and sixty minutes; five, ten, twenty, and twenty-five minutes; and one, five, ten, and fifteen minutes. You can buy them online for approximately twenty-five dollars each.

The Datexx TimeCube works for me because it's easy—I don't have to search for an app on my phone, find a button, or set anything. It's also more elegant than any other timer I've seen, so I have no problem keeping it in plain sight, reminding and inspiring me when I want to start writing or need to clean and organize my closet or a drawer in my kitchen. In these instances, I'll set the timer to twenty-five minutes and get started, telling myself I can do anything for twenty-five minutes. What usually happens, though, is that once I get started, I don't stop writing, cleaning, or organizing for hours.

As ADHDers, our procrastination often stems from the discomfort we feel when we think about starting something when we'd rather do twenty other more interesting things. The TimeCube helps me get over this uncomfortable emotion by jolting me out of my head and into action. I don't have to think about it: I just have to flip over the cube and begin.

was. Every day for a week, she packed up and moved out items from the space for just twenty-five minutes, which made her feel accomplished—positive emotion for the win! Cecilia proved to herself that she was reliable and could show up and keep a commitment to herself, which inspired her to keep going. I shared with her

Frank Sinatra's "Nice 'n' Easy," which is about relaxing and taking things easy, to play during her twenty-five-minute sessions, which she told me made her laugh, helping her stay in positive emotion as she flitted around her storage space. This is how, after ten months of procrastinating and paying a fee that she didn't need to, Cecilia finally cleared out her storage space within a week.

WHAT ABOUT SETTING deadlines for yourself? Deadlines can help you get things done, but they probably won't make you feel better about doing them. They're unlikely to generate positive emotion, especially if you blow one. Deadlines can sometimes have the opposite effect, looming over you and triggering the negative emotion of perceived failure before you even begin. Many of us with ADHD may also just continue to procrastinate when faced with a deadline, waiting until the last hour, which can spike our dopamine as we rush to slide under the wire to get it done on time. While we may be able to do that from time to time and feel good, pulling all-nighters or massive last-minute efforts rachets up our stress hormone cortisol over time, increasing feelings of overwhelm while also impairing physical and mental health. Instead of deadlines, use The Plan and other techniques I've covered so far to limit overwhelm and generate positive emotion.

DEALING WITH IMPOSTER SYNDROME

Dear Tracy,

I want to share an experience with you that I've had repeatedly in my life that I believe impacts my sense of self. Whenever I manage to accomplish something, whether because of looming pressure or driven by my passion

and interest, I don't feel the sense of accomplishment that my friends and peers tell me that they do. I'm almost bewildered by the achievement and not sure I'll be able to do it again. I don't feel as though I can take credit for what I accomplish, which I know makes me less confident than I should be. Does any of this resonate with you?
—Josa

When I received this email from one of my podcast listeners, I immediately thought, *Yes, Josa, it totally resonates with me.* And it resonates with a lot of other ADHD women who have something known as imposter syndrome.

Imposter syndrome describes the feeling many of us have when we doubt our success or can't recognize or celebrate our accomplishments. We may feel like a fraud and that our successes are due to accidents, mistakes, or dumb luck. While plenty of neurotypical people have imposter syndrome, those of us with ADHD are more prone to the mindset for a number of reasons. To begin with, since we often faced or continue to face more struggles in school, at work, or at home, we've never felt as smart, as good, or as worthy as our neurotypical friends, colleagues, or partners. Many of us have spent years trying to hide our ADHD "flaws" and feel like we have to work twice as hard just to keep up, leading us to conclude that we must not be as smart or likable. What's more, we may feel like we don't fit in, increasing the sense that we're just masquerading around in fancy clothes we don't deserve. We may also not trust our success and aren't ever sure if we can re-create it since we don't know how we did it in the first place. We can be so consistently inconsistent that we convince ourselves that our success must have been a mistake.

Surveys conducted by professional networking firms have found that women are more likely to experience imposter syndrome than men. Experts believe that's because women face more hurdles than men to get to the same place in professional situations, have fewer role models whose intellectual (rather than physical) achievements were recognized, and suffer more self-doubt after years of discrimination and being indoctrinated into gender norms. This is particularly true for ADHD women because our neurodivergent traits contradict our gender roles and expectations, as we noted in chapter 3.

I have spoken with so many brilliant women authors, entrepreneurs, doctors, engineers, artists, musicians, scientists, and other professionals or creatives with ADHD who are at the top of their field but can't see, let alone celebrate, their successes.

One of these women is Kristen, an accomplished doctor whom I've interviewed on my podcast. During our time together, she told me that she never felt like she belonged at any academic institution, despite being a star student. In high school, she said, she applied to the US Air Force Academy on a whim. "I didn't realize how difficult it was to get in there until much later, so I always thought they had just made a mistake in accepting me," she noted. The same "mistake" happened again when she was accepted into medical school and again when she did her residency at a renowned hospital. Kristen felt like she got by on good luck or by mistake.

Now, though, after doing the work to understand her ADHD, she sees the strengths rather than weaknesses of her different mind, and she has begun to claim the fact that she's a brilliant, successful woman. She still feels like an imposter from time to time, but she knows now to question these negative thoughts, asking what evidence she has to feel this way while continuing to move ahead in any way she can.

One of the most effective ways to combat imposter syndrome and self-doubt is to work toward conquering the small, everyday tasks we just discussed, using The Plan I outlined earlier. Despite the fact that many of us have achieved significant life successes, we often devalue them because we don't trust ourselves to reach small goals like picking up our kids on time, going to bed before 2 a.m., or finally ticking a tedious chore off our to-do list.

Celebrating our successes, whether big or small, is critical to re-inforcing to ourselves that we're smart, reliable, worthy, and good at what we do. I've emphasized the importance of celebrating our suc-cesses several times already in this chapter, but how do we do it if it makes us feel uncomfortable or hesitant? Or we can't even recognize our successes in the first place?

Any time you accomplish something that you've been dreading or procrastinating, even if it's simply folding laundry that's been sit-ting out for two days, take the time to celebrate it. You don't need to celebrate in a big way. Simply taking the time to acknowledge that you accomplished what you set out to do is oftentimes all you need to generate positive emotion. You can also tell yourself that you're the kind of person who folds laundry rather than letting it clutter up your field of view. Pause, feel pride for what you did, and pat yourself on the back.

As you grow more comfortable and get better at recognizing your smaller successes, begin to celebrate the larger ones by meeting friends or family for a celebratory dinner, or setting aside a day to do whatever you want, whether it's to binge Netflix, take an afternoon yoga class, or spend the entire day reading that book that's been on your booklist for months. When I accomplish a larger success, I also like to create a physical reminder of it by taking a photo or adding something to my house that I'll walk by every day that I can associate with that success.

No matter whether your success is large or small, try also to take a few minutes of silence to bask in the positive emotion of a job well done. This can help cement in you the awareness that you are capable of success and can reliably create many more instances of it. While it may feel difficult at first to celebrate you, once you start doing so, I promise it will generate so much positive emotion that you'll begin to look forward to it.

ADHD women often tell me how surprised they are to discover how adopting a plan to conquer the overwhelm, get things done, and generate positive emotion changes their sense of who they are and what's possible for them. "I don't know how it happened, but after listening to your podcast every week, I started to see all the wonderful things in myself that I'd never seen before and question the negative

No matter whether your success is large or small, try also to take a few minutes of silence to bask in the positive emotion of a job well done.

beliefs about me that I never knew I had permission to question," says Sam, who signed up for Your ADHD Brain Is A-OK after listening to my podcast. "Once I became aware that my procrastination was really about emotion and not time, I started to challenge myself to sit in the discomfort of those emotions rather than react or run away. I could control the overthinking and the overwhelm by learning how to pause and then choosing how to react in a way that better served me and actually made me proud of myself."

8

ADHD-Specific Strategies to Better Manage Your Relationships

When I decided I wanted to marry Rich, now my husband, I didn't wait for him to propose. Instead, I hired a plane to fly over a beach on the North Shore of Massachusetts with a banner that read, "Rich, Marry Me! ♥, Tracy." We'd been dating for only six months and lived on opposite coasts at the time, but I knew that this was the person I wanted to spend the rest of my life with. I took charge and made it memorable.

The day before I proposed was not a good one. We were stranded for hours in a storm on Martha's Vineyard, I was seasick from the ferry ride back to the mainland, and then somebody left a dent but no note on my car in the parking lot. I also had a fleeting thought that maybe I was being impulsive, followed by wondering what the hell I was doing. After all, on our first date, I had made it very clear to Rich that I had no interest in a serious relationship. He almost didn't ask me out again. Now, six months later, here I was, proposing?

We were late to the beach—my fault, of course. As we navigated the dunes down to the water, I tossed Rich a bottle of champagne. The beach was empty that day except for a group of people taking photos with a Polaroid instant camera. When they saw the banner behind the plane, they mouthed the words, looked at me, then pointed at Rich.

"Well, what did he say?" one of them shouted.

He hadn't said anything yet. He was still reading the banner fluttering behind the single-engine Piper. Then his eyes softened with a smile, and he yelled, "Yes!" They cheered, snapped a photo of us, and handed it to me.

Rich then asked me what I had in mind for a wedding. As it turned out, I had plenty in mind. A friend had already helped me secure a date at a church and historic Tudor-style mansion outside of San Francisco. I also had a short list of caterers, musicians, and florists. "All you have to do is show up!" I told Rich. In true ADHD fashion, no one was quicker at executing on an idea, and since parties were my area of extreme interest at the time, it was easy for me to accomplish.

As ADHDers, we can be fun, spontaneous, and full of exciting and creative ideas. But we can also be pains in the asses to live or deal with. The truth is, we can face more interpersonal problems when we have ADHD than neurotypical people do. I'm not being unfair or making generalizations. Research shows that as fun and joyful as we might be, common ADHD traits like distractibility, inattentiveness, hyperactivity, impulsivity, and emotional dysregulation can complicate and impair our interpersonal relationships, both romantic and platonic. We may blurt out whatever we're thinking, refuse to go with the flow, and have to do things our way. To others, our behavior can seem unloving, inconsiderate, or upsetting, even if that's not our intention. Our partners or friends may feel like we never listen or don't care about them because we struggle to pay attention to what they're saying or their interests. We might forget the plans we made, tasks we promised to do, or important dates like anniversaries or birthdays. Or we may drop the ball in helping to manage financial responsibilities or household chores. We might also make hasty financial decisions or decide to switch or cancel social plans at the last minute as we act on our impulsivity.

Just because we may face more conflict in our relationships, however, doesn't mean there aren't effective workarounds we can use to improve how we interact with others. Simply becoming more aware of the ways in which our ADHD traits can impact or hurt our relationships can go a long way in helping us change our behavior or soften others' outlook on how we act.

Before we begin, I want to emphasize that many common ADHD traits, like creativity, spontaneity, curiosity, empathy, intuition, drive, and resourcefulness, make us endearing, attractive, and interesting to others. We never want to quash our "too muchness" because that's what makes us *us*. There's no question that ADHD makes you an amazing partner and friend in many ways too. Our goal here instead is to provide awareness and strategies for navigating your relationships and making them even better.

ROMANTIC RELATIONSHIPS AND ADHD

If you've ever felt like you've struggled more in your love life than those without ADHD, your hunch wasn't only in your head. New research shows that those of us with ADHD dispute more issues, fight more frequently, and fall back on dysfunctional ways to resolve our conflicts more readily in our marriages than those without ADHD. Another study even found that the divorce rate for couples affected by ADHD is nearly twice that of couples unaffected by the condition.

In my role as an ADHD coach, I've heard many clients describe a frustrating parent-child dynamic between themselves and their neurotypical partner—a problem that's also been noted by therapists. The one affected by ADHD feels as though their partner treats them like a child, reminding them what to do or always telling them they need to focus, be on time, or complete a certain task. At the same time, the one unaffected by ADHD feels like they have to parent their partner or nothing will get done. Either way, this creates a push-pull dynamic and power struggle that can be detrimental to any romantic relationship, no matter how loving.

After working with ADHD women for years (and being one myself), I believe that the most important thing we can do for our partners is to learn everything we can about our ADHD so that we're more aware of how our characteristics might impact our relationships and what we need in a relationship to be happy. When we become aware that our behavior is oftentimes due to a differently wired brain rather than a character flaw, it can help ease any shame we may have around how we act with others. We may feel more willing to put ourselves in our partner's shoes and see our behavior from their perspective. We may also be more open to developing effective workarounds that take both people's feelings and desires into account and can help us avoid conflict.

Just as important is encouraging our partner to learn on their own about ADHD, which can help them develop awareness, empathy, and understanding of why we do what we do. They may be able to see, for example, that you're not purposefully being uncaring or careless when you forget, get distracted, can't pay attention, or do something impulsively—it's just how your ADHD brain is wired.

When my friend Sandra was first diagnosed with ADHD, her husband bought the book *ADHD 2.0: New Science and Essential Strategies for Thriving with Distraction* so that he could learn more about how her brain worked. After he finished it, he told Sandra that he felt as though he'd learned a new language that he could use with her. He said he also realized that she wasn't intentionally doing things to upset him. Sandra felt more loved and supported by his interest, which also helped bolster their relationship.

If both partners have ADHD in a romantic relationship, the good news is that you'll likely have more empathy for one another and each other's differences and challenges. You'll also likely have different symptoms, as the condition manifests uniquely in everyone. One partner may struggle more with organization, for example, while the other may have a problem with time management. Recognizing each of your unique symptoms can help you divvy up household responsibilities to the person who may be better suited to handle them. This is why it's so important to learn as much as you can about ADHD and how it shows up for each of you.

Either way, I encourage all my clients, women who join my groups, and those who tune in to my podcast to get curious about their romantic relationships and pay attention when things work well and when they don't. Doing this can help you identify what you might want to change, along with what works for you and your partner when it comes to resolving conflict. Communicate with your partner when you're not fighting or upset with each other so you can calmly and lovingly discuss your conflict styles. Was there an occasion, for example, when you had a difference of opinion but resolved it in a way that made you both feel supported? If so, what did you do and how did you do it? Most importantly, when and how can you leverage the same strategy going forward?

Many of us who have ADHD can often be argumentative and challenging with our partners when it doesn't serve our best interests or the interest of our relationships. If this sounds like your relationship, ask yourself what your intention is. Do you want to feel powerful over your partner or would you rather feel connected to them? Being right may feel good in the moment, but it does little to build empathy or love. Reminding yourself of your intention can help you temper your emotion and reduce the frequency and severity of conflict.

I also believe in learning to celebrate your successes as a couple, even the small ones. Because so many of us ADHD women are perfectionists, we may feel as though we can never reach our relationship goals or get into a really good place with our partners. Recognizing and celebrating the small successes—like when you create a new habit that works well for both of you, or go a whole day actively trying to listen to each other—can help generate positive emotions, which is extremely beneficial to our ADHD brains.

Here are some additional tips to create peace and collaboration in your romantic relationships:

- Create standards by talking about what is acceptable to each of you. For example, what does a clean kitchen look like? Is being five minutes late OK, but ten minutes isn't? Is clutter acceptable on the desk in the family room but not on the coffee table?

- Make a list of each of your strengths and weaknesses. What does your partner do better than you? From this list, divide tasks according to strengths and interests.

- For tasks neither of you wants to do, divide them up to maintain the level of organization or cleanliness you both decide is acceptable.

- Make it fun. You'll be surprised at how doable mundane, boring tasks can be if you're laughing and having fun.

- Adopt a growth mindset. When things don't work out the way you'd like, don't see it as a failure but as an opportunity to pivot and get curious about yourselves and what can be done differently in the future.

In my experience, many ADHD women find themselves attracted to difficult relationships because helping and saving people can stimulate us. Similarly, ADHD experts say that ADHD women often end up in relationships with a partner who gaslights them, which means the other tries to convince them that their feelings, experiences, memories, or even sanity are invalid. Because many ADHD women already struggle with working memory, forgetfulness, rejection, and low self-esteem, we're more susceptible to gaslighting. I always recommend that the women I work with pay attention to how people make you feel and to trust your intuition. When you're around the right people, you will feel accepted, validated, and loved. These are your people and the ones with whom you should spend more time.

Some women ask me what to do if their partner refuses to learn about ADHD or believes the condition doesn't exist or is just an excuse. I always tell them what I'll share with you now: Continue to learn about ADHD and work on yourself, regardless of what your partner will or won't do or what they believe. Focus on your strengths, values, and what generates positive emotion for you. Over time, your partner may begin to see a positive change in you and want to learn more about ADHD. If this doesn't happen, remember that we all deserve relationships in which we feel loved and accepted and have the space to be who we really are.

PARENTING AND ADHD

WANTED:

A mom who will wear many hats daily, including that of wet nurse, housekeeper, cook, chauffeur, administrative assistant, tutor, coach, personal shopper, therapist, part-time party planner, and social coordinator. Never ends. No pay. Little sleep.

While some ADHD women thrive in traditional roles of motherhood, many of us don't. Sure, being a mom is challenging no matter who you are, as you can see from the job description above, but it can be more difficult for those of us with poor executive function skills that hinder our organization, time management, and sense of structure. We may find it impossible to keep a calendar, for example, or we may get easily overwhelmed by what feels like our endless to-do list. We may lose interest easily in repetitive tasks like cooking, laundry, and school pickup—and why wouldn't we, since many of us find them boring and tedious, like we're living a real-life *Groundhog Day*?—or we may show up late or become immersed in an interesting project and "forget" we even have children, which is something I hear often from ADHD women.

At the same time, however, our ADHD brains give us a lot of advantages. We can be more empathetic and readily identify with our children's struggles. We may be able to come up with new or creative solutions to everyday problems while other parents remain stuck. We often share what we like to hyperfocus on with our children, instilling in them a sense of passion and purpose, and because we may be easily energized, we can get enthusiastic about our children and help them celebrate their successes.

In my work with women, I've learned that ADHD mothers function best when we're able to create our own custom parenting role. Many ADHD moms are happier when they don't have to stay at home because having an outside job gives us structure and mental engagement, which is something that ADHD therapist Terry Matlen has also discussed. This was true for me when I was raising two young children. While I've loved being a mom more than any role before or since, I also wanted to continue to work.

No matter your work situation, whether you're a stay-at-home mom or working part-time or in an office every day, here are some tips I've learned as an ADHD mom that can make parenting life a lot easier:

- **NEGOTIATE A DIVISION OF LABOR THAT LEVERAGES YOUR STRENGTHS.** Even before I was diagnosed with ADHD, Rich and I sat down and divided our family's domestic duties among us to make it easier for both our brains to focus on what we enjoyed and did well so that we could get more things done. We agreed that anything related to money, the car, our dogs, and administrative stuff like paperwork for school activities or medical expenses would be in his column. Anything to do with social planning like playdates, birthday parties, vacations, holidays, gifts and entertaining, and homework and school projects was in my column, along with buying the kids' clothes and decorating the house. Otherwise, we shopped, cooked, cleaned, organized, and gardened together, oftentimes as a whole family.

When you don't negotiate domestic duties, they may default to you as the woman, which can be a prescription for resentment, anxiety, and overwhelm. This is a problem for all mothers, of course, but it's a disaster for those of us with ADHD. Dividing up our domestic duties made me feel part of the family rather than the chief household nag or drill sergeant who was constantly trying to run the show.

- **ASK FOR SUPPORT.** I can't emphasize how important it is to ask for support, whether it's from your partner, children, extended family, fellow moms, teachers, coaches, or neighbors. If you ask kindly, I find that most people are happy to help. Plus, there's a reason that the proverb "It takes a village to raise a child" exists . . . because it's true.

  When considering ways to create support for yourself, ask:

  ☛ *What can your partner do to help you? Can they take on responsibilities in the home that may not be your strong suit, like paying bills, while you focus on ones that leverage your ADHD strengths, like organizing activities for the family? As a woman, it's not your job to be the conductor of the household, but you can work together with your partner to create and uphold a system to share responsibilities that works for you as a couple or family.*

  ☛ *What can your children do to help you? Can they pick up their toys, for example, put their dirty clothes in the washer, do the dishes after dinner, et cetera?*

- **FORGET LISTS AND OPT TO AUTOMATE.** Many of us struggle to create systems that can help us get things done. But building systems into your daily life by automating your tasks can help make sure they get done, giving us one less thing to worry about and remember. What can you automate? Consider putting bills on autopay, ordering groceries online and having them delivered weekly, and setting up regular playdates that occur on the same day and at the same time every week.

- **GET CLEANING HELP (AND OTHER HELP IF YOU CAN AFFORD IT).** I highly suggest doing whatever you can to enlist the help of a regular cleaning person—something that therapists who also specialize in ADHD recommend. Every woman who initially told me she couldn't afford to hire help but then found a way has always said how much smoother things are and how much happier she is now that she no longer tells herself what a horrible person she is whenever she sees a dirty kitchen or a pile of laundry.

    There are many ways to make a weekly or biweekly cleaning person part of your budget. You can barter with someone who needs a service that's easy for you to provide or hire a high-school student who will work for less because they're not professional. Or you can get creative like one of my Your ADHD Brain Is A-OK members Avani did. She couldn't afford to hire help so she and another stay-at-home mom who also put off household chores agreed to clean each other's homes together once a week. Meeting for a "cleaning friend date" made it fun and provided accountability while their kids got the added benefit of a weekly playdate.

    If at all possible, I also recommend hiring a nanny or regular babysitter, even if it means making financial sacrifices elsewhere. Despite the fact that women have less social approval for delegating and hiring for domestic jobs that we struggle to do, cutting back on other expenses to pay for a nanny was one of the best decisions we ever made. I struggle with building structure into my day and managing time, and our nanny, Isabel, was a master at both structure and time. She quickly became part of our family and kept us all on a schedule. Just knowing that Isabel would be walking in the door every morning helped me stay on my game, because I didn't want to create more work for her. This did wonders for my mental and emotional well-being, as well as for my children's happiness, allowing me to be more centered and present with them. I was able to focus on what was important, which was them, not any self-perceived failings. It also allowed me to do a better job in my professional life because Isabel provided the structure that ensured my focus wouldn't be divided during work hours.

FRIENDSHIPS AND ADHD

It was 6:00 p.m. when I came flying into the hotel parking lot, gravel bouncing off my tires. This was my third year of being invited by the same group of women to an overnight spa trip, and I was late again. They had all arrived much earlier that day to get facials and massages before having dinner together and spending the night. This year, I had planned to join them in the morning, just as I had planned to for the last two years. But here I was, arriving late for dinner again.

I liked these women. They were smart, interesting, and kind. The reason I kept showing up late had nothing to do with them—just thinking about having to lie quietly during a massage or facial makes me feel like I'm about to jump out of my skin. Since then, I've learned that I really struggle to participate in group events that aren't centered on a common interest. Today, I no longer torture myself by agreeing to these kinds of events, opting instead to catch up with friends over dinner, which I actively enjoy.

To make and sustain friends, we all have to follow social rules, such as showing up (preferably on time) and participating in social get-togethers. It's thoughtful to remember friends' birthdays, drop dinner off when someone is sick, and offer to help out with their children. These social rules can be challenging for ADHD women, though. Like me, many ADHD women I know are terrible at scheduling get-togethers, despite our best intentions. It can take me weeks to schedule anything due to the organizational skills required to make a plan.

I'm also terrible at calling by phone to stay in touch. I know that once I get on the phone, I can happily talk for over an hour—and

I feel like I never have a free hour to schedule a call, so I put it off. What's more, some of us have rejection sensitive dysphoria (RSD) and struggle to regulate our emotions, both of which can negatively impact our friendships.

I've heard from so many other women that simply understanding that friendships may be more difficult for those of us with ADHD increases our positive emotion and improves our relationships. Janet is a content marketing expert, author, and international speaker who runs a multiple-six-figure business in the UK. She also has ADHD and RSD; I met her when she was a guest on my podcast *ADHD for Smart Ass Women*. She said that learning more about both ADHD and RSD and how they might impact her friendships has helped. "I now understand why I do what I do," she reflected. "I understand why my poor working memory might make birthdays difficult for me to remember and why my hyperactivity and inner drive make it so hard for me to show up, relax, and hang with my friends. I know why vacations or lying by a pool with other people is something I just can't do. As a mother and a friend, I should be able to hang out at a pool instead of sitting there thinking, *I'm bored and want to do anything but this.* Now, however, I know that there's nothing wrong with me—I just have a differently wired brain."

Learning to manage social cues and rules

I've heard some experts say that women with hyperactive ADHD lack social skills because we're not good at reading social cues. I think that's hogwash. Because we often have more empathy, meaning we can feel what others are feeling, and are more intuitive, we can be brilliant at reading the room and picking up on social cues. Instead, our impulsivity and natural exuberance can make it difficult for us to care about the social cues. We may get too excited and stand too close, talk too much, and stay on a topic we want to talk about for too long.

Personally, I find it difficult to refrain from gushing about whatever I'm currently excited by or quelling my exuberance to talk about my children. I also don't seem to be able to exercise caution when giving advice. I'm opinionated, passionate, and intense and can sometimes push people's boundaries. I don't apologize for it, however—it's who I am and largely responsible for my sparkle.

Based on my observations, women with the inattentive subtype of ADHD who are generally quieter or less verbally impulsive have an easier time fitting in with friends. Those of us with the combined or hyperactive and impulsive subtype may struggle more socially because we tend to have big personalities and be outspoken, opinionated, and even argumentative. We can talk a lot and have a difficult time holding ourselves back from leading conversations or taking over the direction of social plans, which can be irritating to others in a group dynamic.

I've always been extroverted. Being around people energizes me. But I don't like feeling trapped in a group where I have to exchange social niceties. I dislike meetings, especially on Zoom. On the other hand, I used to love throwing large outdoor parties when my kids were younger: The size of the parties felt challenging to my ADHD brain and kept me focused and engaged. At the same time, I could flit around from person to person and make sure everyone was taken care of. These parties, which almost always revolved around my kids, allowed me to have fun, exercise my creativity, and build family memories.

I'm sharing my experience because I believe it's helpful to be aware of how your ADHD might influence your ability to abide by social rules, as it can help you determine which events you might want to avoid because you'll be too energetic or restless and may be perceived to be impolite. I've also discovered that social rules in friendships are easier to follow when we prioritize spending time with people who share similar values and appreciate us for exactly who we are. While we can all have friends who like certain aspects of us and vice versa, the easiest relationships are formed between people who accept one another unconditionally, in my experience.

Fitting in while being a nonconformist

Another problem many ADHD women face is trying to fit in when our natural inclination is to stand out. We're often incapable of following traditional patterns and prefer to shake things up and make things better, since that's what makes life interesting.

I remember planning my first big event after I was appointed the social coordinator of a local mother's club. The event had been held every year and had always included hot dogs and hamburgers. After I suggested bratwurst on pretzel buns and beef short ribs, which sounded more interesting and more appetizing, you would have thought that I was trying to push beluga caviar and escargot based on the reaction.

Jayne, the hair-styling entrepreneur whom I told you about in chapter 4, noticed she feels socially awkward in many situations because she feels like she doesn't fit in. "I've either felt less than or better than, but never just like 'one of them'—and that's been really hard," she said of her friends. Despite her celebrity status in the hair world, she mentioned, "I don't always get invited to things." Jayne continued, "I don't have a huge group of friends. I also often compare myself to neurotypical people who are able to function in a more temperate, consistent manner."

Jayne said she doesn't enjoy small talk and struggles to listen when others talk about plans they organized six months ago. "I don't look down on it, but I have bigger fish to fry. I just don't function like that," she revealed. "And that's the way that I tell myself that I'm OK." She's learned to accept that she has many other strengths, like running an international business, which prevents her from being able to plan that far in advance even if she wanted to.

Another coping strategy for Jayne: While she has a difficult time getting out the door, she's realized that once she's on her way to meet friends, she feels happier that she's going. She reminds herself of this positive emotion whenever she thinks about backing out of social commitments that she's already made. Transitions can be difficult for us, but once we're out with friends, we're almost always grateful we made the time to see them. Because we tend to be fearless and intuitive and have had different, interesting life experiences, our friends often look up to us and value our opinion when they need advice and inspiration. We can also be a lot of fun, getting those around us to rally and try new things. Always remind yourself that your ADHD gives you unique strengths in life, which extends to friendships.

Coping with justice sensitivity and the need to feel understood

Many women with ADHD have a strong sense of justice and fairness, as we covered in chapter 4. We may struggle when we see discrimination, exclusivity, and dishonesty, and we may have a more difficult time than others interacting with or accepting people when we suspect they're being inauthentic. Because many of us have received daily invalidation for much of our lives for our ADHD traits, we're often more willing to take the side of the underdog and see things from others' point of view. This is one reason why many of us have a deep sense of empathy, which, when combined with our intuition, can help us see people for who they are. Our natural inclination is often to help the underdog win or the scapegoat escape because we know how it feels. Our impulsivity and fearlessness can also cause us to call others out when we think they're being unfair or fake.

While this warrior tendency makes many of us successful in our careers and even more attractive to other people, it can be off-putting, especially since we're women and "should" be polite, accommodating, and supportive. Per society norms, we're supposed to keep our feelings to ourselves and try our best to get along with everyone.

How people are treated has always been so important to me. I will usually stand up for the underdog even if it means alienating a friend or business associate. There are many times when I've asked myself, *Why do you always have to do this? Life would be so much easier if you just kept your mouth shut. Let other people fight their own battles.* But I've also learned the power of being exactly who I am by following through on my actions. I used to spend so much time trying to make sure that people understood who I really was and why I was doing what I was doing. Now I just do it.

At the same time, justice sensitivity and the need to be understood can help us be better friends. "I have this ability to see what is naturally good in people, and since it's so important for me to be understood, I want them to be understood as well," reflected Catherine, who is part of my Your ADHD Brain Is A-OK community.

Mika, who joined my Facebook group, noticed her justice sensitivity makes her more loyal and good at listening and helping people. "I will spend a ridiculous number of days, weeks, and sometimes years trying to help my friends who are struggling with serious life problems," she said. "I know that they will never be able to do the same for me, I will always give more, but for now, I'm OK with that."

Building structure

Maintaining friendships has become harder for me as I've gotten older because I don't have the same structure in my life that I did when I was younger. For example, in college, I saw friends every day in classes, on campus, and at parties. When I was a practicing attorney, office friendships became personal friendships because none of us had children yet. And when I had school-age children, I saw my parent friends all the time at school pickup, sports games, birthday parties, and regular playdates. Sometimes, I'd complain that there were too many other pressing things on the calendar to see friends, but I realize now how good it was for me and my ADHD brain to be pulled away from school or work to socialize with people who forced me to regularly chill out and relax.

Today, I no longer see colleagues in an office or parent friends at Friday night playgroup. These daily and weekly opportunities to socialize never took any planning, but now if I want to maintain my friendships, I have to create more structure in my life. I used to think that online friends weren't "real" friends. Over the years, I've been lucky to have made many very close friends with women I've met online who have similar goals and comparable interests. I've also been able to meet many of them in person on a pretty regular basis. I check in with some of them daily, with a five-minute audio message, text, or DM. With others, I follow up several times a month, with hour-long conversations by phone or Zoom. This makes me feel more connected and makes my days more enjoyable. And because these women have similar schedules and obligations, there are no hard feelings if one of us cancels. I also feel comfortable enough to reach out if I discover I have a spare hour on a Friday afternoon. For in-person get-togethers, I've learned to suggest meeting up in my home rather than at a restaurant, because it feels more relaxed. To help lower the stress of hosting, I'll pick up multi-course meals from a caterer, which don't cost much more than cooking everything myself yet saves me hours of work. My weekdays are busy enough, so I try to schedule in-person get-togethers at night after the workday is over.

Surrounding yourself with like friends

I knew that I had finally met my people when I began my work with other ADHD women, which is a big reason why I started my podcast *ADHD for Smart Ass Women*. By hosting a podcast, I could meet even more ADHD women. I could travel anywhere in the world and always have someone to share a lunch or dinner with. I wanted more women friends who shared my curiosity, drive, and sense of humor! Once I launched my podcast, I met them in spades. They're my guests, listeners, and other podcast hosts. By becoming friends with other ADHD women, I have discovered so many brilliant, interesting friends. I've never had so much fun. I'm often incredulous at how kind, thoughtful, and caring they are. Many of us also marvel at how much we have in common, like our intensity and too-muchness, and we give one another permission to be exactly who we are.

TIPS TO STRENGTHEN YOUR FRIENDSHIPS

- Make sure your friends value who you are. If you feel competitive energy or as though you have to dim your light to keep them happy, find new friends. True friends care about what's going on in one another's lives and celebrate one another's accomplishments and wins.

- Let your friends know that you want to see them while explaining how your brain makes scheduling and follow-up extra difficult. Ask them if they'd be willing to take the lead in these areas if you volunteered to take the initiative on some aspect of your friendship that may be more difficult for them.

- Don't leave a social event without getting the next one on the calendar. Even if you need to reschedule it, begin the planning process so that the initiative is there.

- Sign up or join a club, group, or class that you're both interested in and that has built-in structure, like a book club, workout group, or program where you're learning something together.

9

ADHD-Specific Strategies to Better Manage Time and Planning

I looked at the clock in the kitchen, then jumped into the shower: three hours until I had to meet Rich outside his apartment on our way to see *Swan Lake*. And I was determined not to be late. We had just started dating, and I didn't want to come off as a flake. Three hours meant I had all the time in the world, I thought, so it should be easy.

What seemed like a short time later, after the shower, I went back out into the kitchen to check the time again. I had dried my hair, but I wasn't dressed and hadn't started my makeup yet, and I wanted to be sure I was still on schedule. That's when I saw the digital clock on the kitchen stove flip to 5:51 p.m. What?! I was supposed to meet Rich at 6 p.m., and his apartment was at least a thirty-minute drive from where I was living at the time. How could this have happened? Was the clock wrong or had I read it incorrectly when I first checked? It didn't make sense.

I slapped on some mascara and blush, then dabbed concealer on a bump I had just opened by anxiously scratching my face once I realized I was going to be late (hello, body-focused repetitive behaviors—see page 77 for more info). I threw on a dress, grabbed my purse, and jumped into my car. I then proceeded to stall the thing three times trying to drive up and out my steep driveway because, in my panic, I had somehow forgotten how to drive a clutch. Once out and onto the freeway, I realized that it was Saturday night traffic in San Francisco. I hadn't called Rich to tell him I was running late before I left the house (this was before the advent of cell phones). "Tracy, you need a game plan!" I yelled to myself and smacked the steering wheel. But it was too late to have a plan.

As I drove, I could feel the anxiety wrapping up and around my throat. I liked this guy—and I hated being late, even though it happens often to me. When I finally arrived at his apartment at 6:45 p.m., I found him standing next to a cab, paying the driver. My future husband didn't know anyone who was ever forty-five minutes late, so he had gone out to the theater to see if I was already there, then taken a taxi back home because he was convinced that I must have been in a car accident and wanted to call the area hospitals.

"I forgot the tickets at home and didn't realize it until I was in the car," I started to stumble. "So I had to drive all the way back to get them, and I was so unnerved that I forgot to call you when I got back to my house. When I finally realized it, it was too late . . ." I looked at Rich to see if he was buying my white lie. But he just reached over and hugged me. "I'm just so happy that you weren't in a car accident," he said.

My relief was obvious—he believed me. But the momentary relief didn't solve the bigger problem I felt sinking into me as I realized we had missed the curtain call for *Swan Lake*. Why, oh why, was I always late?

WHY WE STRUGGLE MORE WITH TIME

ADHD challenges our executive function skills, or our cognitive skills related to planning, prioritizing, scheduling, self-regulating, and self-motivating, all of which affect our sense of time and degree of time management. For many of us, our brains feel the most comfortable when we can enjoy an unconstrained flow of time, moving from one thing to another whenever we feel like it.

If you have ADHD, any time management problems you have aren't because you have a character flaw or are an inconsiderate person. Because our brains are wired differently, we can struggle more than neurotypical people with estimating time and how long it takes us to complete tasks and activities, according to research. We can suffer from "time blindness," meaning that we're unaware of the passage of time because we don't pay attention to it and are distracted by other things. And while we may have the best intentions to be more time conscious, we can let shinier tasks, activities, and interests derail us from our best aim unless we have a strategy that works for our ADHD brains.

> *If you have ADHD, any time management problems you have aren't because you have a character flaw or are an inconsiderate person.*

Another reason we may lose track of time is our tendency to hyperfocus on those things that interest us: five hours can feel like fifteen minutes when we're engaged and interested in something while fifteen minutes can feel like five hours when we're not. We may also have issues with our working memory, which can cause us to forget what we're doing or what we wanted to accomplish once we become distracted by something else.

Because many of us don't have a practical understanding of time, we can also struggle with planning and figuring out how many minutes, hours, or days an errand, task, or project might take. For decades, I couldn't predict how long it would take me to get ready in the morning, despite the fact that this was something I did every single day.

Time blindness among those of us with ADHD is on a continuum, meaning that some of us really struggle while others may not have any time management issues at all. I'm terrible with time, for example, while my son, Markus, is never late for anything. No matter what side of the spectrum you're on, learning time management strategies can help you stay on track, remain calm and organized, and generate the positive emotion we all need to be happy and function at our best.

STRATEGIES TO IMPROVE YOUR TIME MANAGEMENT

Use analog clocks

Many of us with ADHD need to *see* time pass to be able to better manage it. When you look at an analog clock—those are the old-school ones with hands that tick from second to second—you can see and feel how long a second, minute, and five minutes takes. For this reason, many experts encourage people with ADHD to install analog clocks throughout their home and office.

After I realized that part of the reason I was always late was because I had no idea what time it was, I put analog clocks everywhere in my home so I wouldn't guesstimate in my ironic efforts to "save" time. Now whenever I look up and see the physical time on an analog clock instead of a jumble of numbers, I'm always surprised how helpful it is at keeping me on schedule.

Invest in a smartwatch

Personally, wristwatches have never helped me better manage my time because they feel like jewelry, causing me to forget that I even have one on. However, smartwatches are pretty hard to forget about, as they use something called haptic feedback, which sounds and feels like a gentle vibrating reminder that doesn't make me pitch it across the room. Better still, you can sync your smartwatch with your online calendar and receive reminders sixty, ten, and five minutes before you need to be somewhere. I also set up a reminder to buzz when an event or meeting actually starts. If this sounds like overkill, I can't tell you how many times I've sat in front of my computer with five minutes to spare before an online meeting, then gotten so engrossed in an email or something else that I forgot about the meeting altogether. If you're struggling to set this up like I did, make the time to call the watch company's support team and have them walk you through the setup. It is worth it to never miss another meeting.

I also use the alarms on my smartwatch to remind me about the laundry I'm washing, the food that I'm cooking, and the bathroom break my dog needs. The beauty of a smartwatch is that you can also hit Snooze instead of Stop if you can't attend to the task at that immediate moment—and trust me, you'll want to do this so that you don't forget the task altogether ten minutes later.

Use timers

For years, no matter how hard I tried, I was always late in the morning to help my husband drop off our kids at their school. That's before I finally invested in countdown timers for my bathroom, which changed how quickly I got ready and slashed the number of times my children yelled for me to hurry up before they'd get yet another tardy because their mother, not them, was late.

Before using timers, I believed that it took me only thirty minutes total to get ready in the morning for my day. That's before I took the time to plan backward, as you'll learn to do on page 139, first breaking the process down into all the individual steps, like how long it took me to shower, dry my hair, put on my makeup, and get dressed. Using timers, I wanted to see exactly how long each step really took me—which was a lot longer than I had assumed for each. For example, the shower I thought took me no more than ten minutes really averaged around twenty-five minutes, with some showers lasting up to forty-five minutes or longer. (I find showers therapeutic: the warm water feels good and increases my creativity.)

After I had gathered realistic estimates of how long each step in my morning routine would take me to complete, I decided to set goals for each increment, like no more than ten minutes for my shower instead of twenty-five minutes. In this way, I could make sure I stayed on track and was out the door in forty-five minutes total.

Although it's not a countdown timer, one of the best timers I've found to help better understand the passage of time is something called the Time Timer, a brand-name device with an analog clock face that's designed specifically for people with ADHD. When you set the timer, a pie-shaped red section appears over the face of the clock showing the number of minutes in your desired increment, then shrinks in size as the timer counts down.

Create a challenge

ADHD brains love a good challenge. To better manage my life, I've learned to develop games to help me meet my time goals. For example, in the morning, I'll make a goal to beat how many minutes it took me to get ready the morning before. I bought a waterproof digital clock for my shower and a second one for my vanity, which suctions to the mirror. In the shower, I set the timer for ten minutes and try to beat it. I set another timer to blow dry my hair in ten minutes, then to get dressed in five minutes after laying out my clothes the night before. (I learned pretty quickly after analyzing how long each step of my morning took me that I could easily spend a whole thirty minutes trying things on and leaving them in piles all over my bedroom floor before taking another ten minutes to put everything away.)

This is how I started getting out of my house in no more than forty-five minutes every morning—something that I can now do without a challenge since it's become part of my regular routine. At the time, though, it was fun and efficient, and the speed kept my distracted brain engaged. More importantly, it helped me create a habit that is now an effortless part of my life.

Create a visible reminder of your time goal

One reason timers worked so well for me was because I put them in visible places to remind me of my intention to streamline my mornings. This means I never lost sight of my goal to get out the door. Whether you keep visible timers around the house like I did or post a piece of paper with your time goal on your computer, refrigerator, or bedroom mirror, these reminders can help you remember your intention to be on time for the activities with which you struggle the most.

Create workarounds

After I realized that I could easily lose forty-five minutes doing my makeup in the morning—something that should take me only fifteen minutes—I started to apply cosmetics in the car while my husband was driving our kids to school. I bought a special cosmetic makeup bag with a drawstring lip so that my products can't fall out, then sat in the passenger seat and used the mirror on the visor to apply. Knowing that we'd pull up in front of the school fifteen minutes after getting into the car meant my makeup routine could only last that long. It worked! While I no longer have a morning ride during which I can do my makeup, knowing that I can efficiently and effectively get it done in fifteen minutes has helped me stick to that time frame, even when I don't have to rush out the door.

Slow down and do it once the right way

As you know from previous chapters (or real life), our ADHD brains are often easily bored, and we don't like to do things that don't interest us. This means that we may skip important steps in processes that will inevitably make time management more difficult. For example, if I had only spent five extra minutes to slowly read the instructions on how to assemble a desk that I had recently bought online, I would have saved myself seventy-two hours of negative emotion cursing the product, trying to return it, then looking for another desk that would come preassembled.

Discover what works for you

Time management is an ongoing process in which you pause, set an intention, create a system, then make that system work better for you. Every brain is wired differently, though, and only you know what is most likely to work for your specific brain. Get creative with your strategies and don't be embarrassed to do what helps you, even if your ideas sound nutty to your family, friends, or colleagues.

STRATEGIES TO BETTER PLAN

Planning when you have ADHD isn't easy because it's one of those executive function skills that we're often deficient in. Most people who are leaving for a weeklong trip on a Friday morning, for example, might start to plan what they'll take and even start to pack earlier in the week, getting more motivated to have everything ready to go by Thursday night. However, most of us with ADHD don't do this. We're not motivated to think about what to pack on Monday, Tuesday, Wednesday, or even Thursday, waiting until Friday morning to think about what we want to take *and* pack, when it's already too late.

Lots of us also bargain with ourselves around scheduling, telling ourselves that we'll do it tomorrow or we'll start in two hours, then postpone again for another four, six, or twenty-four hours. Some of us may also resist scheduling anything in the first place because we worry that we won't feel like doing that activity when the time comes around.

While planning doesn't come easily for many of us with ADHD, learning to do so can help us do what we need to get done, better maintain our work and personal relationships, and make more time to move our bodies, eat better, sleep, and do all the other activities that can boost our ADHD brains. Here are the best strategies that many successful women with ADHD whom I know use to create a plan and stick with it.

Schedule the next event before the current one concludes

Coordinating, planning, and scheduling are challenging enough for our brains, but when we wonder whether we'll feel like doing something two weeks from now, scheduling can become downright off-putting. Eradicate the possibility by always scheduling your next doctor's appointment, yoga class, work meeting, friends' dinner, et cetera, before your current appointment, class, meeting, or dinner finishes. If something comes up or you really don't feel like it in the moment, you can always reschedule. I find, however, that I almost always want to show up and actually do, and when I have these events on the calendar, my brain is able to focus more on the moment than wondering or worrying whether I need to plan a future appointment, workout class, meeting, or dinner.

Plan backward

Instead of focusing on how much time you have before needing to be somewhere or finishing a task, sit down and think about exactly which steps you need to take before that event or deadline. Our ADHD brains rarely think, *Wow, it's going to take a lot of time, so I'd better get on it.* Instead, we jump to, *It's not due for thirty days, so I have plenty of time.* But when we plan backward, we might discover that we don't have thirty days to complete that personal project because we're working in an office three days a week, are on vacation for one week, and have two holidays in the middle of the month, which means we have only seven days instead of thirty.

In my mind, I believe that I can do just about anything in thirty minutes. But if I pause and visualize the necessary steps, I often realize that I can't get ready for an evening out, replant a section of my garden, run an errand, or go to the grocery store in a half hour. By planning backward in the instance of food shopping for example, I'll realize that it takes twenty minutes to drive to the store, five minutes to park, twenty minutes to find the items I need, and five minutes to check out, all of which brings me to fifty minutes total—nearly double the amount of time I would have normally allotted. This estimate also doesn't give me any buffer time in case I run into traffic or a friend at the store, both which can often occur. So if I pad my schedule with more time just in case, I realize that I need an hour to go to the store. By planning backward, I've learned to build more realistic time estimates into my day so I'm not late for my next activity or I don't fall behind schedule.

THREE TIPS FOR BETTER WRITING

1. **TRY BEAR.** This app, designed for iPhones, iPads, and Mac desktops and laptops, helps you organize notes, to-do lists, and other written material all in one place. I'll use the Bear app to start writing an outline for a new podcast episode while waiting in line at the grocery store, jot down a book a friend recommended I read, or store the name and photo of a paint color that I used in a room in the house in case I need to do touch-ups in the future. Everything I write goes into Bear, which has eradicated the anxiety I used to feel about finding pieces of information in old folders, notebooks, or sticky notes. While you can certainly use the Notes app that comes already installed on iPhones and other Apple products, with Bear, you can search for a note using any word. For those who use Android products, try Supernotes, which also works with Windows, Mac, Linux, and IOS.

2. **INSERT MORE PARAGRAPH BREAKS.** I regularly receive emails from podcast listeners telling me how much my work has made a difference in their lives. I love receiving these messages, but they're often pages of straight text without any paragraph breaks, which makes them very difficult to read. To organize your thoughts and increase readability, try breaking up what you write into as many short paragraphs as possible. Doing so creates white space and makes content easier to scan and navigate. Organizing your content into separate paragraphs will also better focus your brain on a specific idea or topic so that you can more easily and clearly communicate your points.

3. **CONSIDER ARTIFICIAL INTELLIGENCE.** I've found apps like ChatGPT or Bard very helpful when I feel overwhelmed and struggle to start writing. Both are artificial-intelligence-based chatbots (meaning you converse with them) that can help you write emails, answer test questions, translate text, or even write song lyrics or poetry. You of course have to verbally tell the app what you want to write about. I'll often use

ChatGPT to create an outline for a writing project by sharing my ideas and asking it to create a simple outline. I'll then ask follow-up questions about specific aspects of my outline or if there's anything I haven't mentioned but should consider, helping me to process my thoughts and clarify which points I want to cover. Once I have an outline, I can start writing, which obviates the initial inertia of a blank page.

Another way I use ChatGPT or Bard is to ask the app to summarize an article, news story, transcript, or research paper before I read it. This provides the overall gist, or big picture, of the material right away, helping me to create a mental roadmap so that I stay engaged and focused on key ideas, while also reducing the likelihood I'll get hung up on an irrelevant idea or lose interest while reading the text. I've used ChatGPT and Bard to break down the steps of an item on my to-do list too.

The great thing about ChatGPT or Bard is that it gets better at understanding you the more you use it, giving you more appropriate or fitting responses. Just remember that both are AI-based tools and that you should always verify and cross-check any information they provide by consulting reliable sources.

To plan backward, sit down when you're not stressed and think about what you need to do before an event or deadline. Break it down into smaller steps. Consider how long each step will take and what you will need to do to complete that action. Moving forward, picture attacking each step individually. Afterward, debrief to assess your estimate's accuracy. Then reassess. For more on task completion, see page 100.

Visualize the end result

When neurotypical people have something they need to get done, for the most part, they set goals and get things done—that's all the motivation they need. For those of us with ADHD, we usually need to visualize the end result or net gain so that we can harness the positive emotion that comes with seeing the reward and use it as inspiration to turn procrastination into action. For example, I really dislike annual doctors' appointments due to the difficulty of scheduling them, the boredom of sitting in the waiting room, and the discomfort of having to be present during the actual appointments. Because I have at least five annual appointments—one with my primary care doctor, one with my ob-gyn, one with my ophthalmologist, et cetera—I'll schedule them all over the course of two consecutive days rather than dragging them out during the full year. For these two days, my only priority is to make sure that I get to those appointments, which can be a slog. But I keep myself focused on how good it will feel when I walk out of the last appointment on day two knowing that I'm done with health appointments for the year. I visualize myself finishing the final appointment and keep that image in my head to inspire myself to keep going. This year I celebrated my success by ordering a mocha and ginger cookie at the kiosk in front of the medical complex where my doctors have their offices.

> *It's our neurobiology, not us, and if we can't plan the way our friends or family do, there's nothing wrong with us.*

UNDERSTANDING THAT OUR ADHD brains struggle more with time management and planning can help us accept that we're not flawed, scatterbrained, or deliberately inconsiderate if we're always late or can't plan like everyone else. Instead, we have a differently wired mind, one that also makes us more creative, empathetic, and unique. If we're often late, it's our neurobiology, not us, and if we can't plan the way our friends or family do, there's nothing wrong with us. We can remind ourselves that we have other talents, like being high-energy and passionate, that we bring to our homes, our work, and our relationships. At the same time, we can learn to develop strategies to keep us on track, meet deadlines, and schedule in advance.

And yes, I eventually did tell Rich the truth about those *Swan Lake* tickets . . . after we were married.

ADHD-Specific Strategies to Better Manage Money

It was December, the week between Christmas and New Year's. I was twenty-three, in law school, and home for the holiday break. From my bedroom, I could hear my parents running frantically up and down the stairs that led to our garage.

"Shut the garage door!" my mother yelled. I peeked out of my bedroom window and saw a man in a mechanic's jumpsuit scanning our property. In the distance, I could see what looked like a tow truck. A familiar feeling of dread formed in the pit of my stomach.

I heard a tapping sound on my bedroom door, followed by my mom's harried whisper, "Open the door." My mom's face was flushed. My dad was right behind her, pragmatic and calm as usual. "Tracy," he began, "a man just rang our doorbell. He said he was from a collections agency sent by the bank to tow your car for nonpayment. Is this true?"

Before I go any further, let me say that my mom and dad have never been late paying a bill. Not even a day. Not ever. For them, being even one day late is unfathomable: financial commitments are written in blood.

While I agree with them, what I didn't understand at the time was how this had happened to me and my car. I had bought it less than a year before after negotiating a killer contract with the dealership that caused the whole place to erupt in applause when I sealed the deal. The manager even came out for the final signature to compliment me on my negotiation skills and offer me a job on his sales floor. After all, I had bargained hard with the dealership for three days under fluorescent lights. This wasn't an impulsive buy, even if the car—an Italian convertible with a less than stellar maintenance record—wasn't the wisest buy for a grad student who had a part-time job as a law clerk.

I don't remember exactly what happened after I bought the car, but I have vague memories of unexpected bills arriving from the dealership. I also remember that the law firm where I was working announced a hiring freeze, cutting my hours and all end-of-year bonuses. Didn't they know I was relying on that bonus to pay off my late car payments?!

Always the optimist, I figured I'd eventually find a way to pay the bills without having to tell my parents I was in trouble. When I first told them about the car, they suggested I wait until I had a real job with a consistent income to buy a potentially problematic vehicle. The last thing I wanted to do was show them they were right.

As I scrambled to figure out a way to save my car from collections, I began to run through my head how I could have kicked this financial time bomb down the road for ninety days—the last time I paid an installment—trashing my credit in the process. Had it really been ninety days? It felt like it had only been a few weeks. Ultimately, I managed to get up-to-date on my car payments and redress the late fees using a combination of an unexpected request to do paid research from one of the partners at the law firm where I clerked and some help from my parents. But until I was finally diagnosed with ADHD, I didn't understand how this had happened and, consequently, I was always too embarrassed to repeat this story.

To this day, I have never balanced my checkbook. Not once. This isn't because I'm flush with money, but because I can't stand doing it. In college, my ADHD workaround was to have two checking accounts so that when one got low or I bounced a check, I'd switch to checking account number two, leaving the first one alone for a couple of weeks in the hope it would recover.

When my husband, a banker who had always balanced his checkbook down to the penny, was still my boyfriend he was aghast at my financial strategies. Once we were married, he asked me to save receipts for everything I bought that cost more than fifty cents. I laughed, rolled my eyes, and said no. Poor banker man didn't know what he was up against.

Money is my nemesis. I struggle with finances. And I'm not alone: many people with ADHD have difficulties managing money. Why? Dealing with financial issues usually requires organization and attention—two traits we often lack. If we procrastinate or have a poor understanding of time, we may delay or not pay our bills altogether, causing repercussions that further exacerbate our financial struggles. Those of us with ADHD are also four times more likely to impulse spend than our neurotypical peers. Studies show that we can also make poor decisions around money and don't understand financial information as well. It's not that we're not smart but more that we're not interested.

Finance, like time, is rooted in numbers, which are certain and limited—the absolute antithesis of how our random, unpredictable, and often creative ADHD brains work. Numbers require precision, monitoring, and follow-up, which are usually not our strengths. It's no wonder then that dealing with money can also generate negative emotion, which ensures we steer clear of doing it in the future. On top of all of this, in my experience most ADHD women are very generous and care more about making a difference and having the freedom to do what they want to do, when they want to do it, than money.

After I was diagnosed with ADHD, I made a targeted decision to take control of my own finances and empower myself to be better with money. To accomplish this goal, I strategized how I could create spontaneity, flexibility, and positive emotion around finances—all attributes that many of us with ADHD need in our attack plans for us to successfully meet a goal. I also recognized that I had to flip the script on the negative emotion I already felt whenever I paid a bill, faced a budget, or heard my husband ask me to reconcile an expense. As long as negative emotions existed around finances, I'd never take control of them—a fact reinforced by every single financial advisor and money coach with ADHD I've spoken to.

TAP YOUR ADHD SUPERPOWERS WITH ENTREPRENEURIALISM

At age eight, I ventured into my first business, selling Christmas cards. Using holiday money, I ordered a sample kit of dozens of boxes of cards and set out to sell them. Door after door closed in my face until one kindly neighbor had the decency to explain to me that my timing was all wrong: no one was thinking about Christmas cards . . . in January.

That's when my craftiness kicked in. Thanks to my mom, I already knew how to sew, and once I got a little older, she taught me how to crochet too. I started knitting and crocheting leg warmers and scarves and selling them to the other girls who went to my ballet school. Shortly after that, I launched into making and peddling my own jewelry (feather earrings, anyone?). In college, after spending the summer after my freshman year working as an aerobics instructor, I enrolled in an entrepreneurial program and started an aerobics company. In graduate school, I wrote a business plan to launch an event management company. I also founded and ran a designer women's wear company that made apparel for high-end department stores such as Neiman Marcus, Saks Fifth Avenue, and Nordstrom. Today, I spend my time teaching my patented program that helps ADHD women discover their passions and superpower strengths.

I thrive around other entrepreneurs. I've amassed female friends from all over the world who run their own businesses. Something about the entrepreneurial personality just feels like home to me. These women have high energy and are bold, fearless, and tenacious, and usually display some hyperactivity, distractibility, and impulsivity.

According to one large-scale study, people with ADHD are 60 to 80 percent more likely to have entrepreneurial intentions than those who don't. In fact, we may be up to 300 percent more likely to start our own companies than neurotypical people, says entrepreneur Garret John LoPorto, author of *The DaVinci Method*. Some experts, like prominent radio talk-show host, ADHD author, and former psychotherapist Thom Hartmann, believe that all entrepreneurs have a degree of ADHD (remember from page 7 that ADHD symptoms can be present on a spectrum). And after meeting thousands of ADHD women and seeing how many are entrepreneurs, I also see the positive association between ADHD and entrepreneurialism.

Why are people with ADHD more entrepreneurial than neurotypical folks? To answer that question, just think about all our amazing superpowers, like our tendency to be hyperactive, passionate, energetic, and creative problem-solvers. We like new, stimulating, and challenging things. While these traits may make traditional school or work more difficult, they're incredible strengths to have when it comes to starting and running a business. Many of us are also nonlinear thinkers, always coming up with new ideas that challenge the status quo. And if we're impulsive, we won't spend a lot of time thinking about whether our idea is a good one—we'll just jump on it, fearlessly and passionately, which is often exactly what's needed to launch a new, successful business.

We can also be resilient optimists: studies show that ADHD entrepreneurs often respond positively to uncertainty and are able to act in the face of the unknown. Being entrepreneurs can fulfill our need for risk-taking and novelty-seeking in a way that better serves us. We can also be impatient and easily bored with the status quo, making the lack of any established routine in running our own business particularly attractive. For all these reasons, entrepreneurs with ADHD exhibit more intuitive cognitive styles and higher levels of "entrepreneurial alertness," according to research published in *Entrepreneurship Theory and Practice* that analyzed years of prior research. Many successful entrepreneurs have been vocal about their ADHD, including Olympic gymnast Simone Biles, singer Solange Knowles, reality TV star Paris Hilton, and billionaire magnate Richard Branson.

If you're curious to explore entrepreneurialism, identify the areas of your life about which you're particularly passionate or have an extreme interest (hint: they're likely the same topics or activities on which you hyperfocus). This is one reason why, as ADHDers, it's so important to know our values, strengths, skills, passions, and purpose. While this is true of everyone, not just those of us who have ADHD, we are most content when we are living our lives in intention and focused on problems that we are interested in solving.

I'm not going to rehash the same advice you've probably heard your entire life, like telling you to track your purchases, automate your bills (although this one you should absolutely do), balance your checkbook, or pay off all your credit cards but freeze one in ice that you can literally break for emergencies (that was actual advice).

I want to be clear: not all women with ADHD struggle with money. Some, like the female investment advisors and financial coaches whom I've interviewed, have shown the world that money is their area of interest. I've used these brilliant women's strategies to change how I think about money, generating positive emotion that has helped me tackle and better manage my own money matters. I've shared their strategies through my podcast and programs with thousand of women who've told me that they've also experienced the same success. Now I want to share them with you.

STRATEGIES TO BETTER MANAGE YOUR MONEY

Decide to take charge of your money

Many women with ADHD have fallen into a pattern of learned help-lessness around our finances. We defer to our partners, family, or paid professionals because we hate dealing with money or have been told that we're terrible or irresponsible with it. After I married a banker, I maintained this "helplessness" for decades, believing that I was incapable of dealing with money. I wouldn't even try to under-stand our finances because Rich was so good at it. *He's the banker. I don't have to do this*, I thought.

At the same time, I hated feeling helpless around money. I also worried about what would happen if something awful occurred to him. I knew I wanted to take control of my money, and I wasn't going to wait for a tragedy. As soon as I made that decision, I felt a huge sense of empowerment. I started generating positive emotion by fi-nally deciding to act, even before I took any concrete action. Since then, I've never looked back.

Create an intention around your life and money

Siw Slevigen, a financial advisor with ADHD who frequently works with ADHD women, tells her clients that the best way to begin to engage with their money is to get clear on and connect with their intention around what they want their life to look like around their finances. She says to start by identifying what's important to you, what's not, and what you're neutral about to help you clarify which items, services, and other areas of your life are worth your money and which are not. This sounds a lot like our values exercise in chapter 5. As part of the process, ask yourself what about your current spend-ing habits you want to change. Are you spending money on things that aren't important to you? Which aspects of your finances trigger negative emotions?

Determine a financial strategy that stimulates positive emotion

The closer many of us get to feeling overwhelmed, the more likely our brains are to shut down in response. But managing money is no different than managing many other realms of our ADHD brain. We don't need to necessarily focus on changing our behavior. Instead, we want to pay attention to our thoughts and emotions around our finances so we can determine how we feel about money. This is why it's important to create strategies that can help you feel a sense of satisfaction, reward, joy, or other positive emotion when it comes to money. Slevignen recommends taking the time to come up with ways to maximize your joy around money and make choices that better serve you.

> *Investing in experiences that create memories rather than material things brings people more joy.*

For example, investing in experiences that create memories rather than material things brings people more joy. Experiment with how you feel when you spend money on self-care or self-improvement, which can help generate positive emotion around money. Or you may feel joy when spending money charitably, or on your family or friends. Pay attention to what sparks the most joy when you spend and deal with finances.

After you identify ways to generate positive emotion around money, you can create a strategy to apply them to as many aspects of your financial responsibilities as possible. For example, whenever I am considering spending money, I pause and ask myself if I'm doing so in a way that creates memories, educates me, or provides self-care or connection with others. I know these all generate positive emotions for me around money. The more of these boxes I can tick, the more likely I will be to make the purchase.

I used to feel irresponsible when spending money on things that might attract the judgment, criticism, or sneers of my friends or colleagues. After I decided to empower myself to be master of my own finances, though, I learned to ignore what others thought. I reminded myself of my intention and the things I had predetermined were important.

For example, my son and daughter now both live in New York City. When my son first arrived there for college, my husband and I decided that we'd pay for the two of them to go out to a nice dinner together every Sunday night. We determined that it was important to us that our children spend time together, stay connected, and always remember that they have each other in a big city that was across the country. Because we buy them dinner once a week, we choose not to spend our money in other areas. Still, I know some people who think that funding our adult children's weekly dinners in New York City is a waste of money—they should buy their own meals or we should put that money in an investment fund for them—but it's what we value. And every Sunday, we feel positive emotion when they FaceTime us together after dinner or text us a photo with their smiling faces.

Switch from impulse spending to impulse saving

If you struggle with impulse buying, Slevigen recommends planning your purchases one day in advance by creating a list of what you're going to buy. Finalize on Monday, for example, exactly what you need to buy Tuesday, and do not deviate from it.

When Slevigen first shared this strategy with me, I recoiled. "That sounds like the exact opposite of anything creative, spontaneous, or fun!" I exclaimed. But then she explained why the plan works: "What this strategy does is show you that you can follow a spending plan to a T for one day if that is your intention. And because you have a plan, you'll be much less likely to get distracted." You'll also feel good because you kept a promise to yourself that you can spend within what you intended, so you're creating positive emotion simply by creating and sticking with your plan.

"But what if you're tempted to buy something that's not on your list?" I asked her. This is where the real genius of Slevigen's plan comes in: if you see something you want and don't buy it, you reward yourself for sticking to the plan by telling yourself that you can add the item to your list the following day if you still want it. To add incentive, Slevigen recommends creating a separate savings account for all the money you *don't* spend on impulse buys, which she has termed "impulse saving." And by saving, you're creating the positive emotion and dopamine hit you would have received from the impulse buy.

For example, if you're in line at the grocery store and see a chocolate bar, you may be tempted to throw it in your cart—you're tired and hungry, and it's been a long day. But then you remember your list, and chocolate's not on it. So, while standing in line, you transfer the money you would have spent on the chocolate bar into your special savings account and tell yourself that you can put the candy bar on your list the following day. Doing so creates the same kind of positive emotion you would have felt from buying the chocolate, reasons Slevigen.

"The brain wants immediate gratification, but it won't take long for you to switch the reward from impulse shopping to impulse saving as long as you do it in a joyful way," she said. "Once you start saving, it will become easier and easier. That's how you start to build new neuropathways in your brain that make impulse saving a fun habit."

This plan applies to both in-store and online shopping. Another strategy I find useful for online shopping is to follow this rule: every online purchase has to sit in your shopping cart for at least twenty-four hours before you can buy it. If you forgot about it over the course of one full day, you probably didn't really need it to begin with.

Start to invest by yourself

Over the years, whenever people told me that I needed to create a budget and track my purchases, I always rolled my eyes—I knew I would never do it. But the repeated suggestion got me to thinking about why people made these suggestions. To build wealth, of course! Then it dawned on me: What if I skipped all the neurotypical steps and jumped right to the building wealth part and did it in a way that worked for my brain? That's how I decided to start investing my own money—a tip that also comes from *New York Times* bestselling author and financial whiz David Bach, author of *Smart Women Finish Rich* and *The Automatic Millionaire*.

Don't worry, I'm not suggesting anyone start day-trading or fire their financial advisor to oversee their own investment funds. What I'm talking about with this tip is saving a small amount of money every day to personally invest. After all, investing money is the ultimate power move that can give you full control over your finances.

After I decided to take charge of my money, I downloaded the investing app Acorns and linked it with my checking account. I have no vested interest in Acorns, but after years of trying to automate investments, this is the first app I've found to be simple and easy to use. Acorns recommends a portfolio of funds for you based on your personalized answers. The app then invests in your individual portfolio by deducting recurring increments of as little as five dollars per week from whichever bank account you link it to.

Why bother to invest your own money, especially if you're only doing so in small amounts? First, the fastest way to stop feeling anxious around your finances is to prove to yourself that you don't need to spend every penny you make. And with this strategy, you'll be saving money every single week. Next, investing your own money, even if it's just a small amount with the aid of an app, can help you feel smarter, more savvy, and more in control around money. Not only are you saving, but you also have the chance to make money on your savings. Investing even small amounts of money can also pique your interest in learning more about finances, as it did for me. I started to seek out and read books about money after I started investing, and the subject began to generate positive emotion in me. My favorite book so far is *Financial Feminist: Overcome the Patriarchy's Bullsh*t to Master Your Money and Build a Life You Love* by money and career expert Tori Dunlap, who saved her first $100,000 by age twenty-five.

While there's no guarantee of growth, the average stock market return for the last thirty years has been approximately 10 percent, as measured by the S&P. Let's say you save $5 a day, or $35 a week and approximately $150 per month. Factoring in compounded interest—the money you make off the interest you earn—and a 10 percent annual return, you'd earn $30,727 in ten years, $339,073 in thirty years, and $948,611 in forty years.

If you believe that investing money is only for the wealthy, I'd encourage you to reconsider your perspective. Investing $5 per day is the cost of a coffee—you could even start with $1 daily. Once you automate your weekly savings and investment transfers, you can also forget about them, which we're prone to do anyway. This means you can start saving and hopefully making extra money with no additional time commitment. Plus, when you automate your investments, you don't need to remember to do anything, which means it's completely painless. I also check my Acorns account several times a month just to remind myself that I can do hard things my own way, which never fails to give me a little hit of dopamine.

Picture your money doing good in the world

For decades, I felt anxiety around paying bills because the steps involved were so boring. This anxiety began in college when, no matter what I did, I always seemed to owe more money than I had. This discomfort, combined with my sunny optimism that led me to believe a sudden windfall was right around the corner, would cause me to kick the can to the next day.

After I decided to take control of my own finances, however, I knew I needed to figure out how to turn this anxiety into positive emotion. One strategy that's worked for me is that I visualize my money doing good in the world whenever I'm paying someone. I picture the other person or an employee in the company paying for groceries, taking their loved ones out to eat, writing a check for their kids' education, or simply living an easier life. By sending positive emotion with my money, I create positive emotion for myself. This has eased my anxiety tremendously and has helped me to be even more generous with those who may not have the same resources as me.

How Physical Movement Can Treat ADHD

The best ADHD treatment I've found is exercise. Moving your body in some way—any way—on a consistent basis can help you manage your ADHD symptoms more easily and effectively. I've seen physical activity overhaul the lives of hundreds of women—including my own life—boosting mood, focus, and productivity.

Exercise has such a positive effect on ADHD symptoms, in fact, that a single workout can immediately increase your attention span, lower your impulsivity, and help you better regulate your emotions. Researchers also call exercise an "effective treatment" for ADHD, capable of balancing brain chemicals as well as or even more effectively than stimulant ADHD medication.

For years, I relied on exercise to help manage my ADHD symptoms without realizing it. When I was seven, I started dancing ballet to a live piano in Antonio Mendez's studio, which I did obsessively until I was thirteen. After that, I discovered running and joined the jogging craze. When I first got to college, I stopped working out, and my focus and productivity dropped precipitously (see page 31 on how I almost flunked out of college after my first year). Then, one Friday night my sophomore year, my boyfriend at the time dragged me into the university weight room, and I've been hooked on strength training ever since. I've also worked as an aerobics instructor, practiced Bikram yoga (a type of hot yoga) religiously for five years, and am a self-described "gym rat."

I always thought that exercise was just a great way to burn calories and look better. After I became an ADHD coach and learned exactly what physical activity can do for our ADHD brains, however, it dawned on me why I always felt compelled to work out and why, when I do, my days are almost always happier, more focused, and more productive. I began to see that physical movement works like a drug in my brain, reduces the unnecessary chatter in my mind, and calms my anxiety. Since then, I've removed as many obstacles as I can from the task of working out so that it's easier for me to initiate.

> *Exercise has such a positive effect on ADHD symptoms, in fact, that a single workout can immediately increase your attention span, lower your impulsivity, and help you better regulate your emotions.*

For example, I invested in a set of weights, a treadmill, and a spin bike for my home, two of which I try to use every morning before doing anything else. During Covid, my husband cut a half-a-mile walking trail outside our property for our family that I continue to use to walk our dogs, Mo and Teddy. On weekends, I like to walk, hike, and garden. When I work out first thing in the morning, I always feel grounded and calm, as if all obstacles to taking on the day have been removed. In this way, my workout acts as an on-ramp to the day, because after I reach my exercise goals in the morning, it generates the momentum to keep me going for the rest of the day.

When I was promoting my most recent online ADHD program, my daughter had just come home to celebrate my birthday. We had lots of social obligations, not to mention a new puppy, and contractors were doing work on our house. Bottom line: I had too much going on. One afternoon in the middle of this madness, I realized that I hadn't gotten anything done. My focus was nonexistent, and whenever I tried to work, I kept getting up because I couldn't stay seated—everything distracted me. When I did manage to sit, I could only spin from one incomplete task to another, incapable of finishing anything.

At first, I blamed my lack of focus on our crazy week, but then I paused and asked myself if there was something else going on. I realized that I had been so focused on taking a shower before the contractors arrived that morning that I had forgotten to work out. By now, it was 3 p.m., but I knew the only way to salvage the day was to get my heart rate up so that my brain could focus. I got on my spin bike for thirty minutes, and five minutes into the workout, I felt more grounded and calm. After twenty minutes, I felt focused and inspired. Once I finished the workout, I knocked out all of the partially completed tasks littering my to-do list. Every task I crossed off inspired me to tackle the next one.

In this chapter, we'll take a look at how exactly exercise can benefit our ADHD brains, along with the most effective ways to move your body to better manage your symptoms and the optimal time of day to be active to boost your productivity.

HOW PHYSICAL ACTIVITY CAN REVAMP YOUR ADHD BRAIN

Knowing how movement impacts my ADHD brain has helped motivate me to exercise when I'd rather do anything else and made it easier for me to make physical activity part of my daily routine. And as an ADHD coach, I always share with the women in my groups the specifics of how exercise can help their ADHD brains. Once they learn and experience it firsthand, they make exercise part of their daily routine. And you can too. Physical activity:

- **SPIKES YOUR DOPAMINE.** If you have ADHD, your brain is deficient in dopamine production, as multiple studies have found. Dopamine is a neurotransmitter, or brain chemical, that increases mood, attention, motivation, and memory, in addition to impacting other functions. How to get more dopamine? Move your body in any way, even if you do so only briefly. Physical activity spikes dopamine, along with norepinephrine, another neurotransmitter that helps regulate attention and mood. Prescription ADHD drugs also boost these two neurotransmitters, although research shows that exercise may do so more effectively than medication because physical activity balances them at the same time. (Note: You should never substitute exercise for ADHD medication without speaking with your provider. If ADHD medication works for you *and* you want to exercise, you'll still reap additional benefits by adding activity to your routine.)

- **IMPROVES EXECUTIVE FUNCTION.** Remember those pesky executive function skills that we oftentimes struggle with if we have ADHD? Exercise can lift them, helping us increase our focus, control our impulses, initiate and complete tasks, switch from task to task, and fine-tune our working memory.

- **CHANGES YOUR BRAIN PHYSICALLY.** Exercise increases production of brain-derived neurotrophic factor (BDNF), a protein that helps promote brain growth, which ADHD doctor John Ratey likens to "Miracle-Gro for the brain." The more you exercise, the more BDNF you produce, bumping up your brain's capacity to grow and adapt. BDNF plays a role in neuroplasticity, which describes our brains' ability to change over our lifetime with exposure to different environments and lifestyle habits. Exercise also stimulates neurogenesis, the production of new brain cells in middle-aged and older adults. Basically, every time you're active in a sustained way, you're helping to grow new brain cells and protect existing ones.

- **INCREASES MEMORY AND LEARNING.** BDNF can also rewire your brain to increase your ability to learn and remember. Multiple studies show that exercise in general boosts learning and memory. Even a two-minute bout of moderate exercise can improve your ability to learn, problem solve, plan, concentrate, and express yourself verbally for up to two hours afterward.

- **IMPROVES EMOTIONAL REGULATION.** Exercise works to regulate our brain's amygdala, the area that processes strong emotions like anxiety, fear, and aggression. According to Ratey, exercise is like taking a bit of the antidepressant Prozac and the ADHD drug Ritalin at the same time, increasing the same neurotransmitters in our brain to help us better control our emotions.

- **HELPS PREVENT AND EASE DEPRESSION AND ANXIETY.** If you've ever felt elated after a workout, you know how much exercise can shift your mood. The impact goes beyond lifting your spirits, however: regular movement can also help treat depression—something that ADHD women often struggle with. Research also shows that consistent exercise can be more effective than prescription drugs in treating the mood disorder and preventing people from relapsing. For this reason, exercise is often used as the first line of defense in depression treatment in Britain before antidepressants are prescribed. (Note: Never substitute exercise for antidepressants without speaking with your provider. There's also nothing wrong with taking antidepressants, which can be lifesaving drugs for many.)

  Similarly, exercise can ease anxiety by distracting you from your thoughts and increasing the production of the stress-easing chemicals like serotonin, dopamine, and gamma-aminobutyric acid (GABA). According to recent research, moderate exercise can even prevent anxiety disorders.

- **HELPS CONTROL HYPERACTIVITY.** For most of us with ADHD, we need to move our bodies to burn off our hyperactivity, whether it's physical or mental. Even for people without ADHD, exercise calms an overactive mind and helps control spinning or ruminative thoughts.

WHAT TO DO IF YOU CAN'T EXERCISE

Exercise has a PR problem in the world today. Whenever I talk about exercise on my podcast or in my group programs, I inevitably get emails, DMs, or questions in person from women asking what "real" people can do if they "can't exercise." Whenever I hear this, I tell my clients to reframe the word *exercise* into *movement*. While exercise for many conjures up the idea of hours on a treadmill, in a spin class, or training for a triathlon, most of us can *move* our body in some way, whether it's by taking a walk, gardening, dancing to your favorite Spotify playlist, or even doing chair aerobics or chair yoga if you have a more serious or limiting health condition or injury (go online to learn how to move while seated—there are some great, free tutorials on YouTube by qualified instructors). The key here is to build awareness around how much better you feel after you move. I recommend that my clients rate the intensity of their discomfort on a scale from zero to ten, with ten being the most extreme. I then ask them to rate how they feel after they've moved their bodies. They typically report feeling calmer, more emotionally regulated, and focused. Connecting movement with feeling good helps them push through the discomfort when they struggle to start.

THE BEST TIME OF DAY TO BE ACTIVE

I used to always exercise at night, but after I was diagnosed with ADHD, I began to experiment with working out first thing in the morning. When I did, I always felt happier and more focused for the rest of the day. It didn't matter how I felt when I woke up. Once I worked out, everything shifted and I felt better, with a greater degree of control over my day. Since then, I've never looked back.

Today, I do everything within my power to exercise in some meaningful way first thing in the morning. Doing so gives me a spike of dopamine that springboards me into my day. It also provides a sense of immediate accomplishment that triggers that positive emotion I've talked so much about in this book, pushing my dopamine levels even higher and making it easier for me to focus on and knock off my next task on my to-do list.

While moving your body at any time of the day can improve your ADHD symptoms, research shows that doing so first thing in the morning will give you the most bang for your buck. Morning exercise resets your mood for the day and increases levels of the feel-good chemicals dopamine, norepinephrine, and serotonin, helping to propel you into a productive and more emotionally regulated afternoon and evening. Moving your body after waking up can also capitalize on the body's levels of the stress hormone cortisol, which are naturally higher in the morning, making you more alert while also boosting physical performance. What's more, if you take ADHD medication, researchers say exercising an hour before you do so can help sustain

QUICK TIPS TO AMPLIFY YOUR ADHD BRAIN WITH EXERCISE

- Do at least thirty minutes of aerobic activity four times per week.

- Find a structured activity that requires complex movements like martial arts, yoga, or rock climbing.

- Make it social by finding an exercise buddy or group class to stay accountable and add a fun factor.

- Take it outside for increased concentration and lower stress levels.

- Choose an extreme or adventurous activity to harness your focus, satisfy impulsivity, and steer off boredom.

the focusing effects of a good workout. You may also discover that you need a lower dose of stimulant medication after adopting a consistent exercise routine. (Note: Never titrate your ADHD meds without speaking with your provider first.)

All this said, if you prefer to work out at night or that's the only time you can fit movement into your routine, you'll still reap plenty of benefits for your ADHD brain. Don't let perfect be the enemy of good, meaning any movement, no matter when you do it, is better than no movement at all.

BEST TYPES OF MOVEMENT FOR MANAGING ADHD

If you've already found a way that you like to move your body—whether it's running, walking, biking, hiking, or hitting the gym—that you do on a consistent basis, congratulations! That's amazing, and it's likely the best type of exercise for you. But if you've struggled to make movement a part of your regular routine, you may want to experiment with more structured types of exercise, such as ballet or barre classes, yoga, martial arts, rock climbing, or even skateboarding or snowboarding. All these activities combine complex movements, which stimulate the brain to focus on what we're doing. Structured exercise also activates multiple parts of the brain required for balancing, timing, and fine motor skills, among other functions, helping to harness our overactive minds.

Finding a regular group exercise class or participating in an adult sport like pickleball can also help hold you accountable. When you have an instructor, trainer, or friends expecting you to show up, you're more likely to do so than when you're responsible for getting yourself to the gym alone in the morning or after work. Team or group activities can also make movement more fun and provide connection, which is important for our ADHD brains.

If you really want to optimize your workout for your ADHD brain, consider taking your workout outside. Research shows that physical activity performed in nature lowers ADHD symptoms more effectively than when we exercise inside. Not only does nature lower cortisol levels, it's also been shown to help reset the brains of both neurodivergent and neurotypical people when we have "attention fatigue," restoring our concentration and cognitive resources when we feel tapped out.

Finally, if you have the access or ability to participate in extreme sports like rock climbing, mountain biking, skiing, or skateboarding, these may help you manage your ADHD symptoms on another level. Experts say these types of sports may be best at harnessing the attention of the ADHD brain because they engage the body's fight-or-flight survival response. You have to remain on high alert and focused for your safety, which motivates you to pay attention. Sports that are adventurous or risky may also sate our impulsivity, if that's one of our traits, in a healthier way than other outlets and prevent us from ever getting bored by what we're doing.

Using Nutrition to Curb ADHD Symptoms

I pushed the last empty box of candy turtles into the trundle under the bunk bed I shared with my sister. It was the twelfth and final box of nutty, chewy, caramel deliciousness that I'd consumed in less than one week. With 12 turtles per box, that's 144 chocolates that I'd shoved into my ten-year-old mouth in less than seven days.

I can't remember what my fifth-grade class was raising money for, but the boxes weren't meant for me to eat—they were meant for me to sell. But I had a sweet tooth, so sweet in fact that even though my dad was a dentist who believed his children didn't eat candy, I spent every spare dime I had on sweets that I stashed in the same trundle. And while small candies like Lemonheads, Jolly Ranchers, and Now and Laters were favorites because they were easy to hide, twelve empty boxes of turtles were not.

It all started innocently enough. My plan was to eat just one box of turtles, then break into my piggy bank, take out a dollar, and add it to the other eleven that I would inevitably receive from selling the remaining boxes. But once I started eating the turtles, I couldn't stop. Every subsequent box I ate, I justified with "Oh, it's just one more," until there were no more boxes to justify.

Did I even have twelve dollars in my piggy bank? Turns out I did. Twelve dollars went promptly to the school, and my parents were none the wiser, even though the highly incriminating evidence of twelve empty turtle boxes was still inside my trundle.

Six months later, my brother gleefully ratted me out. Only decades later do I now understand how my ADHD brain led me down this sugar-coated path of deception and piggy bank crime.

HOW ADHD AFFECTS OUR BEHAVIORS AROUND FOOD

If you've struggled to maintain or lose weight and have ADHD, I want you to give yourself permission to cut yourself some slack. Having ADHD means we're up to ten times more likely than the general population to have issues with our weight. Why? Because our brains are low in dopamine, so we instinctually seek out foods like sugar and carbs that can provide an instant hit of the feel-good chemical—and the more sugar and carbs we eat, the more we need to get the same dopamine hit to feel sated. Our ADHD brains are also low in GABA, a neurotransmitter that makes us feel calm and helps control our inhibition. Without sufficient levels of GABA, we're more likely to reach for seconds or even thirds or say *screw it* when deciding whether to opt for grilled chicken or chocolate cake for dinner. If impulsivity is one of our traits, we may also be more likely to make poor food choices and overeat. Some of us may use eating as a way of procrastinating what we don't want to do, while those of us who suffer from poor emotional regulation may rely on sugar, carbs, or other comfort foods to help self-soothe. And if we have an ADHD comorbidity like depression or anxiety that affects our emotional health, we may also use food to self-medicate.

Another factor that can contribute to overeating is reward

deficiency syndrome, a condition linked to low dopamine levels that's more common in those of us with ADHD. Reward deficiency syndrome causes our brain to instinctually seek out bigger, more immediate, or more repeated rewards through food, drugs, or risky behavior to try to increase our dopamine. If food is our preferred source of dopamine and we have reward deficiency syndrome, we'll be driven to eat more food more often or to choose items that can provide a bigger spike, like junk food or processed carbs. When we have reward deficiency syndrome, we also don't get the same satisfaction from the reward that neurotypicals do, which is also why we go back a second or third time, hoping to get our expected reward.

Not only are we wired to overeat, we may also struggle to initiate and follow through with a healthy eating plan—or any kind of regular eating plan at all. You can blame our impaired executive function skills, which make it challenging to start or maintain a healthy diet, let alone plan, prep, or shop. If we tend to hyperfocus, we may also forget to eat for hours on end, causing us to get ravenous, which usually leads to poor food choices. I'll sometimes get so absorbed by a project that I won't realize I haven't eaten a thing all day until 4 p.m. Other times, I'll feel hungry, but the thought of having to stop to prepare anything seems like too much work. This is how many ADHD women I know end up reaching for fast food or unhealthy convenience items.

Being chronically sleep deprived, as those of us with ADHD often are (see chapter 13), can also affect our weight by increasing our hunger and making us more likely to make unhealthy food choices (and less likely to be physically active).

There's also evidence that people with ADHD are more likely to have an eating disorder, especially binge eating, due to issues in how our brains handle reward processing. Some women with ADHD may be more prone to eating disorders as a way of compensating for the lack of control, adequacy, competence, or accomplishment they feel.

HOW TO USE NUTRITION
TO BOOST OUR ADHD BRAINS

While we may struggle more with weight and healthy eating, we can use smart nutrition to increase our brain function and power while curbing our tendency to overeat or engage in other problematic eating patterns. Here, I've put together a list of realistic, actionable, and implementable strategies to help you use nutrition to boost your ADHD brain rather than derail your cognitive or physical health. These strategies have been recommended by nutritionists who specialize in ADHD and successfully implemented by many of the women I've worked with.

Plan time to shop, prep, and/or cook

Healthy eating is a lot like getting to the gym—it takes some planning and organizing, which can be difficult for our ADHD brains to do. But once you build in time to go to the grocery store and cook, whether it's assembling a simple salad or falling in love with more complex meal prep (hello, new hyperfocus!), it'll become second nature for you to eat better and resist the call of fast or convenient food. For some of us, part of our planning may be to identify healthier quick meal and snack options for those days when our time management skills are less than ideal.

Let go of the "good" versus "bad" food mentality

Many of us grew up with diet culture that dictated the idea that certain foods are "good" and others are "bad." This mentality, though, usually just fuels a restrict-and-binge cycle: the more you tell yourself a food is bad, the more you'll likely crave it. Instead, remind yourself that all food is energy and can keep you alive. Getting rid of the idea that certain foods are good and bad can also help you overcome any fear you might have with feeling out of control around food, which often occurs in women with eating disorders.

Find nourishing foods you love

Given our go-go-go ADHD brains, many of us have never paused long enough to know which foods we really like. Take the time over the next several weeks to consider and experiment with which foods satisfy you *and* make you feel your best, meaning energized, nourished, and healthy after eating them. When weighing different food choices, be sure to think about a food's long-term effects: while sugary and carb-heavy items may make you feel happy when you're eating them, they may not make you feel sated, energized, and nourished in the long run. Pay attention to which foods make you feel good not only while you're eating them but also thirty minutes later.

Limit distractions while you eat

We know that our ADHD brains love distractions. But when we distract ourselves while we eat, we're not focused on our food, reducing how much we enjoy it—some of us may not even feel as though we've eaten when we actually have. For each meal, take the time to sit down and focus on and savor your food, without a laptop, phone, or television. By visually engaging with your meal and staying in the moment, you'll be more mindful and feel more satisfied after eating. If eating without distractions seems too understimulating or uncomfortable, listen to music, a podcast, or an audiobook so that your visual focus remains on what you're eating.

Prioritize two nutrients to boost your ADHD brain

When it comes to nutrition, there are no magic foods or nutrients that can help hack your cognitive health overnight. But there are two foods (or nutritional supplements) that may make it easier for you to maintain a healthy weight, heal disordered eating, and/or boost your brainpower, depending on your goals.

The first are probiotics, which are the healthy bacteria in yogurt, kefir, raw sauerkraut, miso, and other fermented foods. If you think you already know what you need to about probiotics, keep reading: I'm guessing you may not have heard how probiotics can help our ADHD brains. Studies show they have a large positive effect on our symptoms.

You see, the health of our microbiome—the vast community of bacteria, fungi, and yeast that lives in the gut—directly affects the health of our brain via a two-way pathway known as the gut-brain axis. When we improve the health of our gut, we increase the health and function of our brain. And we can improve the health of our microbiome by consuming or supplementing with high-quality probiotics. Research states that consuming or supplementing with probiotics can increase executive function, along with attention, memory, and learning abilities, while also reducing mental stress. Probiotics may also boost mood and curb symptoms of depression, anxiety, and other mental health comorbidities related to ADHD. These healthy gut bugs have also been shown to prevent or treat binge eating and other eating disorders, with researchers even citing probiotics as "novel therapeutic approaches" to disordered eating.

The second nutrient for the ADHD brain is omega-3 fatty acids—specifically the marine omega-3s, eicosapentaenoic acid (EPA) and docosahexaenoic acid (DHA), which are found primarily in fatty fish like salmon, mackerel, tuna, sardines, and anchovies. EPA and DHA are necessary for brain structure, growth, and function, and have been shown to reduce brain inflammation and boost executive function, memory, and learning. Some studies even suggest that EPA and DHA supplements can help reduce ADHD symptoms as effectively as stimulant drugs, and low levels of both marine omega-3s have been associated with the development of ADHD. Like probiotics, EPA and DHA have also been found to increase mood and prevent and treat depression and anxiety, along with borderline personality disorder, obsessive-compulsive disorder, and other mental health conditions.

> *When we improve the health of our gut, we increase the health and function of our brain.*

The problem for most of us, however, is that we don't consume enough fish to have adequate blood levels of marine omega-3s. And while our body can convert a small amount of the omega-3 fats found in plants like chia seeds, brussels sprouts, and walnuts into EPA and DHA, the percentage is too tiny to make a noticeable difference. This is why consuming more fatty fish or taking a high-quality marine omega-3 supplement is essential, according to the National Institutes of Health. I've always eaten a lot of seafood, but since adding a daily omega-3 supplement, I have noticed a considerable uptick in my mood, focus, and memory.

Consider intermittent fasting

Intermittent fasting has become popular in recent years among biohackers, health gurus, and weight-loss experts. Now growing evidence supports that the practice can help limit ADHD symptoms and boost brain function. When you fast intermittently, you choose a consistent time block during which you eat your meals, then fast for the remaining time—usually skipping breakfast and fasting throughout the morning, eating later in the day and evening before stopping at a specific hour. In a 16:8 fast, for example, you eat within an 8-hour window, then fast overnight and into the next morning for the remaining 16 hours.

Intermittent fasting forces your body to burn through all the sugar or glucose in your blood before tapping into your fat stores for energy. Doing so increases BDNF, which helps create new neurons, triggering the brain to grow and change while improving the body's insulin sensitivity needed for optimal cognitive function. According to research, intermittent fasting can improve memory, focus, learning, and overall executive function, and reduce brain inflammation.

I've heard from many ADHD women who say intermittent fasting has helped them overhaul their focus, mood, and mental chatter while also making it easier for them to lose weight. "Thanks to intermittent fasting, my brain fog has cleared, my mood is calmer, and for the first time in twenty years, I have been able to lose and maintain weight loss in a way that has felt effortless and healthy," Katrina wrote me after listening to an episode on intermittent fasting on my podcast.

According to research, intermittent fasting can improve memory, focus, learning, and overall executive function, and reduce brain inflammation.

After hearing these types of success stories, I decided to try intermittent fasting myself a few years ago. After just several days of fasting for sixteen hours daily, I noticed my focus, memory, and overall mood were better and that, for me, feeling full and sluggish in my body translates to feeling the same way in my brain. I love intermittent fasting today because it's so simple: I only have to think about food for eight hours a day, which means less planning and prepping.

If you want to try intermittent fasting, be patient. Your body will likely adapt to your new eating schedule after a week or so. This was my experience. I've never been a morning eater, but when I first tried intermittent fasting, I was always starving by noon, and managing my hunger until 2 p.m., which is when I typically broke my fast. It took some effort. During the first week, I drank a lot of green tea, which helped settle my stomach and curb my appetite, and scheduled several lunches at 2 p.m. at my favorite restaurants as a reward for sticking with my fast. After a week, however, I had acclimated to fasting until 2 p.m. and was no longer hungry before then.

According to the Mayo Clinic, Johns Hopkins Medicine, and other major health organizations, intermittent fasting can reduce inflammation, improve conditions associated with inflammation, and boost thinking and memory, among other benefits, and is generally safe for most people. But before you adopt any fasting program, speak with your physician, as it can interfere with some medical conditions. If you suffer from an eating disorder or disordered eating, intermittent fasting may not be right for you—check first with a licensed practitioner.

Drink more water

If you'd asked me several years ago if I drank enough water, I would have told you that I didn't without getting too upset about the admission. That's before I read *Biohack Your Brain: How to Boost Cognitive Health, Power, and Performance* by Kristen Willeumier and learned that I was chronically dehydrated and it was significantly affecting my cognition and focus.

And I wasn't in the minority. Seventy-five percent of Americans are chronically dehydrated, which means most of us don't consume enough water and other fluids on a consistent basis, which sabotages our mood, memory, attention, and overall cognitive function. As Willeumier points out, when you're dehydrated, your brain has to do more to process the same amount of information. Being dehydrated affects our cognitive structure and volume, causing our brain tissue to actually shrink. Even mild dehydration can impair memory, attention, and mood—one reason why well-hydrated people do better on cognitive tests and have improved memory, motor skills, mental energy, alertness, and concentration.

For these reasons, it's essential for those of us with ADHD to stay hydrated to boost our brain function and power. If you take stimulant medication, you may need to be even more vigilant about your fluid intake, since the drugs have been shown to increase dehydration. According to the Mayo Clinic, women should aim to consume around 11.5 cups of fluid per day, or just over 90 ounces, some of which can come from the water content in food.

After reading Willeumier's book, I decided to set a goal of drinking 64 ounces of water per day. I purchased two 64-ounce glass water bottles so that I could track my fluid intake, keeping one at all times in the fridge chilling with sliced cucumber—you can add slices of orange, lemon, lime, or a handful of berries if you like a flavor pop—so I always have a cold bottle ready to go. With this method, I found it easy to measure and increase my fluid intake, and within weeks, I noticed that I had less brain fog, especially in the afternoons, along with more energy and fewer headaches. My skin has also become clearer, and my eyes are no longer dry and itchy.

13

Overhauling ADHD-Related Sleep Problems

Sleep: it's what we really need to feel organized, focused, calm, and sharp—and it's what we as ADHD women often struggle to get. Women with ADHD may face consistent sleep problems, and according to an unscientific survey I conducted among the 90,000 women who belong to my Facebook group, ADHD for Smart Ass Women, it could be as high as 95 percent. More formal research estimates as many as four out of five adults with ADHD have a sleep disorder that prevents us from falling asleep, staying asleep, and getting the sleep we need. Sleep issues are so common among those of us with ADHD that "restless sleep" was even part of the diagnostic criteria for the condition in the 1980s. (The criteria has since changed because children rarely have sleep issues by age twelve, which is when the *DSM-5* has determined that ADHD symptoms must manifest.)

What do sleep problems look like in those of us with ADHD? For many, it takes us hours to fall asleep because our minds are so hyperactive, causing us to ruminate, catastrophize, or worry. For this reason, up to 70 percent of ADHD adults report that it takes them at least an hour or more to fall asleep, according to Dr. William Dodson, one of the first practitioners to specialize in adult ADHD.

Some of us may be able to fall asleep but can't stay asleep. We get restless in the middle of the night and start tossing and turning—something that's more likely to happen if we have ADHD, according to numerous studies, including one published in *ADHD Attention Deficit and Hyperactivity Disorders* that analyzed years of prior research on ADHD and sleep. And since we can't fall asleep or consistently wake up through the night, many of us also struggle to get up in the morning.

Still other ADHD women, myself included, go to bed much too late because of something sleep experts call revenge bedtime procrastination (RBP). RBP is a real condition in which people procrastinate going to bed to spend time late at night on leisure activities, getting "revenge" for being too busy during the day or because we feel too overwhelmed by working, parenting, or just plain old adulting during normal waking hours. Unfortunately, when we have RBP, what we do at night to procrastinate sleep, whether it's watching TV, scrolling through social media, or online shopping, only serves to undermine our life in general, even though in the moment it may feel fun or even rewarding. And if we have ADHD, we're more likely to have RBP than neurotypical people because we already tend to be procrastinators, who are impulsive in the moment (*Who needs sleep, anyway?*), have trouble managing time (*How's it already two in the morning?*), often don't want to deal with the boring routine of getting ready for bed, and may also want to stall the anticipated discomfort of being unable to fall asleep because we can't turn off our overactive minds.

Some people with ADHD may also deal with intrusive sleep, a problem that occurs when a person falls asleep when it's not appropriate or safe, like during a work meeting or even while driving. While the extent of intrusive sleep is unknown, researchers say those of us with ADHD are more likely to experience the condition because we're often easily bored and chronically sleep deprived, a combination that can cause us to drift off when we really shouldn't.

You may not struggle with intrusive sleep or RBP, but if you have ADHD, I'm guessing that you have experienced problems with sleeping at night or feeling rested enough during the day. In this chapter, we'll take a look at why we ADHDers have more sleep issues and what we can all do to improve our sleep so that we can boost our brain function and better manage our lives.

WHY WE STRUGGLE MORE WITH SLEEP

While researchers agree that those of us with ADHD struggle more with sleep, theories abound on exactly why. Some scientists believe that our brains' different wiring affects our arousal and alertness levels, thereby interfering with our sleep. Other researchers say we have a delayed circadian rhythm, meaning that our body's twenty-four-hour internal clock is set later than neurotypical folks, causing us to be alert later into the evening, which is why we may resist going to sleep or be unable to fall asleep. We also have a higher like-lihood of developing sleep-related comorbidities, like restless leg syndrome, sleep-disordered breathing, and narcolepsy, which can wreak absolute havoc on our shut-eye.

If that's not enough, many of the most common ADHD symptoms like impulsivity, poor time management, and procrastination can prevent us from getting into bed when we should. And for some of us, when we do go to bed, hyperactivity causes us to ruminate or spin through our thoughts. Furthermore, if the idea of going to bed sounds dull and monotonous to us, we might resist because we don't like being bored. Many of us also don't like being told what to do—and that includes getting into bed. And if we take stimulant ADHD medication, the drugs can interfere with our sleep, per the Cleveland Clinic and numerous clinical trials. To add one more element, women with ADHD have to deal with hormonal changes as we get older that can worsen the sleep disorders we already face because of our neurodivergent brains.

But there's hope! There's always hope. A few simple strategies can help you overcome your sleep issues. Keep reading.

FIVE ESSENTIAL HABITS FOR BETTER SLEEP

You likely already know a little something about sleep hygiene, or healthy practices that can help you fall asleep faster, stay asleep through the night, and wake up feeling more restful and refreshed. Before we get to the strategies that can help us ADHDers sleep better at night, make sure these five essential habits are part of your routine.

1. **BE CONSISTENT.** Going to bed at approximately the same time every night and waking up at approximately the same time every morning will help your body establish a routine that becomes easy for you to follow. When you fall into a natural routine, your brain does the work for you, causing you to feel sleepy at night and alert after you get up.

2. **MAKE YOUR BEDROOM DARK, QUIET, AND COLD.** Light interferes with sleep while disruptive noise will wake you up or make it more difficult to sleep, even if you're not consciously aware of the sound (we can still hear sounds during lighter stages of sleep, and they can disrupt our shut-eye without our knowledge). Cooling your bedroom to 60 to 67 degrees Fahrenheit can also help promote sleep, so turn down the thermostat or open windows before you hit the hay.

3. **AVOID CAFFEINE AFTER 4 P.M.** If you're more sensitive to caffeine, you may need to limit your consumption even earlier in the day.

4. **LIMIT ALCOHOL.** You may believe that booze helps you sleep better, but it blocks REM sleep, which is critical for cognition, learning, memory, and emotional and mental health.

5. **SKIP TECHNOLOGY FOR AT LEAST AN HOUR BEFORE BED.** Not only can the blue light emitted by cell phones, laptops, iPads, and other devices throw off your sleep cycle, but technology also stimulates you, activating regions of your brain that prevent you from falling asleep.

HOW SLEEP PROBLEMS IMPACT OUR ADHD BRAINS

- **IMPAIR OUR EXECUTIVE FUNCTION TO AN EVEN GREATER DEGREE.** Just one night of too little shut-eye can diminish your executive function, which is already weakened if you have ADHD. This means your memory, concentration, and problem-solving abilities will suffer even more if you're not getting enough sleep.

- **AFFECT OUR ABILITY TO MEMORIZE AND LEARN.** Sleep is when our brains consolidate memories so that we can recall what we learned or experienced during the day. If we're short on sleep, we shortchange our brains' ability to memorize, which is something that many of us with ADHD already struggle with. Just one night of poor sleep can slash our ability to learn by as much as 40 percent, according to research. I always tell my college-aged kids that they shouldn't pull all-nighters if they want to remember the information they're studying: You're better off ending your study sessions earlier to prioritize sleep. You'll be able to better recall what you learned the day before.

- **WORSEN THE ADHD SYMPTOMS WE ALREADY HAVE.** If you're not getting enough sleep, you'll struggle to focus and make good decisions. Sleep deprivation can also cause or worsen symptoms of low mood, depression, and anxiety. Just one night of sleeplessness can also mess with our amygdala, an area of the brain already impaired in those of us with ADHD, interfering with our ability to regulate our emotions and perceive the world around us clearly and calmly. While it may seem counterintuitive, sleep deprivation can also increase our tendency to be hyperactive.

- **AGGRAVATE ADHD COMORBIDITIES.** Nearly every health condition worsens with too little sleep, including the ones that oftentimes accompany ADHD, such as mental health issues like bipolar disorder and learning disabilities like dyslexia.

- **EXACERBATE RELATIONSHIP ISSUES.** Running low on sleep inevitably increases conflict and tension in our interpersonal relationships. This is true for everyone, but since many of us with ADHD are already prone to experiencing more relationship conflict—see chapter 8—this added layer can worsen an already problematic partnership or friendship.

- **IMPAIR OUR OVERALL HEALTH.** Sleep is so important to immune function, disease prevention, and our overall health that getting fewer than seven hours per night on a regular basis can significantly increase the risk of chronic disease and mental health issues, according to the Mayo Clinic.

EIGHT NEW SLEEP STRATEGIES FOR WOMEN WITH ADHD

Having ADHD means you have a greater tendency of developing certain comorbidities. Common ADHD comorbidities include mental health issues like depression, anxiety, and bipolar disorder; behavioral issues like obsessive-compulsive disorder and oppositional defiant disorder; and tic disorders like Tourette's syndrome. We also have a higher likelihood of developing some physical comorbidities, such as asthma, eczema, epilepsy, chronic obstructive pulmonary disease, and heart disease, among others. We even have a greater chance of having a sleep disorder like sleep apnea or narcolepsy. If left untreated, any of these conditions can seriously interfere with sleep quality and quantity, in which case identifying and treating a mental, physical, or sleep comorbidity may be all that's needed to overhaul your sleep.

1. Reset your circadian clock

Many researchers believe that people with ADHD have a delayed circadian clock, meaning we're biologically programmed to want to go to bed later and wake up later. But we can help reset and refresh our circadian clock, which is critical to do if we have a job or family responsibilities that require an earlier wake-up time.

One of the best ways to reset your circadian clock is by going outside first thing in the morning. Exposing your eyes and skin to natural light after you wake up helps stop your body's production of the sleep hormone melatonin so that you feel more awake and alert. More importantly, morning light exposure will trigger your body to start producing melatonin earlier in the evening, which will help you fall asleep and stay asleep. Unfortunately, you can't just turn on a bunch of bright lights inside and get the same effect. Natural light, even if it's cloudy out, is far more effective at resetting our circadian rhythms than artificial light. If you can't get outside first thing in the morning, spend more time outdoors during the day, which can also help you regulate your circadian clock in addition to boosting levels of vitamin D and the feel-good hormones serotonin and dopamine— all of which can lower fatigue and increase mood.

At nighttime, you'll want to do the opposite, reducing your exposure to bright light, especially those that are artificial, which have been shown to suppress melatonin and interfere with sleep quality. Doing some form of meditation, deep breathing, or other relaxation exercises before you go to bed can also reset your circadian clock by calming your nervous system, helping relax you for sleep.

You can also consider speaking with your physician about whether taking melatonin supplements might be right for you. ADHD experts say taking one milligram of melatonin an hour before bed can help some people with the condition want to go to bed sooner and fall asleep faster.

2. Move your body, preferably in the morning

Incorporating physical activity into your day or working out more frequently if you already exercise is a great way to improve your sleep quality and quantity, no matter how or when you move your body. Exercise is so good at inducing sleep that it's been shown to ease insomnia symptoms as effectively as sleeping pills for some people. Exercise can also increase your mood, reduce your stress, and limit your tendency to ruminate, all of which can prevent anxiety or spinning thoughts from thwarting your ability to fall asleep.

Working out soon after you wake up is the best way to improve sleep since it helps reset your circadian clock by triggering the release of melatonin earlier in the evening. If you're able to exercise outside, you'll do double-time by moving your body while also exposing yourself to natural light.

When I switched to morning workouts, I struggled at first to wake up at an earlier hour to exercise. But after a few weeks, it became much easier for me to get up, and now that it's part of my regular routine, I don't feel any resistance whatsoever. In fact, after I wake up, I look forward to working out because I know that it's a surefire way to feel better in the morning.

3. Do a brain dump

Sometimes we don't want to go to bed at night because we don't want to be alone with our thoughts. Our tendency to ruminate and catastrophize can worsen at night because there's nothing to distract us once we lie down in bed. For this reason, many therapists recommend doing a "brain dump" before bed by writing down all your worries, thoughts, and to-do lists in a journal. This can prevent nighttime rumination by purging your thoughts from your mind, helping you feel as though you've addressed them by getting them out and down on paper. According to one study, people who journal their to-do list for the following day fall asleep up to 37 percent faster than those who journal only about what they have done during the day.

4. Remove resistance to bedtime prep

There's only one thing I hate more than dealing with hair and makeup in the morning and that's dealing with brushing teeth, washing my face, removing my makeup, and moisturizing my skin at night. I dislike getting ready for bed so much that I'll sit on the couch much later than I want to or should simply because I don't want to deal with the process.

To help counter my resistance, I first tried getting ready for bed earlier in the evening, but that did nothing to circumvent my procrastination. My resistance eventually became such a problem, causing me to stay up an hour or more later than I should at times, that I finally had to get creative. I figured out that if I moved my toothbrush and skincare to the bathroom closer to my family room, I'd wash my face and brush my teeth whenever I used the bathroom while spending time with my husband reading or watching TV. And it worked. I still keep all my bedtime products in the family room bathroom and rely on this method to help fight my tendency to indulge in revenge bedtime procrastination.

Another idea is to take a warm shower or bath one hour before bed and brush your teeth, wash your face, and do all your other bedtime prep then. The added bonus is that taking a shower or bath shortly before bed can help drop your core body temp, making it easier for you to fall asleep faster, according to studies.

5. Develop a wake-up plan to feel more alert in the morning

If you have problems waking up in the morning, you need a plan to help you feel more alert and awake after you get out of bed. Some women I work with say they set an alarm an hour before they really have to get up so they can take their ADHD medication with a glass of water beside their bed. Doing this helps them feel more alert and organized when they do get up.

Another strategy is to keep your alarm clock or phone away from your bed so that you physically have to get up and walk across the room to turn it off. Another option is the app Alarmy, which you have to turn off by shaking your phone a certain number of times, solving math problems, typing out motivational quotes, or taking a photo of your front door, all which can help wake up your body and brain.

No matter which strategy you adopt, stop using your Snooze button. Not only does it decrease the amount of solid sleep you get—if you can get up later, simply set your alarm later in order to maximize your slumber time—it's also all too easy to hit Stop instead of Snooze, increasing the likelihood that you'll miss work, family, the gym, or another obligation.

6. Come up with a fun strategy that can motivate you to go to bed

One of the few things my husband and I used to always disagree on was an appropriate bedtime: I always wanted to stay up much later than he did. After I was diagnosed with ADHD and realized that I also had revenge bedtime procrastination, I acknowledged that he was right and started to strategize how I could motivate myself to go to bed when I wanted to do anything but. I knew that fun, funny, and challenging worked for my ADHD brain, so I began to brainstorm ideas that included all three aspects. I started by setting a bedtime for myself that I could consistently maintain, which I determined to be midnight, then I began to think about who else had a deadline of midnight. Cinderella! According to the classic fairy tale, if she's not home by the stroke of midnight, her stagecoach turns into a pumpkin. That sounded like a challenge to me! I set up my Google Alexa to play a message at 11:50 p.m. that said, "Cinderella, you have ten minutes to get to bed or you'll ride in on a pumpkin!" That message motivated me to get up off the couch—my own much less glamorous version of a stagecoach—and run around my living room, closing windows, locking doors, and turning off lights. At 11:55 p.m., I programmed Alexa to play church bells chiming to remind Cinderella that the top of the hour was close.

Yeah, this strategy was ridiculous, but it made me laugh every time, generating the positive emotion I needed to motivate myself to get to bed. I didn't have to play this game with myself for very long, though, before it stuck and became a habit. Pretty soon, I felt so much better getting into bed at a reasonable time that I moved my bedtime to 11 p.m. Even so, right before I get up to go into the bedroom, I can't help but think of Cinderella and beating those church bells, which still causes me to laugh and, more importantly, gets me into bed at the same time. After all, no one wants to end their day on a pumpkin!

7. Try taking your prescription medication

Despite the fact that stimulant medication can disrupt sleep, Dr. William Dodson, one of the leading and most veteran experts on adult ADHD, recommends taking your ADHD medication forty-five minutes before bedtime. Because stimulant meds can calm restlessness, doing so may help some people ease the mental hyperactivity they feel when lying awake in bed. This strategy doesn't work for everyone, however, so speak with your doctor, then be willing to experiment for a few nights while maintaining an open mind.

8. Be the expert on yourself

Some people are night owls, meaning they sleep better when they go to bed later, while others like me are morning larks, who prefer to get up super early. If you're a night owl or morning lark (compared to the majority of people who are hummingbirds and like to go to bed at more "normal" hours), you've probably felt like you don't fit in and may have tried to force yourself to go to bed much earlier or later in order to adhere to a "typical" sleep schedule. But here's the thing: everyone has their own unique circadian clock based on their genetics. If you're forcing yourself to go to bed too early or too late, you could be sabotaging your sleep because you're not slumbering in sync with your biology. If you have flexibility in your schedule, give yourself permission to go to bed later or earlier than everyone else. What's more important than the time you go to bed is adopting a consistent schedule that allows you to get at least seven hours of sleep per night that you can maintain seven days per week.

Because we're each unique creatures in other ways, reflect on the nights you've slept your best and ask yourself what you did during the day or before bed that may have helped you achieve these restful results. Did you exercise during the day or spend more time outside? Did you listen to relaxing music right before bed, read a physical book, or put on some white noise like a box fan? While some sleep experts advocate that you shouldn't have a television in the bedroom, I know many ADHD women who've improved their sleep by playing familiar TV shows at a low noise level or listening to the hum of a soothing podcast or meditation app.

The point here is that you're the expert on you, and if you find a successful strategy, stick with it, even if it contradicts what's "normal" or even recommended. Trust your gut. We're smart, and while we may be different, that's also what makes us amazing problem solvers.

14

Dealing with Learning Differences

Nearly half of all children with ADHD in the United States have a learning disability like dyslexia. While this book is for adult women with ADHD, children don't outgrow learning disabilities, according to the National Center for Learning Disabilities, meaning we have greater odds of having a learning disability. For many of us with ADHD, our learning challenges may not have been detected or diagnosed when we were children, leaving us struggling and wondering for years whether it's just our ADHD or a combination of learning issues.

This is exactly what happened to Juliana, a member of several of my online programs, whose learning disability went undiagnosed. At twenty-nine, Juliana was finally diagnosed with both dyslexia and dysgraphia after I suggested she see a specialist. Juliana said her diagnoses were such a relief as they finally explained her exceptional drive and tenacity. For nearly three decades, she never felt smart in a traditional sense. Her diagnoses also allowed her to start treatment and develop workarounds to address her differences, which slashed her anxiety and boosted her self-esteem.

While ADHD is not classified as a learning disability, its symptoms can impair our learning abilities, especially when we try to grasp information in traditional ways that don't make sense to our neurodivergent brains. For this reason, I believe learning disabilities are really just learning *differences*, an etymological shift that reflects that our brains are simply hardwired to think differently. We have a harder time reading, writing, spelling, and communicating in "standard" ways.

Etymology aside, having both ADHD *and* a learning difference can be that much more challenging. While I'll offer a few workaround strategies here, the real take-home of this chapter is to understand what common learning differences look like so you can investigate whether you might have one and, like Juliana, get diagnosed and begin treatment.

An important note before we begin: Like ADHD, learning differences don't have anything do with intelligence. Many people with learning differences actually have above average intelligence.

THE MOST COMMON LEARNING DIFFERENCES WITH ADHD

Dyslexia

People with dyslexia may read slowly; struggle with pronunciation, reading comprehension, vocabulary, spelling, and writing; or have a combination of several issues. Like ADHD, dyslexia includes a spectrum of symptoms that manifests differently in every individual. What those with dyslexia have in common, however, is that they read using the right side of their brains while non-dyslexics use the left side of their brains. Neither is right or wrong. But since society has set up reading to occur in a certain way—remember, too, that reading in itself is a social construct because no one is born with the ability to read—we're expected to digest words using the left side of our brain, which is unnatural to dyslexics. An estimated 15 to 20 percent of people have symptoms of dyslexia.

People with dyslexia can, however, learn to read in traditional ways. One approach known as Orton-Gillingham has become popular with many dyslexics because it teaches them how to break down words into sounds and letters so they can comprehend text in the same way that those without dyslexia do. You can also experiment with using assistive technologies like Google's Text-to-Speech, which reads aloud text from the screens of Android devices, and NaturalReader, an app designed specifically for dyslexics that reads aloud text via a Chrome extension. Some dyslexics also find that reading on colored paper is much easier than reading black print on white paper. Juliana told me that she had success using Text-to-Speech and NaturalReader while also seeing a professional trained in the Davis Method, a well-known approach that teaches dyslexics how to use their strengths to overcome reading difficulties.

Dyscalculia

Dyscalculia makes it difficult to learn number-related concepts and perform math calculations. It affects approximately 11 percent of children with ADHD. Symptoms include difficulty with counting, multiplication, telling time, reading charts and graphs, and with finances and money management.

Emily, who is part of my Facebook group and has both dyscalculia and ADHD, told me that she needs to know the reason "why" a mathematical formula works before calculating the equation. "I can't simply memorize a method in a vacuum and replicate it in an exam," said Emily. "I need to know why I have to subtract x from both sides— then I can remember what I need to do next." While most of us don't have to do complicated mathematical equations today, women with dyscalculia can still struggle with money issues and other number-related problems. The main strategies I hear from ADHD women with dyscalculia are: (1) use a calculator; (2) outsource financial tasks like taxes, retirement planning, and investment account management if you can; and (3) ask colleagues or develop ways yourself to present data in displays that don't require complex graphs or charts.

Dysgraphia

Dysgraphia is a learning difference that affects written expression. Children with dysgraphia usually have problems with their handwriting, including the inability to write legibly, in a straight line, or with appropriate letter spacing or sizing. They may also grip a pencil awkwardly, have trouble staying within margins, and struggle with sentence structure and grammar when writing. In adults, the condition can show up as hard-to-read handwriting and difficulties with grammar, spelling, syntax, and organizing thoughts into written expression. Filling out forms by hand and activities that require fine motor skills like slicing food or buttoning small buttons are problematic.

Dysgraphia is one of the most frequently missed learning differences, and many adults don't know they have it. Studies suggest that many people with ADHD also have dysgraphia, with estimates ranging as high as 59 percent.

Many women with ADHD and dysgraphia find speech-to-text software helpful. Occupational therapist Vanessa Gorelkin also recommends:

- Practicing mindfulness on a regular basis to reduce anxiety around writing activities.

- Enlisting a friend or family member and alternate drawing letters in each other's palm, which can help you "feel" the shape and method of making the letter.

- Trying to type without looking at the keyboard, which can help enhance literacy, make error corrections less stressful, and encourage hand muscle memory.

THE EYE CONDITION OFTEN MISTAKEN FOR A LEARNING DISORDER

I first heard about a condition called vertical heterophoria from ADHD influencer René Brooks, who started the blog *Black Girl, Lost Keys* to help empower African American women with the condition. She had been living with chronic neck pain, dizziness, anxiety, migraines, and nausea for years, with her symptoms so intense she sometimes was unable to work. That's all before she was diagnosed with vertical heterophoria, a condition that occurs when your eyes are slightly misaligned, causing dizziness, headaches, motion sickness, and eye pain. Testing for vertical heterophoria isn't part of routine eye exams, which is why it often goes undetected in children and adults. That's not great news for those of us with ADHD, as doctors believe there's some link between vertical heterophoria and ADHD. While not a learning difference, the condition is often mistaken for one since it can cause people to struggle with reading, writing, and learning.

After René was diagnosed with vertical heterophoria, her life changed. She was prescribed a pair of glasses with prism lenses, which work to correct eye alignment, and within days, her chronic pain, anxiety, headaches, and nausea were gone. If you're suffering from any of these symptoms, make an appointment with an optometrist who's familiar with the condition and has the equipment needed to diagnose it (not all optometrists do).

Auditory processing disorder (APD)

Auditory processing disorder is a learning difference that affects how the brain receives, organizes, and interprets sound. People with ADP don't have hearing loss. Instead, their ears just aren't in sync with their brain, causing difficulty following directions, listening to multiple speakers, filtering out background noise, discerning the difference between similar-sounding words, and responding to questions.

APD is common in children with ADHD, according to Children and Adults with Attention Deficit/Hyperactivity Disorder (CHADD), a program funded by the CDC. A small study of twelve children with ADHD published in the *International Archives of Otorhinolaryngology* found treating children with the ADHD medication methylphenidate (often prescribed under brand names like Ritalin and Concerta) for six months improved and even reversed symptoms of APD.

Language processing disorder (LPD)

Language processing disorder occurs when people struggle to express or understand language. People with this learning difference often know what they want to say but have trouble finding the right words or understanding or interpreting what others are saying to them, making it difficult to follow and participate in conversations. The difference between ADP and LPD is the former describes an inability to accurately interpret sounds while LPD refers to an inability to interpret meaning from language.

People with ADHD are at a greater risk of having language difficulties. At the same time, symptoms of LPD are also easily confused with ADHD, which is why, if you suspect you might have this learning difference, it's important to get diagnosed and start treatment. A speech or language therapist can assess you for LPD, and therapy can be quite helpful: according to research conducted on children, more than 57 percent improved after just six months of treatment.

What about autism?

Autism spectrum disorder (ASD) is a developmental disability caused by brain differences, according to the official definition from the

THE DISORDER THAT MIMICS DYSLEXIA

I know several women who believed they were dyslexic only to finally figure out that what they suffered from was a visual processing disorder, which is "associated with the delayed capacity to perceive information received through the sense of vision," according to an article published in the *Ophthalmology Open Journal*. This doesn't mean that someone with a visual processing disorder has blurry eyesight or difficulty seeing objects close up or far away. Instead, people with visual processing disorders may confuse words that look similar, lose their place while reading, see double, skip lines or words, reverse letters or numbers, struggle to discern between foreground and background, or have difficulties reading or copying from a chalkboard or a book. Visual processing disorders are often confused with dyslexia and can mimic some of the symptoms of ADHD. A developmental optometrist, neuropsychologist, and ophthalmologist may all be able to diagnose the condition.

Centers for Disease Control. It can affect people of all ages, and while typically diagnosed in childhood, autism, similar to ADHD, is often overlooked or misdiagnosed in females. This is problematic for those of us with ADHD because half of all people with ASD also show signs of ADHD, according to the Children and Adults with Attention-Deficit/Hyperactivity Disorder (CHADD). Symptoms of ASD vary greatly from person to person—that's why it's known as a spectrum disorder—but multiples studies, including research spearheaded by doctors at the Cleveland Clinic's Center for Pediatric Behavioral Health and Center for Autism, show that women manifest symptoms differently than men, with a greater social communication impairment, weaker adaptive skills (meaning those needed to function on a daily basis), and increased "problem behavior." If you suspect you are on the autism spectrum, a psychologist or psychiatrist who specializes in adult autism is necessary, as the diagnostic process for adults, like the one for children, can be arduous and frustrating. But finding out that you have ASD can help reduce shame and overhaul your self-esteem, as you see that the disorder, not you, is responsible for certain traits, and allow you to begin treatment, which can include cognitive behavioral therapy.

GETTING DIAGNOSED WITH A LEARNING DIFFERENCE

If you suspect you may have a learning difference, it's nothing to be embarrassed about or ashamed of. It doesn't mean you can't learn; you just learn differently. The sooner you can get a proper evaluation, the sooner you can start therapy to help you better manage the ways in which your brain thinks differently. To be assessed for a learning disability as an adult, the Learning Disabilities Association of America recommends making an appointment at any of the following:

- The vocational rehabilitation department or agency in your state, many of which offer adult evaluations

- A private psychologist or psychology clinic

- A college or university near you with graduate programs in learning disabilities

- A community mental health center

Most importantly, trust your intuition. ADHD doctors may know a lot about ADHD, but that doesn't mean that they also understand learning differences. If you're questioning whether something else is going on inside your brain beyond ADHD, consider getting tested for learning differences. I've talked with many women who've spent decades blaming ADHD for struggles that were in fact learning differences, all the while wondering why treating their ADHD didn't do as much for them as it did for others. Discovering that you have a learning difference greatly reduces shame and allows you to actively decide what you're good at and *want* to be good at. Remember that no one is good at everything, whether we have ADHD, a learning difference, or none of the above.

If you discover you do have a learning difference, consider the Arrowsmith Program, founded by Canadian entrepreneur Barbara Arrowsmith-Young in 1980 and currently taught in more than one hundred schools worldwide. The program leverages the science of neuroplasticity—the capability of the human brain to change during an individual's lifetime—to help address specific learning disorders and improve a person's capacity to learn. For more information, visit arrowsmithschool.org.

Being yourself feels good and empowers you to explore new ideas, question conventional beliefs and systems, and challenge the status quo.

AS YOU'VE SEEN throughout this book, ADHD is associated with many different conditions and traits, some that can make life more challenging. Developing and using targeted strategies that leverage your ADHD strengths can ease or even obviate these challenges. Even more important is noticing which of your ADHD strengths are superpowers. As a woman with ADHD, harnessing and celebrating your unique superpowers can transform your diagnosis from something you fear into the best thing that's ever happened to you. If you've learned anything throughout these pages, I hope it's to trust yourself, your unique brain, and all your remarkable abilities.

Being yourself feels good and empowers you to explore new ideas, question conventional beliefs and systems, and challenge the status quo. Don't ever reduce your expectations in life, like a psychologist once recommended I do for my son, Markus. Instead, choose to step up to and *raise* your expectations. People with ADHD are often late bloomers, which means it's never too late for your future to be anything you want it to be. I know and see you, brilliant, empathetic, creative, driven, and smart ass woman with ADHD.

Next Steps: Why and How to Work with an ADHD Coach

After five years of practicing as an attorney, I announced I was leaving law entirely. That was in 1994, and at the time, I was bored with law and how slowly legal investigations move. Instead, I wanted to start a luxury women's wear company, even though I had no education or experience in the fashion industry. The idea appealed because it would allow me to call all the shots and build my own business. As a female attorney, I had also experienced a gaping hole in the market for trendy but feminine and still work-appropriate blouses and other women's apparel. After talking with a few store buyers who confirmed that hole, I decided this was where I would begin my life as an entrepreneur. Many people thought I was making a huge mistake. Why would I choose to waste all those years of education and a secure salary for something totally unknown? Others didn't say anything directly to me, but they didn't have to: I could see and feel the disapproval on their faces.

It's important to my story to clarify that I didn't hate working in law. I actually liked being an attorney and am grateful every day for my law school education. What I didn't like, though, was the rigidity of my schedule and the multiple daily meetings with colleagues and clients. If I had had the freedom to make my own hours and just get my work done, I would have stayed in law a lot longer. Also, if I had been practicing the kind of law that interests me now—civil rights, political, or constitutional law—I think I would have worked as a lawyer my entire life, but I hadn't connected the dots at the time. It wasn't until later in life when I identified my values, strengths, skills, passions, and purpose using the six-step program I shared with you on page 57 that I realized these areas of law fascinated me. Instead, what I *did* know at the time was that I wanted to change the world to make it a better place for women—I just didn't know who those women would be at the time.

When I quit law, I was in my early thirties and already married to Rich. We knew we wanted children, but I didn't think I wanted them quite yet. There was still so much that I wanted to accomplish, but I felt the pressure of my ticking biological clock. So five years after I stopped practicing law, I had my daughter and never looked back.

While many of my friends struggled with new motherhood, I loved everything about it. Nowhere did I trust my instincts more. My kids challenged me every day, giving me a whole new definition of what it means to be successful and, in some strange way, appeased my ambition. They also gave me permission to be present, enjoy life, and have fun.

I was having so much fun, in fact, that I didn't realize how hard empty nesting would be for me until my daughter left for college. I was working as a real estate broker at the time and had my son at home, but the lack of hustle and bustle and, frankly, chaos, of everyday family life blindsided me. For years, my life and identity had been wrapped around the family that Rich and I had built, and without two children at home to learn from, banter with, and care for every day, life was too quiet. I knew that I had to build my life around something else. This is how and when my drive and ambition came pummeling back.

By this time in my life, my son had been diagnosed with ADHD, and I had spent the better part of a year reading everything I could about ADHD. I wasn't able to see myself in his diagnosis yet because my symptoms were so different, but I did know that this triggered an unusual number of interests around our education system, how kids learn, what it means to be smart, and why as a society we don't spend more time unearthing our kids' strengths instead of trying to shore up their weaknesses. I also knew that, with all these interests swirling around in my mind, I didn't know which one, if any, I should pursue. This is how I realized that I had to get crystal clear on what my values and my purpose were if I wanted to figure out what to do next. Otherwise, I'd continue to become distracted every time another bright, shiny interest or activity (hello, doing Bikram yoga, breeding Silkie chickens, and cultivating Annabelle hydrangeas) bounded across my horizon.

Many people who go through a similar kind of transition turn to professional self-help, and I was no different—after all, I'd been pursuing self-help my entire life. By then, I had read dozens of self-help books, consulted with a career counselor, and completed multiple seminars, workshops, and courses in my perpetual journey to figure out "who am I really and what I'm meant to do with my life." None of it worked because it didn't connect the dots between who I really was, what was truly important to me, and what I was meant to do with my life.

Right after my son was diagnosed with ADHD, I hired a prominent life coach who was hailed as the coach who coaches other coaches in a last-ditch effort to find my purpose and values. But after multiple sessions together, I still didn't have clarity on what either were. Instead, she asked me questions like, "If you could install two billboards, one on each side of Highway 101 into San Francisco, what would they say?" How was this supposed to help me identify my values and purpose? The only thing this line of questioning did provoke, however, was the consideration that, like my son, I might also have ADHD. I already knew that his brain needed a process, system, structure, or just some way to synthesize and organize all the information that had been rolling around in his mind for years. Sitting there with the life coach, I realized that I needed this too. But after my fruitless experience with her, I began to think that the problem was with me, that I must be uncoachable.

Eight months after Markus was diagnosed, a doctor told me that I too had ADHD. In the interim, it had also become clear to me that my son wasn't receiving the support he needed in school because his teachers and school administrators neither understood ADHD nor knew how to teach students with the condition. Suddenly, I found myself wanting to know more. I signed up for a class called Simply ADHD—fourteen ninety-minute sessions that covered what ADHD looks like and the ways it can impact our lives—that was offered by the ADD Coaching Academy (ADDCA), an internationally recognized and fully accredited organization for ADHD education and coach training. I was interested in the material and found the class so helpful that I kept signing up for more classes with the ADDCA. Before I knew it, I had completed all the organization's general classes and was enrolled in its basic ADHD coach training program. At the time, I had no interest in ADHD coaching because I had had such a poor experience with life coaching. But as I was starting to learn, ADHD coaching is different than life coaching because the former addresses the core challenges that neurodivergents face, like planning, time management, hyperactivity, impulsivity, and emotional self-regulation. What's more, when this kind of guidance is provided for college students, ADHD coaching may improve executive function skills, self-determination, self-esteem, outlook, and overall satisfaction with work or school, according to a review of the findings of nineteen prior studies published in the *Journal of Postsecondary Education and Disability*.

The beauty of ADHD coaching is that a good coach won't tell you what to do—they already know that *won't* work. Instead, they'll help you decide what you'd most like to work on and then assist you in breaking down your to-do list, goals, or ambitions into the smallest steps possible so that you can start to self-determine and get things done. Each one of us already has systems or ways of doing things to reach our goals, yet many of us can't perceive our brain's best practices because we believe or have been told for years that our minds are faulty or flawed. But a good ADHD coach will help you begin to recognize, leverage, and expand upon your own efficient and effective methods. A good coach can also help you realize when you're headed for a mishap and work with you to identify what you may need to do to avoid it. They can also provide a reality check when you don't think through the effects of your actions.

A *great* ADHD coach can also teach you how to celebrate your successes instead of glossing over them, as we're prone to do. With a great coach, you can begin to realize and appreciate all the feats you've already accomplished, which can give you the boost of confidence and positive emotion you often need to accomplish even more in the future.

> *A good ADHD coach will help you begin to recognize, leverage, and expand upon your own efficient and effective methods.*

Most importantly, a great ADHD coach can help you see who you are at your core. Many of us with ADHD focus so much on our weaknesses that we can't see just how unique, special, and brilliant we are, as us, in this very moment. An attuned ADHD coach will help you flip the script to see that even your "weaknesses" have opposing strengths and teach you how to identify and use your inherent superpowers to your advantage. A great coach will also question the stories you tell yourself, facilitating your creation of new narratives that can overhaul your self-image and allow you to tap into your true purpose and values. A great ADHD coach can show you that you're perfect as you are now and, at the same time, help you see the person you want to be. In short, a great ADHD coach can help you reinvent yourself—not into someone different but into the best version of you right now, a true ADHD smart ass woman.

TIPS FOR FINDING A GREAT ADHD COACH

- Look for a coach who makes you feel good (it's all about the positive emotion) and whom you're excited to work with.

- If you live in a small community with few ADHD coaches, consider working with a virtual ADHD coach so that you have access to a wider range of individuals and are able to find the right fit for you.

- Work with a coach who has ADHD because this can offer invaluable lived experience. However, it's important to make sure that you don't share the same weaknesses. If you're disorganized, for example, working with a coach who's also disorganized will not serve you.

- Consider what matters most to you. If humor is really important to you but your coach is humorless, you likely won't make as much progress.

- Consult the online directories of coaches at ADD Coaching Academy (ADDCA), Attention Deficit Disorder Association (ADDA), Children and Adults with Attention-Deficit/Hyperactivity Disorder (CHADD), and the website GetADHDHelp.com.

ACKNOWLEDGMENTS

My blind optimism led me to believe that writing a book couldn't possibly be that hard; after all, millions have done it. I now know that if you've never written a book before, it *is* that hard. Thankfully, so many made this book possible. If any one of you had decamped, this big, messy dream might never have been realized.

Thank you to Allison Lane. Without your deft and sneaky plan of boxing me into a deadline and your sparkle around words, there would have been no book proposal. Who knew that our IRL friendship would be a bonus? Stacey Glick, your expert advice on navigating the traditional book publishing world was invaluable. I knew from our first conversation that you understood my mission and shared it. To my brilliant editor, Sarah Toland, you did much more than edit the gigantic and jumbled manuscript that I hurled at you. With your otherworldly memory for text and your structural sorcery you were exactly what this book needed. Lucky for me, this also came with a side of repartee. Thank you to my meticulous research assistant, Erin Harvey, who always came through even when my requests were last minute and late at night.

Lisa Sharkey, director of creative development at HarperCollins, I am so grateful that you took a chance on me, a first-time author, and believed in my purpose of rescuing smart ass ADHD women trapped in pathology and shame. Thank you to my editor, Maddie Pillari. If I come back in another life, I'm demanding two brains: my own and your pragmatic and uber-organized one. Also on the first-class team at HarperCollins: Brian Moore, Marie Rossi, Andrea Molitor, Iliyah Coles, Lindsey Kennedy, Jeanie Lee, Rachael DeShano, Elina Cohen, and Kelly Dasta—I appreciate all of you.

Dr. Ned Hallowell, thank you for your kindness, generosity, disdain for the word *appropriate*, and the way you championed me to write this book. You made me realize that I could do it; better yet, you made me realize that I *should* do it.

Thank you to my entire Smart Ass team, who kept everything running smoothly during the entire book-writing process: Lyden Charmie Barrun, Grace Bourey, Esther Nagle, Isabelle Baker, and Nicolas Pascal. Catheryn Wreford-holden, thank you for skillfully leading our brilliant team of mods and admins. Without you, our ninety thousand members would have no group. Danielle Knight Englund, Melody Kuphal, Odochi Ibe, Laura Smith Robinson, Andrea Souza, Amber Sarno, and Andonette Martine Wilkinson, I appreciate all of you and am so thankful that you continue to show up. A huge thank-you to Sandra Centorino, my tech expert, Connecticut bestie, and biggest cheerleader. So many of the opportunities that have landed at my feet have roots in your fearlessness. How lucky was I to get to do what I do and meet you in the process? Dr. Christine Li, I love that we share the same mission and that I can always count on your sage advice, calm, kind heart, and focus on what's truly important. Miriam Schulman, my fellow HarperCollins author, thank you for literally walking the path before me and so generously sprinkling and then sharing your bread crumbs. Finally, to Dr. Richard (always Rick to me) Osman. I love that we met on the quiet floor of Struve Hall as teenagers. I also love our decades-long friendship, and I'm so appreciative to you for the years you fought for my patent. Thank you also to my dear friends Angela and Joe Camacho—won't it be great when I'm talking about something besides this book!

Thank you to my family: my beautiful mom, who selflessly offered me the opportunities she never had and always allowed me to be exactly who I am; my father, who made it fun by adding his sardonic wit, while always remaining in positive emotion; my sister, for her extraordinary empathy; my husband, Rich (aka banker man), who, despite my falling in puddle after puddle, remains blind to the fact that I cannot walk on water. To my joyful daughter, Atea, my best friend and all-around dynamo, how was I lucky enough to get the best little girl in the whole world? And of course, to my fearless son, Markus, I am eternally grateful that you've always refused to be anyone but YOU, no matter who demanded it. You have been my greatest teacher. I love you all.

Most of all, a huge thank-you to the Smart Ass community on all continents. Your support of me, my team, and my mission is beyond humbling. This is my life's work and I'm grateful for every minute I've been gifted to do it. I'm so honored to play a small part in making your life better. And finally, thank you to you the reader, for picking up this book and trusting that you deserve more; it just might change your life for the better. As a gift, I'd like to give you complimentary access to my master class What Do I Do with My Life? From Chaos to Confidence, where you will learn more about who you are and how to make faster, more confident decisions. You can find this completely free gift at spyhappy.me/mc.*

---

* Disclaimer: The content is available commencing on or about December 26, 2023, and the author reserves the right to discontinue hosting it at her sole discretion.

EDUCATION AND ADVOCACY ORGANIZATIONS

ADD Resource Center: Organization that provides services and information for and about people with ADHD. https://www.addrc.org/.

ADDA (Attention Deficit Disorder Association): Organization dedicated to helping adults with ADHD improve their lives. https://add.org.

ADDitude: Magazine and website that provides strategies and resources about ADHD and related conditions. https://additudemag.com.

CHADD (Children and Adults with Attention-Deficit/Hyperactivity Disorder): *Attention* magazine, website, and conference that provides information, support, and ADHD advocacy. https://chadd.org.

The Disruptors: Documentary that debunks the most harmful myths about ADHD. https://disruptorsfilm.com/.

Eye to Eye: Founded by David Flink, this organization provides mentors for high school and college kids who learn differently. https://eyetoeye national.org/.

Fair Play: Documentary that features real advice on how to divide household tasks and achieve marital harmony. https://.fairplaylife.com/documentary.

How to ADHD: A YouTube channel created by Jessica McCabe. https ://howtoadhd.com/.

JAN (Job Accommodation Network): Organization that provides free, expert guidance on workplace accommodations and disability employment issues. https://askjan.org.

GADGETS AND APPS

Alarmy app: Get out of bed with this alarm app. https://alar.my/.

Bear app: Never lose another note again. https://bear.app/.

Endel app: Focus, relax, and sleep with soundscapes backed by neuroscience .https://endel.io/.

Healthy Minds Program app: Learn the science of meditation while meditating. https://hminnovations.org/meditation-app.

Insight Timer app: Build healthy habits and create a well-being routine. https://insighttimer.com/individuals.

Supernotes app: A Bear app alternative for Windows and Android users. https://supernotes.app/alternative-to-bear.

The Tapping Solution app: Learn how to tap. https://thetappingsolution.com.

Time Timer: See the passage of time with this timer. https://www.timetimer.com/.

TimeCube by Datexx: Flip the cube to set the timer. https://www.instagram .com/datexxinc.

Zero app: Track intermittent fasting progress. https://zerolongevity.com.

NUTRITION AND INTERMITTENT FASTING

Aleta Storch, MS, RDN, LMHC: Nutrition therapist specializing in ADHD. https://wiseheartnutrition.com.

Nicole DeMasi, MS, RDN, CDCES: Founder of the Eating with ADHD online program and community. https://nicoledemasi.com/adhd.

Rebecca King, MS, RDN, LDN: ADHD nutritionist. https://instagram.com /adhd.nutritionist.

PROFESSIONAL DIRECTORIES

ACO International (ADHD Coaches Organization): https://acoo .memberclicks.net/directory-of-coaches.

ADDA (Attention Deficit Disorder Association): https://add.org/professional -directory.

ADDCA (ADD Coach Academy): https://addca.com/adhd-coach-training/adhd-coaches/.

ADDitude: https://directory.additudemag.com/.

CHADD (Children and Adults with Attention-Deficit/Hyperactivity Disorder): https://chadd.org/professional-directory/.

Get ADHD Help: https://getadhdhelp.com.

PAAC (Professional Association for ADHD Coaches): https://paaccoaches.org/find-a-coach/.

WEBSITES

ADHD Women's Palooza: Linda Roggli interviews ADHD experts who understand what ADHD looks like in women. https://adhdpalooza.com/women-2/.

Black Girl, Lost Keys: René Brooks's blog empowers black women with ADHD. https://blackgirllostkeys.com.

Caroline Maguire: Caroline Maguire, MEd, offers practical, real-world solutions to improve social skills and learn how to relate better to others. https://carolinemaguireauthor.com.

Dr. Hallowell/The Hallowell ADHD Centers: Edward Hallowell, MD, diagnoses and treats ADHD using a strength-based and connectedness philosophy. https://drhallowell.com.

Dr. Sharon Saline: Sharon Saline, PsyD, specializes in managing ADHD and anxiety in women. https://drsharonsaline.com.

eDiagnostic Learning: Laurie Peterson, MEd, MA, LPC, provides educational testing and ADHD diagnoses. https://ediagnosticlearning.com/.

Make Time for Success: This podcast, by Dr. Christine Li, PhD, offers simple strategies to improve productivity, self-esteem, and confidence. https://maketimeforsuccesspodcast.com/.

Marker Learning: Emily Yudofsky provides learning challenge and ADHD diagnoses. https://markerlearning.com/.

Swellhead: Roxanne Jarrett, MA, CPC, works with you to start and finish anything. https://swellhead.com/.

Thrive with Dr. Grace: Dr. Grace Essan, MD, consults with and advises women with ADHD. https://www.thrivewithdrgrace.com/.

VIA Character Strengths Survey: Free scientific survey on character strengths. https://www.viacharacter.org/survey/account/register.

SUPPORT HOTLINES

Crisis Text Line: Text HOME to 741741.

LGBT National Hotline: 1-888-843-4564.

National Domestic Violence Hotline: 1-800-799-7233.

Substance Abuse and Mental Health Services Administration National Helpline: 1-800-662-HELP (4357).

Suicide and Crisis Lifeline: 988.

Trans Lifeline: 877-565-8860.

FURTHER READING

Arrowsmith-Young, Barbara. *The Woman Who Changed Her Brain: How I Left My Learning Difficulties Behind and Other Stories of Cognitive Transformation.* New York: Simon & Schuster, 2012.

This book details the author's journey with learning disabilities and how she invented cognitive exercises to "change" her own brain and yours too.

Dunlap, Tori. *Financial Feminist: Overcome the Patriarchy's Bullsh*t to Master Your Money and Build a Life You Love.* New York: Dey Street Books, 2022.

This book teaches women different principles for paying off debt, spending on things you value, saving money, and investing.

Frances, Allen, MD. *Saving Normal: An Insider's Revolt Against Out-of-Control Psychiatric Diagnosis, "DSM-5," Big Pharma, and the Medicalization of Ordinary Life.* New York: William Morrow, 2013.

This book explores the idea that categorizing a healthy person as "mentally ill" leads to unnecessary medications, limited potentials, a misallocation of medical resources, and the drainage of personal assets.

Greene, Ross W., PhD. *The Explosive Child: A New Approach for Understanding and Parenting Easily Frustrated, Chronically Inflexible Children.* New York: HarperCollins, 1998.

This book uses neuroscience research to build a conceptual framework for understanding children with social, emotional, and behavioral challenges using problem-solving methods.

Hallowell, Edward M., MD, and John J. Ratey, MD. *ADHD 2.0: New Science and Essential Strategies for Thriving with Distraction—from Childhood Through Adulthood.* New York: Ballantine Books, 2021.

Using the latest research, this book provides strategies for minimizing negative symptoms and maximizing the upsides of ADHD.

Hartmann, Thom. *Adult ADHD: How to Succeed as a Hunter in a Farmer's World.* Rochester, VT: Park Street Press, 2016.

This book relates ADHD traits to the hunter-gatherer society of our ancestors and teaches how to maximize ADHD hunter potential in day-to-day life.

Maté, Gabor, MD, and Daniel Maté. *The Myth of Normal: Trauma, Illness & Healing in a Toxic Culture.* New York: Avery, 2022.

This book discusses how Western cultures perpetuate chronic illness and ill health by neglecting the effects of trauma, stress, and the pressures of modern-day living on our bodies. The authors provide a guide for the health and healing of the whole body.

Nadeau, Kathleen G., PhD; Ellen B. Littman, PhD; and Patricia O. Quinn, MD. *Understanding Girls with ADHD: How They Feel and Why They Do What They Do.* Chevy Chase, MD: Advantage Books, 2016.

This book examines the complexities and misunderstandings of girls and women with ADHD.

Nerenberg, Jenara. *Divergent Mind: Thriving in a World That Wasn't Designed for You.* New York: HarperOne, 2020.

This book shares real stories from neurodivergent women, dispels common misconceptions, and offers practical changes for supporting neurodivergent minds.

Orlov, Melissa. *The ADHD Effect on Marriage: Understand and Rebuild Your Relationship in Six Steps.* Weston, FL: Specialty Press, 2020.

This book guides couples in which one of the partners has ADHD through potential issues in their relationships. It offers practical advice on how to fix patterns of behavior that could negatively impact the relationship.

Ortner, Nick. *The Tapping Solution: A Revolutionary System for Stress-Free Living.* Carlsbad, CA: Hay House, 2013.

This book examines how tapping can help improve your life physically, mentally, and emotionally.

Perry, Bruce D., MD, PhD, and Oprah Winfrey. *What Happened to You? Conversations on Trauma, Resilience, and Healing.* New York: Flatiron Books, 2021.

The discussions in this book shift the focus of trauma conversations from "What's wrong with you?" to "What happened to you?" through personal conversations about youth trauma and adversity.

Ratey, John J., MD, and Eric Hagerman. *Spark: The Revolutionary New Science of Exercise and the Brain.* Boston: Little, Brown, 2008.

This book examines how exercise can help remodel our brain in defense against ADHD, depression, and more.

Rosier, Tamara, PhD. *Your Brain's Not Broken: Strategies for Navigating Your Emotions and Life with ADHD.* Grand Rapids, MI: Revell, 2021.

This book explains how ADHD affects every aspect of one's life. The author offers practical tips for improving your life and relationships.

Saltz, Gail, MD. *The Power of Different: The Link Between Disorder and Genius.* New York: Flatiron Books, 2017.

This book uses research, profiles of famous neurodivergent people, and stories from others to share how specific deficiencies in certain areas can lead to great successes in others.

Solden, Sari, MS, LMFT. *Women with Attention Deficit Disorder: Embrace Your Differences and Transform Your Life.* Ann Arbor, MI: Introspect Press, 2012.

This book explores the unique challenges that women with ADHD have and includes treatment and counseling options.

Stapleton, Peta, PhD. *The Science Behind Tapping: A Proven Stress Management Technique for the Mind and Body.* Carlsbad, CA: Hay House, 2019.

This book presents the research and evidence behind tapping in addition to client experiences.

Stephens, Gin. *Fast. Feast. Repeat.: The Comprehensive Guide to Delay, Don't Deny Intermittent Fasting.* New York: St. Martin's Griffin, 2020.

This book explores the latest medical research on intermittent fasting and offers ways to work it into your life.

Walker, Matthew, PhD. *Why We Sleep: Unlocking the Power of Sleep and Dreams.* New York: Scribner, 2017.

This book examines the science behind sleep and how it affects our physical and mental health.

Willeumier, Kristen, PhD. *Biohack Your Brain: How to Boost Cognitive Health, Performance & Power.* New York: William Morrow, 2020.

This text provides ways to alter your brain by making simple changes to your diet and lifestyle that are supported by science.

Zylowska, Lydia, MD. *The Mindful Prescription for Adult ADHD: An 8-Step Program for Strengthening Attention, Managing Emotions, and Achieving Your Goals.* Boulder, CO: Trumpeter Books, 2012.

This book educates the reader about ADHD and teaches them how to use mindfulness to build focus and confidence.

ADHD (ATTENTION-DEFICIT/HYPERACTIVITY DISORDER): A common brain developmental condition that may include traits like hyperactivity (physical or mental) and difficulties focusing, managing time, motivating, and completing tasks, in addition to increased creativity, intuition, empathy, and the ability to hyperfocus.

ADHD COACH: A trained professional who helps people with ADHD better manage their lives and symptoms.

BODY-FOCUSED REPETITIVE BEHAVIORS: A tendency to engage in compulsive activities that can harm the body, such as obsessively biting nails or cuticles, picking at pimples or other skin imperfections, or pulling out hair or eyelashes.

COGNITIVE BEHAVIORAL THERAPY (CBT): A popular form of talk therapy that can help people with ADHD better regulate their emotions and manage symptoms.

COMBINED ADHD: One of three subtypes of ADHD in which people exhibit symptoms of both hyperactive and impulsive ADHD and inattentive ADHD.

COMORBIDITIES: The presence of two or more existing medical conditions, which is common among people with ADHD.

DEFAULT MODE NETWORK (DMN): An interconnected group of areas in the brain used when not focused on a conversation, task, or situation that may be more active in people with ADHD.

DIALECTICAL BEHAVIOR THERAPY (DBT): A form of cognitive behavioral therapy that focuses on developing skills to improve emotional regulation.

DOPAMINE: A neurotransmitter (brain chemical) that helps regulate pleasure and attention, among other attributes, and that may be lower in people with ADHD.

DSM-5: Short for *The Diagnostic and Statistical Manual of Mental Disorders, Fifth Edition*, which practitioners use to diagnose ADHD.

EMOTIONAL DYSREGULATION: An inability to regulate or control emotions.

EMOTIONAL FREEDOM TECHNIQUE (EFT): Also known as *tapping*, a type of psychotherapy in which a person taps certain pressure points on their body in a certain sequence to help better manage emotions and ease anxiety.

EXECUTIVE FUNCTION: A set of mental skills that includes planning, organizing, self-motivating, managing time, problem solving, and retaining working memory that is often affected by ADHD.

EYE MOVEMENT DESENSITIZATION AND REPROCESSING (EMDR) THERAPY: A type of psychotherapy in which a practitioner leads a patient through certain eye movements to evoke painful memories and events in order to help address and heal trauma.

HYPERACTIVE AND IMPULSIVE ADHD: One of three subtypes of ADHD marked by symptoms like impatience, restlessness, and emotional dysregulation.

INATTENTIVE ADHD: One of three subtypes of ADHD marked by difficulties focusing on tasks, organizing, and paying attention to detail or instructions.

MINDFULNESS: A practice in which a person uses self-soothing techniques like meditation to remain in the moment. It has been shown to ease anxiety, anger, depression, and other unpleasant emotional states.

NEURODIVERGENT: A term used to describe people whose brains work differently than what's considered standard.

NEUROTYPICAL: A term used to describe people with what's considered standard neurological patterns and behaviors.

POSITIVE EMOTION: Any emotional reaction that triggers a positive effect, often occurring when a person reaches a goal, mitigates or obviates a threat, or feels content about their current situation.

REJECTION SENSITIVE DYSPHORIA (RSD): A condition common among ADHD women that causes them to be acutely sensitive to what others say and do or to constantly be fearful of criticism or rejection.

REVENGE BEDTIME PROCRASTINATION (RBP): A condition in which a person frequently procrastinates their bedtime to spend time on leisure activities.

REWARD DEFICIENCY SYNDROME: A condition marked by low dopamine levels that causes the brain to instinctually seek out bigger, more immediate, or more repeated rewards through food, drugs, or risky behavior.

TASK POSITIVE NETWORK (TPN): An interconnected group of areas in the brain used when focusing on a conversation, task, or situation that people with ADHD may have difficulty engaging.

NOTES

INTRODUCTION

xvi *ADHD is often passed down from parent to child:* "Causes," Attention Deficit Hyperactivity Disorder (ADHD), National Health Services, December 24, 2021, https://www.nhs.uk/conditions/attention-deficit-hyperactivity-disorder-adhd /causes/.

xvi *are misdiagnosed with mental health conditions:* "Women and Girls," Children and Adults with Attention-Deficit/Hyperactivity Disorder (CHADD), accessed April 7, 2023, https://chadd.org/for-adults/women-and-girls/.

xvi *as many as 75 percent:* Caralee Adams, "Girls and ADHD: Are You Missing the Signs?," *Instructor* 94, no. 6 (2007): 31–35, https://www.researchgate.net /publication/234712960_Girls_and_ADHD_Are_You_Missing_the_Signs.

xvii *creativity is simply impulsivity gone right:* Diane O'Reilly, "Stifled Creativity and Its Damaging Impact on the ADHD Brain," *ADDitude*, August 12, 2022, https://www.additudemag.com/adhd-creativity-brain-health/.

xvii *Leonardo da Vinci:* Cristina Margolis, "Kids' Creations: The Art of Having ADHD," *ADDitude*, November 7, 2019, https://www.additudemag.com/what-it -feels-like-to-have-adhd-art/.

xx *their daily function and life:* "Coaching," Children and Adults with Attention-Deficit/Hyperactivity Disorder (CHADD), accessed April 7, 2023, https://chadd .org/about-adhd/coaching/.

xxi *eminent media outlets:* Kitty Ruskin, "For Some Women with ADHD, TikTok Is the First Place They Felt Heard," *Time*, September 12, 2022, https://time .com/6211695/adhd-tiktok-women/.

xxii *42 percent of all adults with ADHD:* Esme Fuller-Thomson et al., "Flourishing Despite Attention-Deficit Hyperactivity Disorder (ADHD): A Population Based Study of Mental Well-Being," *International Journal of Applied Positive Psychology* 7 (2022): 227–50, https://doi.org/10.1007/s41042-022-00062-6.

CHAPTER 1: WHAT ADHD *REALLY* IS

4 *won't easily shift our attention elsewhere:* Brandon K. Ashinoff and Ahmad Abu-Akel, "Hyperfocus: The Forgotten Frontier of Attention," *Psychological Research* 7, no. 1 (2021): 1–19, https://doi.org/10.1007/s00426-019-01245-8.

4 *in the instance of elite athletes:* Nathaly Pensantez, "Olympians, Professional Athletes, and Sports Legends with ADHD," *ADDitude*, October 3, 2022, https://www.additudemag.com/slideshows/athletes-with-adhd-sports-legends-role-models/.

4 *studies showing that hyperfocus allows those with ADHD: ADDitude* Editors, "The Good, the Bad, and the Ugly of Hyperfocus," *ADDitude*, April 8, 2021, https://www.additudemag.com/hyperfocus-symptoms-positives-negatives-strategies/.

4 *lose all track of time: ADDitude* Editors, "The Good, the Bad, and the Ugly of Hyperfocus."

5 *describes people with typical neurological patterns and behavior:* Jane Ann Sedgwick, Andrew Merwood, and Philip Asherson, "The Positive Aspects of Attention Deficit Hyperactivity Disorder: A Qualitative Investigation of Successful Adults with ADHD," *ADHD Attention Deficit and Hyperactivity Disorders* 11 (2019): 241–53, https://doi.org/10.1007/s12402-018-0277-6.

5 *ADHD is one of the most common:* "What Is ADHD?," Attention Deficit/Hyperactivity Disorder (ADHD), Centers for Disease Control and Prevention, accessed September 26, 2022, https://www.cdc.gov/ncbddd/adhd/facts.html.

5 *less than 20 percent of adults with the condition: ADDitude* Editors, "ADHD Statistics: New ADD Facts and Research," *ADDitude*, July 13, 2022, https://www.additudemag.com/statistics-of-adhd/.

5 *up to 75 percent of all girls with ADHD remaining undiagnosed:* Caralee Adams, "Girls and ADHD: Are You Missing the Signs?," *Instructor* 116, no. 6 (2007): 31–35, https://www.researchgate.net/publication/234712960_Girls_and_ADHD_Are_You_Missing_the_Signs.

5 *while only 3.2 percent of women have:* "Attention-Deficit/Hyperactivity Disorder (ADHD)," National Institute of Mental Health, accessed April 10, 2023, https://www.nimh.nih.gov/health/statistics/attention-deficit-hyperactivity-disorder-adhd.

5 *ADHD is underdiagnosed in adults, especially women:* Eunice Sigler, "ADHD Looks Different in Women. Here's How—and Why," *ADDitude*, November 17, 2022, https://www.additudemag.com/add-in-women/.

5 *replaced by the ADHD diagnosis in 1987:* Dave Anderson, "What Is the Difference Between ADD and ADHD," Child Mind Institute, March 3, 2023, https://childmind.org/article/what-is-the-difference-between-add-and-adhd/.

6 *our never-ending thoughts:* Kate Moryoussef, "'9 Calming Strategies for a Racing, Restless Mind,'" *ADDitude*, July 9, 2022, https://www.additudemag.com/how-to-relax-your-mind-adhd-overthinking/.

6   *increased four times faster than those in children:* Winston Chung et al., "Trends in the Prevalence and Incidence of Attention-Deficit/Hyperactivity Disorder Among Adults and Children of Different Racial and Ethnic Groups," *JAMA Network Open* 2, no. 11 (2019): e1914344, https://doi.org/ 10.1001/jama networkopen.2019.14344.

6   *was developed for children:* ADDitude Editors, "ADHD Statistics: New ADD Facts and Research."

6   *are usually intensely curious, persistent, and lifelong learners:* Sedgwick, Merwood, and Asherson, "The Positive Aspects of Attention Deficit Hyperactivity Disorder."

6   *the condition itself is* not *a learning disorder:* "ADHD," Learning Disabilities Association of America, accessed April 10, 2023, https://ldaamerica.org/disabilities /adhd/.

7   *the existence and impact of ADHD:* "The Science of ADHD," Children and Adults with Attention-Deficit/Hyperactivity Disorder (CHADD), accessed September 26, 2022, https://chadd.org/about-adhd/the-science-of-adhd/.

7   *a number of mental skills:* Russell Barkley, "What Is Executive Function? 7 Deficits Tied to ADHD," *ADDitude*, August 10, 2022, https://www.additude mag.com/7-executive-function-deficits-linked-to-adhd/.

7   *we face impairments to executive function:* "Executive Function Skills," Children and Adults with Attention Deficit/Hyperactivity Disorder (CHADD), accessed April 10, 2023, https://chadd.org/about-adhd/executive-function -skills/.

7   *wide range in the type and severity:* Joel Nigg, "Is ADHD a Spectrum Disorder?," *ADDitude*, September 29, 2022, https://www.additudemag.com/adhd-is -spectrum-disorder/.

8   *how practitioners classify the condition's severity:* "About ADHD—Overview," Children and Adults with Attention Deficit/Hyperactivity Disorder (CHADD), accessed April 10, 2023, https://chadd.org/about-adhd/overview/.

8   *whatever trauma or traumatic stress:* Tanya E. Froehlich et al., "Update on Environmental Risk Factors for Attention-Deficit/Hyperactivity Disorder," *Current Psychiatry Reports* 12, no. 5 (2011): 333–44, https://doi.org/10.1007 /s11920-011-0221-3.

8   *around 40 percent of children with ADHD:* Martina Starck, Julia Grünwald, and Angelica A. Schlarb, "Occurrence of ADHD in Parents of ADHD Children in a Clinical Sample," *Neuropsychiatric Disease and Treatment* 12 (2016): 581–88, https://doi.org/10.2147/NDT.S100238.

8   *environmental factors:* Froehlich et al., "Update on Environmental Risk Factors."

10   *rely on today to diagnose ADHD:* "Symptoms and Diagnosis," Centers for Disease Control and Prevention, August 9, 2022, https://www.cdc.gov/ncbddd /adhd/diagnosis.html.

10 *ADHD is characterized by:* American Psychiatric Association, "Neurodevel-opmental Disorders," in *The Diagnostic and Statistical Manual of Mental Disorders*, 5th ed. (Washington, DC: American Psychiatric Association, 2013), 59–65.

10 *diagnosed with this subtype:* Penny Williams, "What Are the 3 Types of ADHD?," *ADDitude*, January 21, 2023, https://www.additudemag.com/3-types -of-adhd/.

11 *Those with inattentive ADHD:* Williams, "What Are the 3 Types of ADHD?"

11 *diagnosed with the inattentive subtype:* Ortal Slobodin and Michael Davido-vitch, "Gender Differences in Objective and Subjective Measures of ADHD Among Clinic-Referred Children," *Frontiers in Human Neuroscience* 13 (2019): Article 441, https://doi.org/10.3389/fnhum.2019.00441.

11 *the symptoms can look similar:* *ADDitude* Editors, "Why ADHD in Women Is Routinely Dismissed, Misdiagnosed, and Treated Inadequately," *ADDitude*, July 11, 2022, https://www.additudemag.com/adhd-in-women-misunderstood -symptoms-treatment/.

11 *the most common subtype:* American Psychiatric Association, "Neurodevel-opmental Disorders," 60.

11 *10 percent of children diagnosed with ADHD overcome it:* Margaret H. Sibley et al., "Variable Patterns of Remission from ADHD in the Multimodal Treatment Study of ADHD," *American Journal of Psychiatry* 179 (2022): 142–51, https://doi .org/10.1176/appi.ajp.2021.21010032.

11 *obsessing over thoughts:* William Dodson, "Secrets of Your ADHD Brain," *ADDitude*, August 24, 2022, https://www.additudemag.com/secrets-of-the -adhd-brain/.

11 *According to the DSM-5:* American Psychiatric Association, "Neurodevelop-mental Disorders," 59–60.

12 *For adults to be diagnosed with any subtype:* American Psychiatric Association, "Neurodevelopmental Disorders," 59–60.

12 *developed from research conducted on children:* Russell Barkley, "ADHD in Adults Looks Different. Most Diagnostic Criteria Ignores This Fact," *ADDitude*, May 19, 2022, https://www.additudemag.com/adhd-in-adults-new-diagnostic -criteria/.

13 *one of the DSM-5's symptoms for hyperactive and impulsive ADHD:* Substance Abuse and Mental Health Services Administration, *DSM-5 Changes: Implications for Child Serious Emotional Disturbance* (Rockville, MD: Substance Abuse and Mental Health Services Administration, 2016).

13 *include problems that affect executive function:* Barkley, "ADHD in Adults Looks Different."

13 *show some symptoms before age twelve:* American Psychiatric Association, "Neurodevelopmental Disorders," 60.

13 *ADHD education and research:* Barkley, "ADHD in Adults Looks Different."

CHAPTER 2: WHY WOMEN STRUGGLE TO GET DIAGNOSED AND WHAT TO DO ABOUT IT

17 *just as likely to have the condition as boys and men:* Eunice Sigler, "ADHD Looks Different in Women. Here's How—and Why," *ADDitude*, November 17, 2022, https://www.additudemag.com/add-in-women/.

17 *American men with ADHD:* "Attention-Deficit/Hyperactivity Disorder (ADHD)," National Institute of Mental Health, accessed September 28, 2022, https://www.nimh.nih.gov/health/statistics/attention-deficit-hyperactivity -disorder-adhd.

17 *as many as 75 percent of girls with ADHD go undiagnosed:* Caralee Adams, "Girls and ADHD: Are You Missing the Signs?," *Instructor* 116, no. 6 (2007): 31–35, https://www.researchgate.net/publication/234712960_Girls_and_ADHD_ Are_You_Missing_the_Signs.

17 *misdiagnosed with a mood disorder:* Edward Hallowell, "When Depression and Anxiety Are Really ADHD," *ADDitude*, March 31, 2022, https://www.additude mag.com/depression-adhd-symptoms-misdiagnosis/.

17 *their child is diagnosed:* Nicole Crawford, "ADHD: A Women's Issue," *Monitor on Psychology* 34, no. 2 (2003): 28, https://www.apa.org/monitor/feb03 /adhd.

18 *a woman's prognosis is far better:* Alaa M. Hamed, Aaron J. Kauer, and Hanna E. Stevens, "Why the Diagnosis of Attention Deficit Hyperactivity Disorder Matters," *Frontiers in Psychiatry* 6 (2015): Article 168, https://doi.org/10.3389 /fpsyt.2015.00168.

18 *The research establishing the diagnostic criteria:* ADDitude Editors, "Why ADHD in Women is Routinely Dismissed, Misdiagnosed, and Treated Inadequately," *ADDitude*, February 15, 2023, https://www.additudemag.com/adhd-in -women-misunderstood-symptoms-treatment/.

19 *most likely to suggest the possibility of ADHD to parents and healthcare providers:* Leonard Sax and Kathleen J. Kautz, "Who First Suggests the Diagnosis of Attention-Deficit/Hyperactivity Disorder," *Annals of Family Medicine* 1, no. 3 (2003): 171–74, https://doi.org/10.1370/afm.3.

19 *more likely to "internalize" their symptoms:* Ellen Littman, "Women with ADHD: No More Suffering in Silence," *ADDitude*, November 17, 2022, https://www .additudemag.com/gender-differences-in-adhd-women-vs-men/.

19 *talking too much or excessively ruminating:* "Symptoms of ADHD in Women and Girls," Children and Adults with Attention-Deficit/Hyperactivity Disorder (CHADD), accessed April 11, 2023, https://chadd.org/for-adults/symptoms-of -adhd-in-women-and-girls/.

19 *excessive talking is typical in adults with ADHD:* "Being Social and Making Friends as an Adult with ADHD," Children and Adults with Attention-Deficit/ Hyperactivity Disorder (CHADD), accessed April 11, 2023, https://chadd.org /adhd-weekly/being-social-and-making-friends-as-an-adult-with-adhd/.

20 *automatically think of ADHD:* Maureen Connolly, "ADHD in Girls: The Symptoms That Are Ignored in Females," *ADDitude*, January 20, 2023, https://www.additudemag.com/adhd-in-girls-women/.

20 *can also appear shy, forgetful, disorganized, and distracted:* Connolly, "ADHD in Girls."

21 *two or more medical conditions simultaneously:* Cæcillie Ottosen et al., "Sex Differences in Comorbidity Patterns of Attention-Deficit/Hyperactivity Disorder," *Journal of the American Academy of Child & Adolescent Psychiatry* 58, no. 4 (2019): 412–22.E3, https://doi.org/10.1016/j.jaac.2018.07.910.

21 *Common comorbidities for those with ADHD:* Larry Silver, "When It's Not Just ADHD: Symptoms of Comorbid Conditions," *ADDitude*, March 28, 2023, https://www.additudemag.com/when-its-not-just-adhd/.

21 *ADHD women are much more likely:* Ottosen et al., "Sex Differences in Comorbidity Patterns of Attention-Deficit/Hyperactivity Disorder."

21 *anxiety, depression, and other emotional problems:* Susan Young et al., "Females with ADHD: An Expert Consensus Statement Taking a Lifespan Approach Providing Guidance for the Identification and Treatment of Attention-Deficit/Hyperactivity Disorder in Girls and Women," *BMC Psychiatry* 20 (2020): Article 404, https://doi.org/10.1186/s12888-020-02707-9.

21 *providers often mistake common ADHD symptoms for a mood disorder:* Patricia O. Quinn and Manisha Madhoo, "A Review of Attention-Deficit/Hyperactivity Disorder in Women and Girls: Uncovering This Hidden Diagnosis," *Primary Care Companion for CNS Disorders* 16, no. 3 (2014): Article PCC.13r01596, https://doi.org/10.4088/PCC.13r01596.

21 *when girls and women are treated for ADHD:* Edward Hallowell, "What Does ADHD Look Like in Women? Many Doctors Are Still Getting It Wrong," *ADDitude*, June 1, 2022, https://www.additudemag.com/what-does-adhd-look-like-in-women-misdiagnosis/.

21 *to be judged as atypical:* Brynne Calleran, "Attention Deficit/Hyperactivity Disorder and Women: Closing the Gender Gap" (poster presentation, APNA 34th Annual Conference, Lake Buena Vista, FL, September 30–October 4, 2020).

21 *boys are more likely to be referred for treatment:* Mark J. Sciutto, Cara J. Nolfi, and Carla Bluhm, "Effects of Child Gender and Symptom Type on Referrals for ADHD by Elementary School Teachers," *Journal of Emotional and Behavioral Disorders* 12, no. 4 (2004): 247–53, https://doi.org/10.1177/10634266040120040501.

22 *Stereotypes and gender norms:* "ADHD in Women and Girls: Why Female Symptoms Slip Through Diagnostic Cracks," International Board of Credentialing and Continuing Education Standards, accessed April 11, 2023, https://ibcces.org/learning/adhd-in-women-and-girls-why-female-symptoms-slip-through-diagnostic-cracks/.

23 *Ninety-three percent:* William Dodson, "'You Couldn't Possibly Have ADHD!,'" *ADDitude*, January 3, 2021, https://www.additudemag.com/adhd-diagnosis-mistakes/.

23 *some doctors who don't believe in ADHD at all:* Richard Saul, "Doctor: ADHD Does Not Exist," *Time*, March 14, 2014, https://time.com/25370/doctor-adhd-does-not-exist/.

23 *recognized by all major medical groups:* Camille Noe Pagán, "Is ADHD Real," WebMD, August 29, 2017, https://www.webmd.com/add-adhd/childhood-adhd/features/adhd-critics.

23 *internalize hyperactivity with racing thoughts and emotional dysregulation:* Margaret Weiss and Jacqueline Weiss, "A Guide to the Treatment of Adults with ADHD," *Journal of Clinical Psychiatry* 64, suppl. 3 (2004): 27–37, https://www.psychiatrist.com/wp-content/uploads/2021/02/13791_guide-treatment-adults-adhd.pdf.

24 *medical, physical, or genetic test for ADHD:* "Diagnosis of ADHD in Adults," Children and Adults with Attention-Deficit/Hyperactivity Disorder (CHADD), accessed August 20, 2022, https://chadd.org/for-adults/diagnosis-of-adhd-in-adults/.

25 *something known as the QbTest:* "Assessment," Child Mental Health Clinic, accessed August 20, 2022, https://www.cmhclinic.co.uk/assessment/.

26 *tools can be expensive:* "19 Tips for Finding Low-Cost ADHD Treatment," Children and Adults with Attention-Deficit/Hyperactivity Disorder (CHADD), accessed August 20, 2022, https://chadd.org/attention-article/19-tips-for-finding-low-cost-adhd-treatment/.

28 *For approximately 20 percent of ADHD women:* Dusan Kolar et al., "Treatment of Adults with Attention-Deficit/Hyperactivity Disorder," *Neuropsychiatric Disease and Treatment* 4, no. 2 (2008): 389–404, https://doi.org/10.2147/ndt.s6985.

CHAPTER 3: WHY ADHD WOMEN FACE MORE ISSUES

34 *American women handle most of the essential household chores:* Megan Brenan, "Women Still Handle Main Household Tasks in the U.S.," Gallup, January 29, 2020, https://news.gallup.com/poll/283979/women-handle-main-household-tasks.aspx.

34 *to care for elders:* National Center on Caregiving at Family Caregiver Alliance, "Women and Caregiving: Facts and Figures," Family Caregiver Alliance, accessed April 13, 2023, https://www.caregiver.org/resource/women-and-caregiving-facts-and-figures/.

34 *women are more likely to be negatively judged:* Claire Cain Millar, "Why Women, but Not Men, Are Judged for a Messy House," *New York Times*, June 11, 2019, https://www.nytimes.com/2019/06/11/upshot/why-women-but-not-men-are-judged-for-a-messy-house.html.

35 *they judged it as dirtier:* Sarah Thébaud, Sabino Kornrich, and Leah Ruppanner, "Good Housekeeping, Great Expectations: Gender and Housework and Norms," *Sociological Methods & Research* 50, no. 3 (2021): 1186–214, https://doi.org/10.1177/0049124119852395.

36 *ashamed of their ADHD symptoms:* Mira Elise Glaser Holthe and Eva Langvik, "The Strives, Struggles, and Successes of Women Diagnosed with ADHD as Adults," *SAGE Open* (2017): 1–12, https://doi.org/10.1177/2158244017701799.

37 *more likely to suffer from low self-esteem:* Holthe and Langvik, "The Strives, Struggles, and Successes of Women Diagnosed with ADHD as Adults."

37 *greater propensity toward self-harm:* Holthe and Langvik, "The Strives, Struggles, and Successes of Women Diagnosed with ADHD as Adults."

37 *One surprising study:* Esme Fuller-Thompson et al., "The Dark Side of ADHD: Factors Associated with Suicide Attempts Among Those with ADHD in a National Representative Canadian Sample," *Archives of Suicide Research* 26, no. 3 (2022): 1122–40, https://doi.org/10.1080/13811118.2020.1856258.

38 *impetuous, ill-fated decisions:* Sinclaire M. O'Grady and Stephen P. Hinshaw, "Long-Term Outcomes of Females with ADHD: Increased Risk for Self-Harm," *British Journal of Psychiatry* 218, no. 1 (2021): 4–6, https://doi.org/10.1192/bjp.2020.153.

40 *women have been historically excluded from clinical trials:* "History of Women's Participation in Clinical Research," National Institutes of Health, accessed September 23, 2022, https://orwh.od.nih.gov/toolkit/recruitment/history#.

40 *influence ADHD symptoms and the medications commonly used:* Laura Flynn McCarthy, "Women, Hormones, and ADHD," *ADDitude*, March 24, 2023, https://www.additudemag.com/women-hormones-and-adhd/.

40 *can improve mood, concentration, motivation:* Claudia Barth, Arno Villringer, and Julia Sacher, "Sex Hormones Affect Neurotransmitters and Shape the Adult Female Brain During Hormonal Transition Periods," *Frontiers in Neuroscience* 9, no. 37 (2015): Article 37, https://doi.org/10.3389/fnins.2015.00037.

40 *increased cognitive and executive function:* Victoria N. Luine, "Estradiol and Cognitive Function: Past, Present, and Future," *Hormones and Behavior* 66, no. 4 (2014): 602–18, https://doi.org/10.1016/j.yhbeh.2014.08.011.

40 *may even improve the efficacy of ADHD medications:* "ADHD and Estrogen," Edge Foundation, accessed April 13, 2023, https://edgefoundation.org/adhd-and-estrogen/.

40 *ADHD women during times of lower estrogen:* "ADHD and Estrogen."

41 *hormone-related mood disorders:* Farangis Dorani et al., "Prevalence of Hormone-Related Mood Disorder Symptoms in Women with ADHD," *Journal of Psychiatric Research* 133 (2021): 10–15, https://doi.org/10.1016/j.jpsychires.2020.12.005.

41 *whether or not they have ADHD:* Jeanette Wasserstein, "Menopause, Hormones & ADHD: What We Know, What Research Is Needed," *ADDitude*, March 24, 2023, https://www.additudemag.com/menopause-hormones-adhd-women-research/.

41 *One survey of 1,500 women with ADHD:* ADDitude Editors, "ADHD Impairment Peaks in Menopause, According to ADDitude Reader Survey," *ADDitude*, July 11, 2022, https://www.additudemag.com/menopause-symptoms-adhd-survey/.

41 *no research exists on the phenomenon:* Wasserstein, "Menopause, Hormones & ADHD."

CHAPTER 4: TURNING ADHD TRAITS INTO SUPERPOWERS

43 *a common trait among people with ADHD:* Jane Ann Sedgwick, Andrew Merwood, and Philip Asherson, "The Positive Aspects of Attention Deficit Hyperactivity Disorder: A Qualitative Investigation of Successful Adults with ADHD," *ADHD Attention Deficit and Hyperactivity Disorders* 11 (2019): 241–53, https://doi.org/10.1007/s12402-018-0277-6.

43 *cause us to be unrealistic:* Laura E. Knouse and John T. Mitchell, "Incautiously Optimistic: Positively-Valenced Cognitive Avoidance in Adult ADHD," *Cognitive and Behavioral Practice* 22, no. 2 (2015): 192–202, https://doi.org/10.1016/j.cbpra.2014.06.003.

44 *Drs. Edward M. Hallowell and John Ratey:* Edward M. Hallowell and John R. Ratey, *ADHD 2.0: New Science and Essential Strategies for Thriving with Distraction—from Childhood Through Adulthood* (New York: Ballantine Books, 2022).

45 *people who are easily distracted, hyperactive, or impulsive:* Nathalie Boot, Barbara Nevicka, and Matthijs Baas, "Creativity in ADHD: Goal-Directed Motivation and Domain Specificity," *Journal of Attention Disorders* 24, no. 13 (2020): 1857–66, https://doi.org/10.1177/1087054717727352.

45 *according to Dr. Hallowell:* Diane O'Reilly, "Stifled Creativity and Its Damaging Impact on the ADHD Brain," *ADDitude*, August 12, 2022, https://www.additudemag.com/adhd-creativity-brain-health/.

45 *tasks that require divergent thinking:* Holly A. White and Priti Shah, "Uninhibited Imaginations: Creativity in Adults with Attention-Deficit/Hyperactivity Disorder," *Personality and Individual Differences* 40, no. 6 (2006): 1121–31, https://doi.org/10.1016/j.paid.2005.11.007.

46 *hyperfocus like people with ADHD regularly do:* Brandon K. Ashinoff and Ahmad Abu-Akel, "Hyperfocus: The Forgotten Frontier of Attention," *Psychological Research* 85 (2021): 1–19, https://doi.org/10.1007/s00426-019-01245-8.

47 *hyperactivity can lead to extreme restlessness:* Mikka Nielsen, "ADHD and Temporality: A Desynchronized Way of Being in the World," *Cross-Cultural Studies in Health and Illness* 36, no. 3 (2017): 260–72, https://doi.org/10.1080/01459740.2016.1274750.

48 *Numerous studies have found:* Rachel Shoham et al., "ADHD-Associated Risk Taking Is Linked to Exaggerated Views of the Benefits of Positive Outcomes," *Scientific Reports* 6 (2016): 34833, https://doi.org/10.1038/srep34833.

48 *One study published:* Rachel Shoham et al., "What Drives Risky Behavior in ADHD: Insensitivity to Its Risk or Fascination with Its Potential Benefits," *Journal of Attention Disorders* 25, no. 14 (2021): 1988–2002, https://doi.org/10.1177/1087054720950820.

48 *to cover human rights violations and other atrocities:* Katherine Ellison, "Bio," Katherine Ellison, accessed April 13, 2023, https://katherineellison.com/bio/.

49 *people with ADHD produce more relaxing theta brain waves:* Marios Adamou, Tim Fullen, and Sarah L. Jones, "EEG for Diagnosis of Adult ADHD: A Systematic Review with Narrative Analysis," *Frontiers in Psychiatry* 25 (2020): 871, https://doi.org/10.3389/fpsyt.2020.00871.

50 *doesn't adhere to traditional social conduct:* "ADHD and Disruptive Behavior Disorders," Children and Adults with Attention-Deficit/Hyperactivity Disorder (CHADD), accessed April 13, 2023, https://chadd.org/about-adhd/disruptive-behavior-disorders/.

50 *a lower tolerance for repetitiveness and monotony:* Valentino Antonio Pironti et al., "Personality Traits in Adults with Attention-Deficit Hyperactivity Disorder and Their Unaffected First-Degree Relatives," *BJPsych Open* 2, no. 4 (2016): 280–85, https://doi.org/10.1192/bjpo.bp.116.003608.

50 *"outsider's identity":* Sedgwick, Merwood, and Asherson, "The Positive Aspects of Attention Deficit Hyperactivity Disorder."

50 *spark innovation, improve performance, and increase personal status:* Francesca Gino, "Let Your Workers Rebel," *Harvard Business Review*, October 24, 2016, https://hbr.org/2016/10/let-your-workers-rebel.

50 *boost our self-efficacy and well-being:* Bas Kodden, Ramon van Ingen, and Stijn Langeweg, "Non-conformism as Precursor for Self-Efficacy and Well-Being Among Schoolteachers in the Netherlands," *Humanities and Social Sciences Communications* 7 (2020): Article 56, https://doi.org/10.1057/s41599-020-00551-6.

50 *make us sexier to other people, as per one survey:* Amanda Chatel, "Nonconformists Are the Sexiest, Says Study," Bustle, March 31, 2015, https://www.bustle.com/articles/73272-nonconformists-are-more-attractive-and-the-best-partners-says-awesome-science.

50 *American conservationist Aldo Leopold:* "Aldo Leopold: Quotable Quotes," Goodreads, accessed April 13, 2023, https://www.goodreads.com/quotes/509185-nonconformity-is-the-highest-evolutionary-attainment-of-social-animals.

50 *accredited representative:* "Representation of Others," 8 CFR 1292.1 (2017), 1136–37, https://www.govinfo.gov/app/details/CFR-2017-title8-vol1/CFR-2017-title8-vol1-sec1292-1.

52 *hypersensitivity is a common trait:* Zoë Kessler, "My Hypersensitivity Is Real: Why Highly Sensitive People Have ADHD," *ADDitude*, January 21, 2023, https://www.additudemag.com/hypersensitivity-disorder-with-adhd/.

52 *sensory overload: ADDitude* Editors, "Why ADHD in Women is Routinely Dismissed, Misdiagnosed, and Treated Inadequately," *ADDitude*, July 11, 2022, https://www.additudemag.com/adhd-in-women-misunderstood-symptoms -treatment/.

53 *better able to feel and relate to others' emotions:* "Why Does Everything in the World Affect Me So Much," ADDept, accessed April 13, 2023, https:// www.addept.org/living-with-adult-add-adhd/doomscrolling-adhd-and-justice -sensitivity.

53 *Studies show that justice sensitivity:* Thomas Schäfer and Thomas Krane-burg, "The Kind Nature Behind the Unsocial Semblance: ADHD and Justice Sensitivity—A Pilot Study," *Journal of Attention Disorders* 19, no. 8 (2015): 715– 22, https://doi.org/10.1177/1087054712466914.

54 *when we rely on our intuition:* "Intuition—It's More Than a Feeling," Asso-ciation for Psychological Science, April 21, 2016, https://www.psychological science.org/news/minds-business/intuition-its-more-than-a-feeling.html.

54 *more intuitive than neurotypical people:* "ADHD Superpowers," Minnesota Neu-ropsychology, August 12, 2020, https://www.mnneuropsychology.com/articles /ADHD_Superpowers.html.

54 *Our brains tend to focus on the connections:* Lara Honos-Webb, *The Gift of Adult ADD: How to Transform Your Challenges and Build on Your Strengths* (Oak-land: New Harbinger Publications, 2008), 135.

54 *lean on our intuition:* Emil Persson et al., "Using Quantitative Trait in Adults with ADHD to Test Predictions of Dual-Process Theory," *Scientific Reports* 10 (2020): Article 20076, https://doi.org/10.1038/s41598-020-76923-4.

54 *increase our intuitive powers:* Elayne Daniels, "Why So Many People Wonder, 'Are Highly Sensitive People Psychic?,'" Dr. Elayne Daniels, September 16, 2021, https://www.drelaynedaniels.com/why-so-many-people-wonder-are-highly -sensitive-people-psychic/.

CHAPTER 5: HOW TO FIND YOURSELF, YOUR PASSIONS, AND YOUR PURPOSE

57 *we experience life more passionately than neurotypical people do:* William Dodson, "How Adults with ADHD Think: Uncomfortable Truths About the ADHD Nervous System," *ADDitude*, July 11, 2022, https://www.additudemag .com/adhd-in-adults-nervous-system/.

59 *spending time in nature:* Frances E. Kuo and Andrea Faber Taylor, "A Potential Natural Treatment for Attention-Deficit/Hyperactivity Disorder: Evidence from a National Study," *American Journal of Public Health* 94, no. 9 (2004): 1580–86, https://doi.org/10.2105/ajph.94.9.1580.

60 *they create positive emotions in and around you:* Ryan M. Niemiec and Robert E. McGrath, *The Power of Character Strengths: Appreciate and Ignite Your Positive Personality* (Cincinnati: VIA Institute on Character, 2019), 11–12.

CHAPTER 6: BIG EMOTIONS, TRAUMA, AND HOW TO BETTER MANAGE BOTH

70 *RSD is strongly associated with ADHD:* William Dodson, "New Insights into Rejection Sensitive Dysphoria," *ADDitude,* July 11, 2022, https://www.additude mag.com/rejection-sensitive-dysphoria-adhd-emotional-dysregulation/.

70 *lead us to be more easily excitable:* Alan P. Brown, "Why We Feel So Much— and Ways to Overcome It," *ADDitude,* July 13, 2022, https://www.additudemag .com/adhd-emotion-setback-to-positive-energy/.

70 *"significantly greater rates":* Reid J. Robinson et al., "Gender Differences in 2 Clinical Trials of Adults with Attention-Deficit/Hyperactivity Disorder: A Retrospective Data Analysis," *Journal of Clinical Psychiatry* 69, no. 2 (2008): 213–21, https://doi.org/10.4088/jcp.v69n0207.

70 *be ashamed of our emotional outbursts or other behaviors:* Frank W. Paulus et al., "Emotional Dysregulation in Children and Adolescents with Psychiatric Disorders. A Narrative Review," *Frontiers in Psychiatry* 12 (2021): Article 628252, https://doi.org/10.3389/fpsyt.2021.628252.

70 *80 percent of all people with ADHD:* Martin A. Katzman et al., "Adult ADHD and Comorbid Disorders: Clinical Implications of a Dimensional Approach," *BMC Psychiatry* 17 (2017): Article 302, https://doi.org/10.1186/s12888-017-1463-3.

71 *American Psychiatric Association's diagnostic criteria for years:* Philip Shaw et al., "Emotional Dysregulation and Attention Deficit Hyperactivity Disorder," *American Journal of Psychiatry* 171, no. 3 (2014): 276–93, https://doi.org/10.1176 /appi.ajp.2013.13070966.

71 *we respond to external stimuli more quickly:* William Dodson, "The ADHD- Depression Link: Symptom Parallels and Distinctions," *ADDitude,* July 8, 2022, https://www.additudemag.com/adhd-depression-link-symptoms-diagnosis -treatments/.

71 *divergent from the norm:* Shaw et al., "Emotional Dysregulation and Attention Deficit Hyperactivity Disorder."

71 *more apt to remember the negative things people say and do:* Sharone Saline, "5 Tips for Adults with ADHD to Overcome Negative Thinking," *Psychology Today,* October 12, 2022, https://www.psychologytoday.com/us/blog/your-way -adhd/202210/5-tips-adults-adhd-overcome-negative-thinking.

71 *more emotionally excitable in general:* Brown, "Why We Feel So Much—and Ways to Overcome It."

72 *nervous system dysregulation:* Center for Substance Abuse Treatment, "Chapter 3: Understanding the Impact of Trauma," in *Trauma-Informed Care in Behavioral Health Sciences* (Rockville, MD: Substance Abuse and Mental Health

Services Administration, 2014), 59–90, https://www.ncbi.nlm.nih.gov/books /NBK207191/.

73 *stores all memories from infancy onward:* Isabel A Vöhringer et al., "The Development of Implicit Memory from Infancy to Childhood: On Average Performance Levels and Interindividual Differences," *Child Development* 89, no. 2 (2018): 370–82, https://doi.org/10.1111/cdev.12749.

73 *If we didn't feel safe in infancy:* Bessel van der Kolk, *The Body Keeps the Score: Brain, Mind, and Body in the Healing of Trauma* (New York: Penguin Books, 2015), 120.

73 *If our early care:* Bruce Perry and Oprah Winfrey, *What Happened to You? Conversations on Trauma, Resilience, and Healing* (New York: Flatiron Books, 2021), 116.

73 *childhood trauma can increase the likelihood of developing ADHD:* Janna N. Vrijsen et al., "ADHD Symptoms in Healthy Adults Are Associated with Stressful Life Events and Negative Memory Bias," *ADHD Attention Deficit and Hyperactivity Disorders* 10, no. 2 (2018): 151–60, https://doi.org/10.1007 /s12402-017-0241-x.

73 *Thirty-four percent of women with ADHD:* Esme Fuller-Thomson and Danielle A. Lewis, "The Relationship Between Early Adversities and Attention-Deficit/ Hyperactivity Disorder," *Child Abuse & Neglect* 47 (2015): 94–101, https://doi .org/10.1016/j.chiabu.2015.03.005.

73 *symptoms of trauma can mimic ADHD:* Anna Chaves McDonald and Kida Ejesi, "When Trauma Mimics ADHD," in *ADHD in Adolescents*, ed. Alison Schonwald (Springer Cham, 2020), 171–85, https://doi.org/10.1007/978-3-030 -62393-7_13.

73 *Rumination is one way:* Elif B. Koş Yalvaç and Keith Gaynor, "Emotional Dys-regulation in Adults: The Influence of Rumination and Negative Secondary Ap-praisals of Emotion," *Journal of Affective Disorders* 282 (2021): 656–61, https://doi .org/10.1016/j.jad.2020.12.194.

73 *by being active in their minds:* William Dodson, "How Adults with ADHD Think: Uncomfortable Truths About the ADHD Nervous System," *ADDitude*, July 11, 2022, https://www.additudemag.com/adhd-in-adults-nervous-system/.

74 *women with the inattentive subtype:* Joseph W. Fredrick et al., "Sluggish Cognitive Tempo and ADHD Symptoms in Relation to Task-Unrelated Thought: Examining Unique Links with Mind-Wandering and Rumination," *Journal of Psychiatric Research* 123 (2020): 95–101, https://doi.org/10.1016/j.jpsy chires.2020.01.016.

74 *increase the risk of depression:* Stacey Colino, "The Hazards of Rumination for Your Mental and Physical Health," *U.S. News & World Report*, March 14, 2018, https://health.usnews.com/wellness/mind/articles/2018-03-14/the-hazards -of-rumination-for-your-mental-and-physical-health.

74   *common side effects of emotional dysregulation:* WebMD Editorial Contributors, "What Is Emotional Dysregulation?" WebMD, June 22, 2021, https://www.webmd.com/mental-health/what-is-emotional-dysregulation.

74   *more likely than men to suffer from both:* Cæcilie Ottosen et al., "Sex Differencs in Comorbidity Patterns of Attention-Deficit/Hyperactivity Disorder," *Journal of the American Academy of Child and Adolescent Psychiatry* 58, no. 4 (2019): 412–22.e3, https://doi.org/10.1016/j.jaac.2018.07.910.

74   *When we simultaneously have ADHD and emotional dysregulation:* Martin A. Katzman et al., "Adult ADHD and Comorbid Disorders: Clinical Implications of a Dimensional Approach," *BMC Psychiatry* 17 (2017): Article 302, https://doi.org/10.1186/s12888-017-1463-3.

74   *symptoms are blamed on our ADHD rather than a mood issue:* Roberto Olivardia, "Anxiety? Depression? Or ADHD? It Could Be All Three," *ADDitude*, March 31, 2022, https://www.additudemag.com/adhd-anxiety-depression-the-diagnosis-puzzle-of-related-conditions/.

74   *ADHD, depression, and anxiety share similar symptoms:* Olivardia, "Anxiety? Depression? Or ADHD? It Could Be All Three."

75   *There's no official criteria:* "Rejection Sensitive Dysphoria (RSD)," Cleveland Clinic, August 30, 2022, https://my.clevelandclinic.org/health/diseases/24099-rejection-sensitive-dysphoria-rsd.

75   *up to 99 percent:* Stephanie Watson, "What Is Rejection Sensitive Dysphoria?" WebMD, October 3, 2022, https://www.webmd.com/add-adhd/rejection-sensitive-dysphoria.

75   *You may constantly feel disappointed:* William Dodson, "Emotional Regulation and Rejection Sensitivity," *Attention*, October 2016, https://chadd.org/wp-content/uploads/2016/10/ATTN_10_16_EmotionalRegulation.pdf.

76   *Women are three times more likely to have OCD than men:* "Anxiety Disorders—Facts & Statistics," Anxiety & Depression Association of America, October 28, 2022, https://adaa.org/understanding-anxiety/facts-statistics.

76   *an even greater probability of OCD than neurotypical people:* Silvia Brem et al., "The Neurobiological Link Between OCD and ADHD," *ADHD Attention Deficit and Hyperactivity Disorders* 6, no. 3 (2014): 175–202, https://doi.org/10.1007/s12402-014-0146-x.

77   *body-focused repetitive behaviors:* Katharine Anne Phillips and Dan J. Stein, "Body-Focused Repetitive Behavior Disorder," *Merck Manual*, September 1, 2022, https://www.merckmanuals.com/home/mental-health-disorders/obsessive-compulsive-and-related-disorders/body-focused-repetitive-behavioral-disorder.

77   *there's a link between the conditions:* Roberto Olivardia, "Overview of Body-Focused Repetitive Behaviors: Types, Treatments & ADHD Links," *ADDitude*, July 13, 2022, https://www.additudemag.com/body-focused-repetitive-behaviors-adhd-anxiety/.

77 *an inability to regulate emotions like anxiety:* "What Is a BFRB?," The TLC Foundation for Body-Focused Repetitive Behaviors, accessed April 15, 2023, https://www.bfrb.org/your-journey/what-is-a-bfrb.

77 *oppositional defiant disorder:* Janice Rodden, "Study: Oppositional Defiant and Conduct Disorders Far More Common in Girls with ADHD," *ADDitude*, March 31, 2022, https://www.additudemag.com/oppositional-defiant-disorder -in-adhd-girls/.

78 *Borderline personality disorder severely impacts:* "Borderline Personality Disorder," National Institute of Mental Health, accessed September 2, 2022, https:// www.nimh.nih.gov/health/topics/borderline-personality-disorder.

78 *a cycle of sabotage-and-amend within their relationships:* "Borderline Personality Disorder," Mayo Clinic, accessed September 2, 2022, https://www.mayoclinic .org/diseases-conditions/borderline-personality-disorder/symptoms-causes /syc-20370237.

78 *Borderline personality disorder is diagnosed more frequently:* Randy A. Sansone and Lori A. Sansone, "Gender Patterns in Borderline Personality Disorder," *Innovations in Clinical Neuroscience* 8, no. 5 (2011): 16–20, https://www.ncbi.nlm .nih.gov/pmc/articles/PMC3115767/.

78 *Bipolar disorder is a mental health condition:* "Bipolar Disorder," National Institute of Mental Health, accessed April 15, 2022, https://www.nimh.nih.gov /health/topics/bipolar-disorder.

78 *bipolar disorder develops in their late teens or early adulthood:* "Bipolar Disorder," National Alliance on Mental Illness, accessed August 30, 2022, https:// www.nami.org/About-Mental-Illness/Mental-Health-Conditions/Bipolar -Disorder.

78 *affects both men and women equally:* Saloni Dattani, Hannah Ritchie, and Max Roser, "Mental Health," Our World in Data, accessed August 30, 2022, https://ourworldindata.org/mental-health.

78 *there is no blood test:* "Bipolar Disorder."

78 *Up to 20 percent of people with ADHD have bipolar disorder:* Ronald C. Kessler et al., "The Prevalence and Correlates of Adult ADHD in the United States: Results from the National Comorbidity Survey Replication," *American Journal of Psychiatry* 163, no. 4 (2006): 716–23, https://doi.org/10.1176/appi .ajp.163.4.716.

79 *can lead to misdiagnosis:* Janice Rodden and Robert Olivardia, "The Physician's Guide for Distinguishing Bipolar Disorder and ADHD," *ADDitude*, July 11, 2022, https://www.additudemag.com/adhd-vs-bipolar-a-guide-to -distinguishing-look-alike-conditions/.

80 *just twelve sessions of CBT:* Xiaoli Wang et al., "The Effects of Cognitive-Behavioral Therapy on Intrinsic Functional Brain Networks in Adults with Attention-Deficit/Hyperactivity Disorder," *Behaviour Research and Therapy* 76 (2016): 32–39, https://doi.org/10.1016/j.brat.2015.11.003.

80 *can help reduce hyperactivity:* "Cognitive-Behavioural Therapy for Attention Deficit Hyperactivity Disorder (ADHD) in Adults," Cochrane, accessed April 15, 2023, https://www.cochrane.org/CD010840/BEHAV_cognitive-behavioural-therapy-attention-deficit-hyperactivity-disorder-adhd-adults.

81 *CBT is also called cognitive restructuring:* Rebecca Joy Stanborough, "How to Change Negative Thinking with Cognitive Restructuring," Healthline, February 4, 2020, https://www.healthline.com/health/cognitive-restructuring#how-does-it-work.

82 *reduce symptoms of emotional dysregulation and other ADHD traits:* Pierre Cole et al., "CBT/DBT Skills Training for Adults with Attention Deficit Hyperactivity Disorder (ADHD)," *Psychiatria Danubina* 28, suppl. 1 (2016): 103–7, https://pubmed.ncbi.nlm.nih.gov/27663817/.

83 *an outlet for their emotional tensions:* Kin-ya Kubo, Mitsuo Iinuma, and Huayue Chen, "Mastication as a Stress-Coping Behavior," *BioMed Research International* (2015): Article 876409, https://doi.org/10.1155/2015/876409.

83 *reduced the stress hormone cortisol:* Akiyo Sasaki-Otomaru et al., "Effect of Regular Gum Chewing on Levels of Anxiety, Mood, and Fatigue in Healthy Young Adults," *Clinical Practice & Epidemiology in Mental Health* 7 (2011): 133–39, https://doi.org/10.2174/1745017901107010133.

83 *cognitive function by increasing alertness:* Serge V. Onyper et al., "Cognitive Advantages of Chewing Gum. Now You See Them, Now You Don't," *Appetite* 57 (2011): 321–28, https://doi.org/10.1016/j.appet.2011.05.313.

84 *tapping lowers rates of anxiety:* Donna Bach et al., "Clinical EFT (Emotional Freedom Techniques) Improves Multiple Physiological Markers of Health," *Journal of Evidence-Based Integrative Medicine* 24 (2019): Article 2515690X18823691, https://doi.org/10.1177/2515690X18823691.

84 *forces you to do certain eye movements:* "What Is EMDR?," EMDR Institute, Inc., accessed April 15, 2023, https://www.emdr.com/what-is-emdr/.

84 *EMDR has been shown:* "EMDR Therapy," Cleveland Clinic, accessed September 3, 2022, https://my.clevelandclinic.org/health/treatments/22641-emdr-therapy.

84 *EMDR helps lessen the symptoms of ADHD:* "Is EMDR Effective for Treating ADHD?," PESI, accessed April 15, 2023, https://www.pesi.com/blog/details/2105/is-emdr-effective-for-treating-adhd.

85 *physically change our brains through neuroplasticity:* Anna Lardone et al., "Mindfulness Mediation Is Related to Long-Lasting Changes in Hippocampal Functional Topology During Resting State: A Magnetoencephalography Study," *Neural Plasticity* (2018): Article 5340717, https://doi.org/10.1155/2018/5340717.

86 *mindfulness can increase multiple aspects of self-regulation:* Lidia Zylowka et al., "Mindful Awareness and ADHD," in *Clinical Handbook of Mindfulness*, ed. Fabrizio Didonna (New York: Springer, 2009), 323.

86 *Long-term meditators have been found:* Sara W. Lazar et al., "Meditation Experience Is Associated with Increased Cortical Thickness," *Neuroreport* 16, no. 17 (2005): 1893–97, https://doi.org/10.1097/01.wnr.0000186598.66243.19.

86 *mediation practice can help you improve your attentional blink:* Sara van Leeuwen, Notger G. Müller, and Lucia Melloni, "Age Effects on Attentional Blink Performance in Meditation," *Consciousness and Cognition* 18, no. 3 (2009): 593–99, https://doi.org/10.1016/j.concog.2009.05.001.

86 *five minutes of meditation daily:* Amy G. Lam, Sean Sterling, and Edward Margines, "Effects of Five-Minute Mindfulness Meditation on Mental Health Care Professionals," *Journal of Psychology & Clinical Psychiatry* 2, no. 3 (2015): Article 00076, https://doi.org/10.15406/jpcpy.2015.02.00076.

86 *five consecutive days of practice:* Yi-Yuan Tang et al., "Short-Term Meditation Training Improves Attention and Self-Regulation," *Proceedings of the National Academy of Sciences* 104, no. 43 (2007): 17512–16, https://doi.org/10.1073/pnas.0707678104.

87 *the branch of our brain:* Chloe Williams, "Cold Water Plunges Are Trendy. Can They Really Reduce Anxiety and Depression?," *New York Times*, February 20, 2022, https://www.nytimes.com/2022/02/20/well/mind/cold-water-plunge-mental-health.html.

87 *a ten-minute foot massage:* Wendy Moyle et al., "The Effect of Foot Massage on Long-Term Care Staff Working with Older People with Dementia: A Pilot, Parallel Group, Randomized Controlled Trial," *BMC Nursing* 12 (2013): Article 5, https://doi.org/10.1186/1472-6955-12-5.

87 *how long experts say it takes:* Moreno Zugaro, "How to Free Yourself from Negative Emotions in 90 Seconds," Medium, August 29, 2020, https://medium.com/the-authentic-man/how-to-free-yourself-from-negative-emotions-in-90-seconds-cc83199d82c9.

88 *the health of our relationships:* Perry and Winfrey, *What Happened to You?*, 258.

88 *form and maintain healthy social connections:* Jessica Martino, Jennifer Pegg, and Elizabeth Pegg Frates, "The Connection Prescription: Using the Power of Social Interactions and the Deep Desire for Connectedness to Empower Health and Wellness," *American Journal of Lifestyle Medicine* 11, no. 6 (2017): 466–75, https://doi.org/10.1177/1559827615608788.

89 *positive emotion is any emotional reaction:* "Positive Emotion," American Psychological Association, accessed April 16, 2023, https://dictionary.apa.org/positive-emotion.

89 *weakens the prefrontal cortex:* Amy F. T. Arnsten, "Stress Weakens Prefrontal Networks: Molecular Insults to Higher Cognition," *Natura Neuroscience* 18 (2015): 1376–85, https://doi.org/10.1038/nn.4087.

CHAPTER 7: WAYS TO END OVERTHINKING, OVERWHELM, AND SELF-DOUBT

93 *six thousand thoughts per day:* Julie Tseng and Jordan Poppenk, "Brain Meta-State Transitions Demarcate Thoughts Across Task Contexts Exposing the Mental Noise of Trait Neuroticism," *Nature Communications* 11 (2020): Article 3480, https://doi.org/10.1038/s41467-020-17255-9.

94 *don't toggle so easily:* Jonathan Hassall, "Adult ADHD and Emotions," *Attention,* October 2020, https://chadd.org/adhd-news/adhd-news-adults/adult-adhd-and-emotions/.

95 *4-7-8 technique:* Ana Gotter, "What Is the 4-7-8 Breathing Technique?" Healthline, April 20, 2018, https://www.healthline.com/health/4-7-8-breathing.

95 *things that spike our dopamine:* Nora D. Volkhow et al., "Evaluating Dopamine Reward Pathway in ADHD," *Journal of the American Medical Association* 302, no. 10 (2009): 1084–91, https://doi.org/10.1001/jama.2009.1308.

95 *things that may scare or excite us:* Katherine Brooks, "Want to Break Out of the Blues? Try Something New," Right as Rain by UW Medicine, January 10, 2022, https://rightasrain.uwmedicine.org/well/health/try-something-new.

97 *Feeling overstimulated:* Josh Geffen and Kieran Forster, "Treatment of Adult ADHD: A Clinical Perspective," *Therapeutic Advances in Psychopharmacology* 8, no. 1 (2018): 25–32, https://doi.org/10.1177/2045125317734977.

97 *ADHD psychologist Ari Tuckman:* Ari Tuckman, "Sense of Time: It Can't Be 5:00 Already," April 20, 2009, in *More Attention, Less Deficit,* podcast, 4:32, https://adultadhdbook.com/more-attention-podcast/.

98 *bored with mundane tasks:* Ela Malkovsky et al., "Exploring the Relationship Between Boredom and Sustained Attention," *Experimental Brain Research* 221 (2012): 59–67, https://doi.org/10.1007/s00221-012-3147-z.

100 *predictable or repetitive tasks:* Katherine A. Johnson et al., "Dissociation in Performance of Children with ADHD and High-Functioning Autism on a Task of Sustained Attention," *Neuropsychologia* 45, no. 10 (2007): 2234–45, https://doi.org/10.1016/j.neuropsychologia.2007.02.019.

100 *We procrastinate boring tasks:* J. Russell Ramsay, "Why the ADHD Brain Chooses the Less Important Task—and How CBT Improves Prioritization Skills," *ADDitude,* April 12, 2023, https://www.additudemag.com/how-to-prioritize-tasks-adhd-adults/.

108 *Imposter syndrome:* Sanne Feenstra et al., "Contextualizing the Impostor 'Syndrome,'" *Frontiers in Psychology* 11 (2020): Article 575024, https://doi.org/10.3389/fpsyg.2020.575024.

108 *more prone to the mindset for a number of reasons:* Russell Ramsay, "'I Feel Like a Fraud Hiding in Plain Sight,'" *Psychology Today,* February 4, 2021, https://www.psychologytoday.com/us/blog/rethinking-adult-adhd/202102/i-feel-fraud-hiding-in-plain-sight.

108 *women are more likely to experience imposter syndrome than men:* "KPMG Study Finds 75% of Female Executives Across Industries Have Experienced Imposter Syndrome in Their Careers," KPMG, accessed April 16, 2023, https://info.kpmg.us/news-perspectives/people-culture/kpmg-study-finds-most-female-executives-experience-imposter-syndrome.html.

108 *women face more hurdles than men:* Sheryl Nance-Nash, "Why Imposter Syndrome Hits Women and Women of Colour Harder," BBC, July 27, 2020, https://www.bbc.com/worklife/article/20200724-why-imposter-syndrome-hits-women-and-women-of-colour-harder.

CHAPTER 8: ADHD-SPECIFIC STRATEGIES TO BETTER MANAGE YOUR RELATIONSHIPS

113 *complicate and impair our interpersonal relationships:* Burcu Kahveci Öncü and Şennur Tutarel Kişlak, "Marital Adjustment and Marital Conflict in Individuals Diagnosed with ADHD and Their Spouses," *Archives of Neuropsychiatry* 29, no. 2 (2022): 127–32.

114 *fall back on dysfunctional ways:* Öncü and Kişlak, "Marital Adjustment and Marital Conflict in Individuals Diagnosed with ADHD and Their Spouses."

114 *the divorce rate for couples affected by ADHD:* ADDitude Editors, "How ADHD Impacts Sex and Marriage," *ADDitude*, July 28, 2021, https://www.additude mag.com/adhd-marriage-statistics-personal-stories/.

114 *parent-child dynamic:* Melissa Orlov, "ADHD Relationships: When Helping Out Hurts Your Partnership," *Psychology Today*, January 16, 2014, https://www.psychologytoday.com/us/blog/may-i-have-your-attention/201401/adhd-relationships-when-helping-out-hurts-your-partnership.

117 *ADHD women often end up in relationships:* Stephanie Sarkis, "The Gaslighting Risk: Why Adults with ADHD Are Particularly Vulnerable to Manipulation," *ADDitude*, August 18, 2021, https://www.additudemag.com/gaslighting-adhd-adults-women-risk/.

119 *ADHD therapist Terry Matlen has also discussed:* Ralina Harvey-Smith, "What It's Like Parenting with ADHD Symptoms: 'It Felt Like My Head Was Going to Explode,'" *Washington Post*, January 8, 2021, https://www.washington post.com/lifestyle/2021/01/08/parenting-with-adhd/.

121 *enlist the help of a regular cleaning person:* Sari Solden, "Overwhelmed Mom Syndrome—It's a Real Thing," *ADDitude*, July 22, 2021, https://www.additude mag.com/overwhelmed-mom-with-adhd/.

123 *our impulsivity and natural exuberance:* "Relationships & Social Skills," Children and Adults with Attention-Deficit/Hyperactivity Disorder (CHADD), accessed August 16, 2022, https://chadd.org/for-adults/relationships-social-skills/.

126 *justice and fairness:* Rebecca Bondü and Günter Esser, "Justice and Rejection Sensitivity in Children and Adolescents with ADHD Symptoms," *European*

Child & Adolescent Psychiatry 24 (2015): 185–98, https://doi.org/10.1007/s00787
-014-0560-9.

CHAPTER 9: ADHD-SPECIFIC STRATEGIES TO BETTER MANAGE TIME AND PLANNING

132 *estimating time and how long it takes us:* Radek Ptacek et al., "Clinical Implications of the Perception of Time in Attention Deficit Hyperactivity Disorder (ADHD): A Review," *Medical Science Monitor* 25 (2019): 3918–24, https://doi.org/10.12659/MSM.914225.

132 *we're unaware of the passage of time:* Mareen Dennis, "'7 Reasons Why You Need Analog Clocks,'" *ADDitude*, January 21, 2022, https://www.additudemag.com/analog-clocks-adhd-time-blindness-benefits/.

133 see *time pass:* Dennis, "'7 Reasons Why You Need Analog Clocks.'"

135 *designed specifically for people with ADHD:* "Time Timer Original," Time Timer, accessed April 16, 2023, https://www.timetimer.com/pages/time-timer-original?cmp_id=1027706542&adg_id=53290208129&kwd=time%20timer&device=c&gclid=Cj0KCQiA_bieBhDSARIsADU4zLcAESBHw3m_3yOjrpOrhiS1u5Brtb8pj4LkpDYNymIr45EjFhsQSRcaAn47EALw_wcB.

CHAPTER 10: ADHD-SPECIFIC STRATEGIES TO BETTER MANAGE MONEY

146 *difficulties managing money:* Chi Liao, "ADHD Symptoms and Financial Distress," *Review of Finance* 25, no. 4 (2021): 1129–210, https://doi.org/10.1093/rof/rfaa013.

146 *four times more likely to impulse spend than our neurotypical peers:* Rupert Jones, "'Shopping Is a Nightmare': How ADHD Affects People's Spending Habits," *The Guardian*, June 25, 2022, https://www.theguardian.com/money/2022/jun/25/shopping-adhd-spending-habit.

146 *we're not interested:* Janneke Koerts et al., "Financial Judgment Determination in Adults with ADHD," *Journal of Neural Transmission* 128 (2021): 969–79, https://doi.org/10.1007/s00702-021-02323-1.

148 *60 to 80 percent more likely to have entrepreneurial intentions:* Daniel A. Lerner, Ingrid Verheul, and Roy Thurik, "Entrepreneurship and Attention Deficit/Hyperactivity Disorder: A Large-Scale Study Involving the Clinical Condition of ADHD," *Small Business Economics* 53 (2019): 381–92, https://doi.org/10.1007/s11187-018-0061-1.

148 *300 percent more likely:* Garret LoPorto, *The DaVinci Method: Break Out & Express Your Fire* (Concord, MA: Media for Your Mind, 2005).

148 *Thom Hartmann:* Thom Hartmann, *ADHD: A Hunter in a Farmer's World* (Rochester, VT: Healing Arts Press, 2019).

148 *new, stimulating, and challenging things:* Linda Roggli, "Entrepreneurship and ADHD: Fast Brain, Fast Company?," *ADDitude*, June 15, 2022, https://www.additudemag.com/entrepreneurship-adhd-business-research-traits-stories.

148 *ADHD entrepreneurs often respond positively:* Johan Wiklund et al., "ADHD, Impulsivity and Entrepreneurship," *Journal of Business Venturing* 32, no. 6 (2017): 627–56, https://doi.org/10.1016/j.jbusvent.2017.07.002.

149 *more intuitive cognitive styles:* Curt B. Moore, Nancy H. McIntyre, and Stephen E. Lanivich, "ADHD-Related Neurodiversity and the Entrepreneurial Mindset," *Entrepreneurial Theory and Practice* 45, no. 1 (2021): 64–91, https://doi.org/10.1177/1042258719890986.

151 *investing in experiences that create memories:* Jeff Haden, "How Happier People Spend Their Money, Backed by Considerable Science," *Inc.*, January 22, 2021, https://www.inc.com/jeff-haden/how-happier-people-spend-their-money-backed-by-considerable-science.html.

155 *the average stock market return:* Rebecca Lake, "What Is the Average Stock Market Return," SoFi Learn, March 13, 2022, https://www.sofi.com/learn/content/average-stock-market-return/.

155 *a 10 percent annual return:* "The Automatic Millionaire, by David Bach," Sweat Your Assets, accessed April 16, 2023, https://sweatyourassets.biz/the-automatic-millionaire/.

CHAPTER 11: HOW PHYSICAL MOVEMENT CAN TREAT ADHD

157 *Exercise has such a positive effect on ADHD symptoms:* Aylin Mehren et al., "Physical Exercise in Attention Deficit Hyperactivity Disorder—Evidence and Implications for the Treatment of Borderline Personality Disorder," *Borderline Personality Disorder and Emotion Dysregulation* 7 (2020): 1, https://doi.org/10.1186/s40479-019-0115-2.

160 *deficient in dopamine production:* Kenneth Blum et al., "Attention-Deficit-Hyperactivity Disorder and Reward Deficiency Syndrome," *Neuropsychiatric Disease and Treatment* 4, no. 5 (2008): 893–918, https://doi.org/10.2147/ndt.s2627.

160 *Physical activity spikes dopamine:* Mehren et al., "Physical Exercise in Attention Deficit Hyperactivity Disorder."

160 *physical activity balances them at the same time:* John Ratey, "The ADHD Exercise Solution," *ADDitude*, February 8, 2023, https://www.additudemag.com/the-adhd-exercise-solution/.

160 *Exercise can lift them:* Mehren et al., "Physical Exercise in Attention Deficit Hyperactivity Disorder."

160 *"Miracle-Gro for the brain":* John J. Ratey and Eric Hagerman, *Spark: The Revolutionary New Science of Exercise and the Brain* (Boston: Little, Brown, 2008).

160 *the more BDNF you produce:* Adrián De la Rosa et al., "Long-Term Exercise Training Improves Memory in Middle-Aged Men and Modulates Peripheral Levels of BDNF and Cathepsin B," *Scientific Reports* 9 (2019): Article 3337, https://doi.org/10.1038/s41598-019-40040-8.

160 *Exercise also stimulates neurogenesis:* Patrick Z. Liu and Robin Nusslock, "Exercise-Mediated Neurogenesis in the Hippocampus via BDNF," *Frontiers in Neuroscience* 12 (2018): Article 52, https://doi.org/10.3389/fnins.2018.00052.

161 *BDNF can also rewire your brain:* Liu and Nusslock, "Exercise-Mediated Neurogenesis in the Hippocampus via BDNF."

161 *two-minute bout of moderate exercise:* Peter Blomstrand and Jan Engvall, "Effects of a Single Exercise Workout on Memory and Learning Functions in Young Adults—A Systematic Review," *Translational Sports Medicine* 4, no. 1 (2020): 115–27, https://doi.org/10.1002/tsm2.190.

161 *the area that processes strong emotions:* Ratey, "The ADHD Exercise Solution."

161 *exercise is like taking:* Ratey and Hagerman, *Spark*.

161 *consistent exercise can be more effective:* James A. Blumenthal et al., "Effects of Exercise Training on Older Patients with Major Depression," *Archives of Internal Medicine* 159, no. 19 (1999): 2349–56, https://doi.org/10.1001/archinte.159.19.2349.

161 *depression treatment in Britain:* "Depression in Adults: Draft for Consultation," National Institute for Health and Care Excellence, November 2021, https://www.nice.org.uk/guidance/ng222/documents/draft-guideline-4.

161 *exercise can ease anxiety:* John J. Ratey, "Can Exercise Help Treat Anxiety?," Harvard Health Publishing, October 24, 2019, https://www.health.harvard.edu/blog/can-exercise-help-treat-anxiety-2019102418096.

161 *prevent anxiety disorders:* Martina Svensson et al., "Physical Activity Is Associated with Lower Long-Term Incidence of Anxiety in a Population-Based, Large-Scale Study," *Frontiers in Psychiatry* 12 (2021): Article 714014, https://doi.org/10.3389/fpsyt.2021.714014.

162 *exercise calms an overactive mind:* Eli Puterman et al., "Physical Activity Moderates Stressor-Induced Rumination on Cortisol Reactivity," *Psychosomatic Medicine* 73, no. 7 (2011): 604–11, https://doi.org/10.1097/PSY.0b013e318229e1e0.

163 *the most bang for your buck:* Betsy Hoza et al., "A Randomized Trial Examining the Effects of Aerobic Physical Activity on Attention-Deficit/Hyperactivity Disorder Symptoms in Young Children," *Journal of Abnormal Child Psychology* 43 (2015): 655–67, https://doi.org/10.1007/s10802-014-9929-y.

163 *boosting physical performance:* Dae Yun Seo et al., "Morning and Evening Exercise," *Integrative Medicine Research* 2, no. 4 (2013): 139–44, https://doi.org/10.1016/j.imr.2013.10.003.

163 *sustain the focusing effects of a good workout:* Ratey, "The ADHD Exercise Solution."

163 *thirty minutes of aerobic activity four times per week:* ADDitude Editors, "Exercise and the ADHD Brain: The Neuroscience of Movement," *ADDitude*, April 14, 2022, https://www.additudemag.com/exercise-and-the-adhd-brain/.

164 *combine complex movements:* Michael Lara, "The Exercise Prescription," *Attention*, June 2012, https://chadd.org/wp-content/uploads/2018/06/ATTN_06_12 _Exercise.pdf.

164 *Structured exercise:* Ratey, "The ADHD Exercise Solution."

165 *physical activity performed in nature:* Frances E. Kuo and Andrea Faber Taylor, "A Potential Natural Treatment for Attention-Deficit/Hyperactivity Disorder: Evidence from a National Study," *American Journal of Public Health* 94, no. 9 (2004): 1580–86, https://doi.org/10.2105/ajph.94.9.1580.

165 *restoring our concentration:* Carl Sherman, "Green Time: A Natural Remedy for ADHD Symptoms," *ADDitude*, February 8, 2023, https://www.additudemag .com/green-time-natural-adhd-remedy/.

165 *fight-or-flight survival response:* Ratey, "The ADHD Exercise Solution."

165 *prevent us from ever getting bored by what we're doing:* Florence Williams, "ADHD Is Fuel for Adventure," *Outside*, January 21, 2016, https://www.outside online.com/outdoor-adventure/exploration-survival/adhd-fuel-adventure/.

CHAPTER 12: USING NUTRITION TO CURB ADHD SYMPTOMS

167 *to have issues with our weight:* John P. Fleming, L. D. Levy, and R. D. Levitan, "Symptoms of Attention Deficit Hyperactivity Disorder in Severely Obese Women," *Eating and Weight Disorders—Studies on Anorexia, Bulimia and Obesity* 10 (2005): 10–13, https://doi.org/10.1007/BF03354661.

167 *the same dopamine hit to feel sated:* Karen A. Patte et al., "A Behavioral Genetic Model of the Mechanisms Underlying the Link Between Obesity and Symptoms of ADHD," *Journal of Attention Disorders* 24, no. 10 (2016): 1425–36, https://doi.org/10.1177/1087054715618793.

167 *helps control our inhibition:* Richard A. E. Edden et al., "Reduced GABA Concentration in Attention-Deficit/Hyperactivity Disorder," *Archives of General Psychiatry* 69, no. 7 (2012): 750–53, https://doi.org/10.1001/archgenpsychiatry .2011.2280.

168 *a condition linked to low dopamine levels:* Kenneth Blum et al., "Attention-Deficit-Hyperactivity Disorder and Reward Deficiency Syndrome," *Neuropsychiatric Disease and Treatment* 4, no. 5 (2008): 893–918, https://doi.org/10.2147 /ndt.s2627.

168 *Reward deficiency syndrome causes our brain:* Ellen Littman, "Never Enough? Why ADHD Brains Crave Stimulation," *ADDitude*, May 18, 2022, https://www .additudemag.com/brain-stimulation-and-adhd-cravings-dependency-and -regulation/.

168 *junk food or processed carbs:* Jenil Patel, "Processed Carbohydrates Are Addictive, Brain Study Suggests," WKU News, July 4, 2013, https://www.wku.edu /news/articles/index.php?view=article&articleid=2332.

168 *our impaired executive function skills:* Roberto Olivardia, "Is Your ADHD Brain Hard-Wired for Weight Gain?" *ADDitude*, March 31, 2022, https://www .additudemag.com/adhd-and-obesity-hard-wired-for-weight-gain.

168 *unhealthy convenience items:* Kathleen Nadeau, "Are You 'Chemically Wired' to Gain Weight?," *ADDitude*, March 31, 2022, https://www.additudemag.com /adhd-weight-gain.

168 *more likely to have an eating disorder:* Shauna P. Reinblatt, "Are Eating Disorders Related to Attention Deficit/Hyperactivity Disorder?," *Current Treatment Options in Psychiatry* 2, no. 4 (2015): 402–12, https://doi.org/10.1007 /s40501-015-0060-7.

168 *how our brains handle reward processing:* Bruce Jancin, "Binge Eating in ADHD May Not Be Impulsivity-Related," *Clinical Psychiatry News*, September 25, 2020, https://www.mdedge.com/psychiatry/article/229104/adhd/binge -eating-adhd-may-not-be-impulsivity-related.

170 *By visually engaging with your meal:* "Mindful Eating," The Nutrition Source, Harvard T. H. Chan School of Public Health, accessed April 16, 2023, https://www.hsph.harvard.edu/nutritionsource/mindful-eating/.

171 *probiotics can help our ADHD brains:* Anna Kalenik et al., "Gut Microbiota and Probiotic Therapy in ADHD: A Review of Current Knowledge," *Progress in Neuro-Psychopharmacology and Biological Psychiatry* 110, no. 30 (2021): Article 110277, https://doi.org/10.1016/j.pnpbp.2021.110277.

171 *consuming or supplementing with high-quality probiotics:* Chong-Su Kim et al., "Probiotic Supplementation Improves Cognitive Function and Mood with Changes in Gut Microbiota in Community-Dwelling Older Adults: A Randomized, Double-Blind, Placebo-Controlled, Multicenter Trial," *Journals of Gerontology: Series A* 76, no. 1 (2021): 32–40, https://doi.org/10.1093/gerona /glaa090.

171 *Probiotics may also boost mood:* Fereshteh Ansari et al., "The Effects of Probiotics and Prebiotics on Mental Disorders: A Review on Depression, Anxiety, Alzheimer, and Autism Spectrum Disorders," *Current Pharmaceutical Biotechnology* 21, no. 7 (2020): 555–65, https://doi.org/10.2174/13892010216662001071 13812.

171 *"novel therapeutic approaches" to disordered eating:* Elisabet Navarro-Tapia et al., "Effects of Microbiota Imbalance in Anxiety and Eating Disorders: Probiotics as Novel Therapeutic Approaches," *International Journal of Molecular Sciences* 22, no. 5 (2021): Article 2351, https://doi.org/10.3390/ijms22052351.

171 *reduce brain inflammation:* Clemens von Schacky, "Importance of EPA and DHA Blood Levels in Brain Structure and Function," *Nutrients* 13, no. 4 (2021): Article 1074, https://doi.org/10.3390/nu13041074.

172 *EPA and DHA have also been found:* David Mischoulon, "Omega-3 Fatty Acids for Mood Disorders," Harvard Health Publishing, October 27, 2020,

https://www.health.harvard.edu/blog/omega-3-fatty-acids-for-mood-disorders
-2018080314414.

172 *we don't consume enough fish:* Yanni Papanikolaou et al., "U.S. Adults Are
Not Meeting Recommended Levels for Fish and Omega-3 Fatty Acid Intake:
Results of an Analysis Using Observational Data from NHANES 2003–2008,"
Nutrition Journal 13 (2014): Article 31, https://doi.org/10.1186/1475-2891-13-31.

172 *the percentage is too tiny to make a noticeable difference:* Mélanie Plourde and
Stephen C. Cunnane, "Extremely Limited Synthesis of Long Chain Polyunsat-
urates in Adults: Implications for Their Dietary Essentiality and Use as Supplements," *Applied Physiology, Nutrition, and Metabolism* 32, no. 4 (2007): 619–32,
https://doi.org/10.1139/H07-034.

172 *consuming more fatty fish:* "Omega-3 Fatty Acids: Fact Sheet for Health
Professionals," National Institutes of Health Office of Dietary Supplements,
February 15, 2023, https://ods.od.nih.gov/factsheets/Omega3FattyAcids-Health
Professional/.

173 *In a 16:8 fast:* "Intermittent Fasting: What Is It, and How Does It Work?,"
Johns Hopkins Medicine, accessed April 17, 2023, https://www.hopkinsmed
icine.org/health/wellness-and-prevention/intermittent-fasting-what-is-it-and
-how-does-it-work.

173 *forces your body to burn through all the sugar:* "Intermittent Fasting: What Is
It, and How Does It Work?"

173 *Doing so increases BDNF:* Mark P. Mattson et al., "Intermittent Metabolic
Switching, Neuroplasticity and Brain Health," *Nature Reviews Neuroscience* 19,
no. 2 (2018): 63–80, https://doi.org/10.1038/nrn.2017.156.

173 *intermittent fasting can improve memory:* Liaoliao Li, Zhi Wang, and Zhiyi
Zuo, "Chronic Intermittent Fasting Improves Cognitive Functions and Brain
Structures in Mice," *PLOS ONE* 8, no. 6 (2013): Article e66069, https://doi
.org/10.1371/journal.pone.0066069.

174 *According to the Mayo Clinic:* Manpreet Mundi, "What Is Intermittent Fasting? Does It Have Health Benefits?," Mayo Clinic, May 5, 2022, https://www
.mayoclinic.org/healthy-lifestyle/nutrition-and-healthy-eating/expert-answers
/intermittent-fasting/faq-20441303.

174 *Johns Hopkins Medicine:* "Intermittent Fasting: What Is It, and How Does It
Work?"

174 *Seventy-five percent of Americans are chronically dehydrated:* Jennifer Wei-
gel, "Doctors Say Most Americans Are Dehydrated," *Chicago Sun-Times*, November 8, 2018, https://chicago.suntimes.com/2018/11/8/18455701/doctors-say
-most-americans-are-dehydrated.

175 *sabotages our mood:* Na Zhang et al., "Effects of Dehydration and Rehy-
dration on Cognitive Performance and Mood Among Male College Students
in Cangzhou, China: A Self-Controlled Trial," *International Journal of Envi-*

ronmental Research and Public Health 16, no. 11 (2019): Article 1891, https://doi.org/10.3390/ijerph16111891.

175 *causing our brain tissue to actually shrink:* Matthew J. Kempton et al., "Dehydration Affects Brain Structure and Function in Healthy Adolescents," *Human Brain Mapping* 32, no. 1 (2011): 71–79, https://doi.org/10.1002/hbm.20999.

175 *mild dehydration can impair memory:* Ana Adan, "Cognitive Performance and Dehydration," *Journal of the American College of Nutrition* 31, no. 2 (2012): 71–78, https://doi.org/10.1080/07315724.2012.10720011.

175 *well-hydrated people do better:* Kristen Willeumier, *Biohack Your Brain: How to Boost Cognitive Health, Performance & Power* (New York: William Morrow, 2020), 126.

175 *shown to increase dehydration:* Elliott B. Martin and Paul G. Hammerness, "Thirsty: ADHD, Stimulant Medication, and Dehydration," *Attention*, August 2014, 26–27, https://www.chadd.org/wp-content/uploads/2018/06/ATTN_08_14_Thirsty.pdf.

175 *11.5 cups of fluid per day:* Mayo Clinic Staff, "Water: How Much Should You Drink Every Day?," Mayo Clinic, October 12, 2022, https://www.mayoclinic.org/healthy-lifestyle/nutrition-and-healthy-eating/in-depth/water/art-20044256.

CHAPTER 13: OVERHAULING ADHD-RELATED SLEEP PROBLEMS

176 *four out of five adults with ADHD:* "ADHD and Sleep Disorders," Children and Adults with Attention-Deficit/Hyperactivity Disorder (CHADD), April 17, 2023, https://chadd.org/about-adhd/adhd-and-sleep-disorders/.

176 *part of the diagnostic criteria:* Craig H. Surman and Daniel M. Walsh, "Managing Sleep in Adults with ADHD: From Science to Pragmatic Approaches," *Brain Sciences* 11, no. 10 (2021): 1361–72, https://doi.org/10.3390/brainsci11101361.

176 *up to 70 percent of ADHD adults report:* William Dodson, "ADHD and Sleep Problems: This Is Why You're Always Tired," *ADDitude*, July 11, 2022, https://www.additudemag.com/adhd-sleep-disturbances-symptoms/.

177 *years of prior research on ADHD and sleep:* Allan Hvolby, "Associations of Sleep Disturbance with ADHD: Implications for Treatment," *ADHD Attention Deficit and Hyperactivity Disorders* 7, no. 1 (2015): 1–18, https://doi.org/10.1007/s12402-014-0151-0.

177 *RBP is a real condition:* Eric Suni, "What Is 'Revenge Bedtime Procrastination'?," Sleep Foundation, August 29, 2022, https://www.sleepfoundation.org/sleep-hygiene/revenge-bedtime-procrastination.

177 *stall the anticipated discomfort:* Tracy Otsuka, "How to Break the Exhausting Habit of Revenge Bedtime Procrastination," *ADDitude*, February 7, 2023, https://www.additudemag.com/revenge-bedtime-procrastination-sleep-problems-adhd/.

177 *intrusive sleep:* Dodson, "ADHD and Sleep Problems."

178 *our arousal and alertness levels:* Danielle Pacheco, "ADHD and Sleep," Sleep Foundation, March 17, 2023, https://www.sleepfoundation.org/mental-health/adhd-and-sleep.

178 *twenty-four-hour internal clock:* Jessica R. Lunsford-Avery and Scott H. Kollins, "Delayed Circadian Rhythm Phase: A Cause of Late-Onset Attention-Deficit/Hyperactivity Disorder Among Adolescents," *Journal of Child Psychology and Psychiatry* 59, no. 12 (2018): 1248–51, https://doi.org/10.1111/jcpp.12956.

178 *higher likelihood of developing sleep-related comorbidities:* Dafna Wajszilber, José Arturo Santiseban, and Reut Gruber, "Sleep Disorders in Patients with ADHD: Impact and Management Challenges," *Nature and Science of Sleep* 14, no. 10 (2018): 453–80, https://doi.org/10.2147/NSS.S163074.

178 *per the Cleveland Clinic:* "ADHD Medication," Cleveland Clinic, October 6, 2022, https://my.clevelandclinic.org/health/treatments/11766-adhd-medication.

178 *numerous clinical trials:* Penny Corkum et al., "The Effects of Extended-Release Stimulant Medication on Sleep in Children with ADHD," *Journal of the Canadian Academy of Child and Adolescent Psychiatry* 29, no. 1 (2020): 33–43, https://pubmed.ncbi.nlm.nih.gov/32194650/.

179 *hear sounds during lighter stages of sleep:* Jennifer G. Mayer, "Can You Hear While Sleeping?" South Shore Hearing Center, January 20, 2023, https://sshc.com/patient-resources/can-you-hear-while-sleeping/.

179 *60 to 67 degrees Fahrenheit:* Danielle Pacheco, "Best Temperature for Sleep," Sleep Foundation, March 2, 2023, https://www.sleepfoundation.org/bedroom-environment/best-temperature-for-sleep.

179 *it blocks REM sleep:* Danielle Pacheco, "Alcohol and Sleep," Sleep Foundation, October 26, 2022, https://www.sleepfoundation.org/nutrition/alcohol-and-sleep.

179 *technology also stimulates you:* Jessica Schmerler, "Q&A: Why Is Blue Light Before Bedtime Bad for Sleep?," *Scientific American*, September 1, 2015, https://www.scientificamerican.com/article/q-a-why-is-blue-light-before-bedtime-bad-for-sleep/.

180 *can diminish your executive function:* Albertas Skurvydas et al., "One Night of Sleep Deprivation Impairs Executive Function but Does Not Affect Psycho-motor or Motor Performance," *Biology of Sport* 37, no. 1 (2010): 7–14, https://doi.org/10.5114/biolsport.2020.89936.

180 *when our brains consolidate memories:* "Sleep on It: How Snoozing Strengthens Memories," *NIH News in Health*, April 2013, https://newsinhealth.nih.gov/2013/04/sleep-it.

180 *cause or worsen symptoms:* "How Sleep Deprivation Impacts Mental Health," Columbia University Department of Psychiatry, March 16, 2022, https://www.columbiapsychiatry.org/news/how-sleep-deprivation-affects-your-mental-health.

180 *perceive the world around us clearly and calmly:* Eti Ben Simon et al., "Losing Neutrality: The Neural Basis of Impaired Emotional Control Without Sleep," *Journal of Neuroscience* 35, no. 38 (2015): 13194–205, https://doi.org/10.1523 /JNEUROSCI.1314-15.2015.

180 *increase our tendency to be hyperactive:* Vatsal Thakkar, "How Sleep Deprivation Looks a Lot Like ADHD," *ADDitude*, March 31, 2022, https://www .additudemag.com/symptoms-of-insomnia/.

180 *mental health issues like bipolar disorder:* "Sleep Disorders and Mental Illness Go Hand in Hand," UT Southwestern Medical Center MedBlog, May 22, 2017, https://utswmed.org/medblog/sleep-disorders-mental-illness/.

180 *learning disabilities like dyslexia:* Zahavit Paz, "Sleep Deprivation and Importance of Sleep for Dyslexia, LD and ADHD," LD Resources Foundation Action, accessed April 17, 2023, https://www.ldrfa.org/importance-of-sleep -for-people-with-adhd-learning-disabilities/.

181 *increases conflict and tension in our interpersonal relationships:* Cassie Shortsleeve, "How Sleep Affects Your Relationships, According to Science," *Time*, August 3, 2018, https://time.com/5348694/how-sleep-affects-relationships/.

181 *the risk of chronic disease:* Eric J. Olson, "How Many Hours of Sleep Are Enough for Good Health?" Mayo Clinic, February 21, 2023, https://www.mayo clinic.org/healthy-lifestyle/adult-health/expert-answers/how-many-hours-of -sleep-are-enough/faq-20057898#.

181 *Common ADHD comorbidities:* Larry Silver, "When It's Not Just ADHD: Symptoms of Comorbid Conditions," *ADDitude*, March 28, 2023, https://www .additudemag.com/when-its-not-just-adhd/.

181 *developing some physical comorbidities:* Ebba Du Rietz et al., "Mapping Phenotypic in Aetiological Associations Between ADHD and Physical Conditions in Adulthood in Sweden: A Genetically Informed Register Study," *The Lancet Psychiatry* 8, no. 9 (2021): 774–83, https://doi.org/10.1016/S2215 -0366(21)00171-1.

182 *production of the sleep hormone melatonin:* Eric Suni, "Light and Sleep," Sleep Foundation, April 6, 2023, https://www.sleepfoundation.org/bedroom -environment/light-and-sleep.

182 *start producing melatonin earlier:* M. Nathaniel Mead, "Benefits of Sunlight: A Bright Spot for Human Health," *Environmental Health Perspectives* 116, no. 4 (2008): A160–67, https://doi.org/10.1289/ehp.116-a160.

182 *resetting our circadian rhythms than artificial light:* Carla Davis, "Shining Light on What Natural Light Does for Your Body," NC State University Sustainability, March 24, 2014, https://sustainability.ncsu.edu/blog/change yourstate/benefits-of-natural-light/.

182 *suppress melatonin and interfere with sleep quality:* YongMin Cho et al., "Effects of Artificial Light at Night on Human Health: A Literature Review of Observational and Experimental Studies Applied to Exposure Assessment,"

NOTES **249**

Chronobiology International 35, no. 9 (2015): 1294–310, https://doi.org/10.3109/07
420528.2015.1073158.

182 *helping relax you for sleep:* Rob Newsom, "Relaxation Exercises to Help
Fall Asleep," Sleep Foundation, April 1, 2022, https://www.sleepfoundation.org
/sleep-hygiene/relaxation-exercises-to-help-fall-asleep.

182 *go to bed sooner and fall asleep faster:* Fran Golden, "Better Sleep for Adults
with ADHD," *Everyday Health*, November 14, 2017, https://www.everyday
health.com/emotional-health/adhd/better-sleep-adults-with-adhd/.

182 *improve your sleep quality and quantity:* "Exercising for Better Sleep," Johns
Hopkins Medicine, April 17, 2023, https://www.hopkinsmedicine.org/health
/wellness-and-prevention/exercising-for-better-sleep.

183 *ease insomnia symptoms:* Giselle Soares Passos et al., "Is Exercise an Alternative
Treatment for Chronic Insomnia?," *Clinics* 67, no. 6 (2012): 653–59, https://doi
.org/10.6061/clinics/2012(06)17.

183 *prevent anxiety or spinning thoughts:* Serge Brand et al., "Acute Bouts of Exercising Improved Mood, Rumination and Social Interaction in Inpatients with
Mental Disorders," *Frontiers in Psychology* 9 (2018): 249, https://doi.org/10.3389
/fpsyg.2018.00249.

183 *prevent nighttime rumination:* Sarah Jackson, "I Tried Doing a 'Brain
Dump' Every Day for a Week to Declutter My Mind, Manage Racing
Thoughts, and Improve Focus. It's Way Better Than Its Name Suggests,"
Business Insider, January 24, 2022, https://www.businessinsider.com/i-tried
-brain-dump-technique-to-reduce-distractions-build-focus-2022-1.

183 *journal their to-do list:* Michael K. Scullin et al., "The Effects of Bedtime
Writing on Difficulty Falling Asleep: A Polysomnographic Study Comparing
To-Do Lists and Completed Activity Lists," *Journal of Experimental Psychology:
General* 147, no. 1 (2018): 139–46, https://doi.org/10.1037/xge0000374.

184 *taking a shower or bath shortly before bed:* Danielle Pacheco, "Showering Before
Bed," Sleep Foundation, April 19, 2022, https://www.sleepfoundation.org/sleep
-hygiene/shower-before-bed.

185 *the app Alarmy:* "Alarmy," Alarmy, accessed April 17, 2023, https://alar.my/.

186 *taking your ADHD medication forty-five minutes before bedtime:* Dodson, "ADHD
and Sleep Problems."

187 *slumbering in sync with your biology:* Teddi Nicolaus, "Night Owl or Morning Lark? Better Rest Is in Your Genes," *The Nation's Health*, October 2021,
https://www.thenationshealth.org/content/51/8/16.

CHAPTER 14: **DEALING WITH LEARNING DIFFERENCES**

188 *Nearly half of all children:* "Coexisting Conditions," Children and Adults with
Attention-Deficit/Hyperactivity Disorder (CHAAD), accessed August 25, 2022,
https://chadd.org/about-adhd/coexisting-conditions/.

188 *greater odds of having a learning disability:* News Room, "The State of LD: Understanding the 1 in 5," National Center for Learning Disabilities, May 2, 2017, https://www.ncld.org/news/newsroom/the-state-of-ld-understanding-the-1-in-5/.

189 *have above average intelligence:* Amanda Morin, "Learning Disabilities: What They Are and Aren't," Understood, April 17, 2023, https://www.understood.org/en/articles/learning-disabilities-what-they-are-and-arent.

189 *People with dyslexia may read slowly:* "Dyslexia," National Institute of Neurological Disorder and Stroke, accessed August 25, 2022, https://www.ninds.nih.gov/health-information/disorders/dyslexia.

189 *An estimated 15 to 20 percent:* "Dyslexia Basics," International Dyslexia Association, accessed April 17, 2023, https://dyslexiaida.org/dyslexia-basics/.

190 *Orton-Gillingham:* Kristin L. Sayeski et al., "Orton Gillingham: Who, What, and How," *TEACHING Exceptional Children* 51, no. 3 (2018): 240–49, https://doi.org/10.1177/0040059918816996.

190 *11 percent of children with ADHD:* Neelkamal Soares and Dilip R. Patel, "Dyscalculia," *International Journal of Child and Adolescent Health* 8 no. 1 (2015): 15–26, https://psycnet.apa.org/record/2015-29454-003.

190 *difficulty with counting:* ADDitude Editors, "Dyscalculia Test for Adults: Screening for Signs of Learning Disabilities," *ADDitude,* June 6, 2022, https://www.additudemag.com/self-test-for-dyscalculia-in-adults/.

191 *Dysgraphia is a learning difference:* Devon Frye, "What Does Dysgraphia Look Like in Adults?," *ADDitude,* April 28, 2021, https://www.additudemag.com/dysgraphia-in-adults-recognizing-symptoms-later-in-life/.

191 *most frequently missed learning differences:* ADDitude Editors, "[Screener] Dysgraphia in Adults," *ADDitude,* June 6, 2022, https://www.additudemag.com/screener-dysgraphia-symptoms-test-adults/.

191 *many people with ADHD also have dysgraphia:* Susan D. Mayes et al., "High Prevalence of Dysgraphia in Elementary Through High School Students with ADHD and Autism," *Journal of Attention Disorders* 23, no. 8 (2019): 787–96, https://doi.org/10.1177/1087054717720721.

192 *link between vertical heterophoria and ADHD:* Marissa Zimmerman, "Vertical Heterophoria & ADHD: Calming the Visual Chaos," Neurovisual Center of New York, accessed April 17, 2023, https://www.nvcofny.com/eye-care/vertical-heterophoria-adhd-calming-the-visual-chaos/.

192 *it can cause people to struggle with reading, writing, and learning:* "Maybe It's a Learning Disability—Or Maybe It's BVD," Vision Specialists of Michigan, accessed April 17, 2023, https://www.vision-specialists.com/blog/maybe-its-a-learning-disability-or-maybe-its-bvd/.

192 *prescribed a pair of glasses:* René Brooks, "Vertical Heterophoria: The ADHD Related Eye Condition You've Never Heard Of," *Black Girl, Lost Keys* (blog), August 6, 2019, https://blackgirllostkeys.com/adhd/vertical-heterophoria/.

192 *ears just aren't in sync:* Beverly Holden Johns, "What Is Auditory Processing Disorder? Symptoms, Comorbidities, and Exercises," *ADDitude,* July 25, 2022, https://www.additudemag.com/what-is-auditory-processing-disorder-symptoms-exercises/.

193 *APD is common in children with ADHD:* "When They Respond 'What?' 'Huh?' It Could Be Auditory Processing Disorder," *ADHD Weekly,* February 2, 2023, https://chadd.org/adhd-weekly/when-they-respond-what-huh-it-could-be-auditory-processing-disorder/.

193 *reversed symptoms of APD:* Bianca Pinheiro Lanzetta-Valdo et al., "Auditory Processing Assessment in Children with Attention Deficit Hyperactivity Disorder: An Open Study Examining Methylphenidate Effects," *International Archives of Otorhinolaryngoly* 21, no. 1 (2017): 72–78, https://doi.org/10.1055/s-0036-1572526.

193 *difficult to follow and participate in conversations:* "What Is Language Processing Disorder? The Complete Guide," LD Resources Foundation Action, accessed August 25, 2022, https://www.ldrfa.org/what-is-language-processing-disorder/.

193 *greater risk of having language difficulties:* Carroll W. Hughes et al., "Differentiating ADHD from Oral Language Difficulties in Children: Role of Movements and Effects of Stimulant Medication," *BMC Psychiatry* 14 (2014): Article 370, https://doi.org/10.1186/s12888-014-0370-0.

193 *six months of treatment:* Jan Bloomfield and Barbara Dodd, "Is Speech and Language Therapy Effective for Children with Primary Speech and Language Impairment? Report of a Randomized Control Trial," *International Journal of Language & Communication Disorders* 46, no. 6 (2011): 628–40, https://doi.org/10.1111/j.1460-6984.2011.00039.x.

194 *a visual processing disorder:* "What Is Visual Processing Disorder?," Churchill Center & School, accessed April 17, 2023, https://www.churchillstl.org/learning-disability-resources/visual-processing-disorder/.

194 *A developmental optometrist:* "Visual Processing Disorder," Invision Optometry, accessed April 17, 2023, https://invisioncare.com/visual-processing-disorder/.

194 *neuropsychologist:* "Visual Processing Disorder," White Swan Foundation, January 16, 2019, https://www.whiteswanfoundation.org/disorders/neurodevelopmental-disorders/visual-processing-disorder.

194 *ophthalmologist:* "Visual Processing," Advanced Vision Therapy Center, accessed April 17, 2023, https://www.advancedvisiontherapycenter.com/assessments/visual_processing/.

194 *overlooked or misdiagnosed in females:* Robert McCrossin, "Finding the True Number of Females with Autistic Spectrum Disorder by Estimating the Biases in Initial Recognition and Clinical Diagnosis," *Children* 9, no. 2 (2022), https://doi.org/10.3390/children9020272.

194 *half of all people with ASD:* "ADHD and Autism Spectrum Disorder," Children and Adults with Attention-Deficit/Hyperactivity Disorder (CHADD), ac-

cessed November 4, 2022, https://chadd.org/about-adhd/adhd-and-autism-spec trum-disorder/.

194 *women manifest symptoms differently:* Thomas W. Frazier et al., "Behavioral and Cognitive Characteristics of Females and Males with Autism in the Simons Simplex Collection," *Journal of the American Academy of Child and Adolescent Psychiatry* 53, no. 3 (2014): 329–40.e3, https://doi.org/10.1016/j.jaac.2013.12.004.

195 *arduous and frustrating:* Claire Barnett, "'Could I Be Autistic, Too?' Signs of Autism in Women with ADHD," *ADDitude*, January 20, 2023, https://www .additudemag.com/autism-in-women-adhd-signs-symptoms-treatment/.

195 *Learning Disabilities Association of America:* "The Adult Learning Disability Assessment Process," Learning Disabilities Association of America, accessed April 17, 2023, https://ldaamerica.org/info/adult-learning-disability-assessment -process/.

EPILOGUE

202 *nineteen prior studies:* Elizabeth Ahmann et al., "A Descriptive Review of ADHD Coaching Research: Implications for College Students," *Journal of Postsecondary Education and Disability* 31, no. 1 (2018): 17–39, https://eric.ed.gov /?id=EJ1182373.

TRACY OTSUKA is a certified ADHD coach and attorney and is the podcast host of *ADHD for Smart Ass Women*, which ranks in the top 0.05 percent of all podcasts on any subject worldwide with more than five million downloads, and streams in 156-plus countries.

After being diagnosed with ADHD as an adult, Otsuka started her podcast to help women learn about their ADHD brains and how they worked. Before her ADHD epiphany, she was a practicing attorney investigating cases for the U.S. Securities and Exchange Commission; a designer of high-end women's wear sold in Saks Fifth Avenue, Neiman Marcus, and Nordstrom; and a real estate broker selling countless foreclosed properties.

Tracy leads brilliant, driven, high-ability ADHD women (diagnosed or suspecting) to see their symptoms as strengths rather than weaknesses. Her patented six-step program, Your ADHD Brain Is A-OK, teaches women to trust themselves by discovering their strengths, stepping into their purpose, and living to their potential.

Tracy lives with her husband, two kids, two dogs, and seven chickens in Sonoma County, outside San Francisco.